THE RESISTING MUS
POPULAR MUSIC AND SOCIAL PROTEST

To my mother

The Resisting Muse:
Popular Music and Social Protest

Edited by
IAN PEDDIE
West Texas A&M University, USA

ASHGATE

Published by
Ashgate Publishing Limited
Gower House
Croft Road
Aldershot
Hants GU11 3HR
England

Ashgate Publishing Company
Suite 420
101 Cherry Street
Burlington, VT 05401-4405
USA

Ashgate website: http://www.ashgate.com

British Library Cataloguing in Publication Data
The resisting muse : popular music and social protest. – (Ashgate popular and folk music series)
  1. Protest songs – History and criticism 2. Popular music – Social aspects
  3. Popular music – Political aspects 4. Popular music – History and criticism
  5. Subculture
  I. Peddie, Ian
  306.4'8424

Library of Congress Cataloging-in-Publication Data
The resisting muse : popular music and social protest / edited by Ian Peddie.
        p. cm.—(Ashgate popular and folk music series)
    Includes bibliographical references and index.
    ISBN 0-7546-5113-4 (hardback: alk. paper)—ISBN 0-7546-5114-2 (pbk.: alk. paper)
    1. Popular music—Social aspects. 2. Popular music—Political aspects. 3. Protest songs—History and criticism. I. Peddie, Ian. II. Series.

    ML3918.P67R47 2005
    306.4'8424—dc22

                                                                        2005012323

ISBN-10: 0 7546 5113 4 (HBK)
ISBN-10: 0 7546 5114 2 (PBK)

Typeset in Times by Express Typesetters Ltd, Farnham
Printed and bound in Great Britain by TJ International, Padstow, Cornwall

There are the mud flowers of dialect
And the immortelles of perfect pitch
And that moment when the bird sings very close
To the music of what happens.

Seamus Heaney

Contents

Part Three   The Problems of Place

Part Four   The Paradox of Anti-Social Protest

List of figures

List of contributors

Ian Peddie is Assistant Professor of English at West Texas A&M University. Ian has taught classes on popular music and social protest, cultural studies, and modern British and American literature. His publications include 'Poles Apart? Ethnicity, Race, Class and Nelson Algren' (*Modern Fiction Studies*, Spring 2001); 'Love of Labor: Billy Bragg and the Labor Movement' (*PopPolitics 2*, 2000), in addition to essays on Amy Clampitt, Thomas McGrath and Langston Hughes. Ian is also criticism editor of *New Texas: A Journal of the Arts* and is currently working on a book about Scottish author Irvine Welsh.

Peter Dunbar-Hall is Chair of Music Education at Sydney Conservatorium of Music, University of Sydney (Australia). His doctoral research was a study of the implications of popular music stylistic choices among Australian Aboriginal musicians. This forms the basis of a forthcoming text, *Deadly Sounds, Deadly Places – Contemporary Aboriginal Music in Australia* (with Chris Gibson; University of NSW Press). Peter's other research interests include the role of creativity in music teaching and learning, the position of Aboriginal music in Australian education systems, Australian cultural history and the pedagogies of Balinese *gamelan* music. The last of these is based on fieldwork in Bali and regular performances as a member of the Sydney-based Balinese *gamelan gong kebyar*, Sekaa Gong Tirta Sinar. Peter is the author of the biography of Australian theatre performer, Strella Wilson, published by Redback Press. His research appears in numerous journals including *Australian Aboriginal Studies*, *Australian Journal of Indigenous Education*, *Ethnomusicology*, *International Journal of Music Education*, *International Review of the Aesthetics and Sociology of Music*, *Journal of Intercultural Studies*, and *Popular Music and Society*.

Steven Hamelman is a professor in the English Department at Coastal Carolina University, where he teaches American literature and composition. He also plays drums in Virtue Trap, a rock band comprising of other Coastal professors (www.virtuetrap.com). Hamelman has published many scholarly essays on early American fiction, as well as articles on rock music. In 2004 he won the R. Serge Denisoff Award for the best article published in Popular Music and Society. Appearing the same year from the University of Georgia Press was *But Is It Garbage? On Rock and Trash*, Hamelman's study of the function of the 'trash trope' in rock music and culture.

Kimberly Jackson completed her PhD in Comparative Literature at SUNY, Buffalo, and is currently Assistant Professor of English at Florida Gulf Coast University. Her dissertation, 'Performing Infancy: Transmitting/Transmuting the Inhuman in Evolutionary and Technological Gothic', explores, through gothic literature and film, the relationship between techno-science and humanity's various figurations of itself from the end of the nineteenth century to the present. She is currently working on a project on the reality TV series, *The Swan*, which explores the relationship set up by the show between the viewer and the viewed.

Sean K. Kelly is an Assistant Professor of English and philosophy at Florida Gulf Coast University and a 2001 graduate of Binghamton University's Philosophy, Literature, and Criticism Program. He has published articles in *Arizona Quarterly* ('A Reading of *As I Lay Dying*: Another Proposal for Thinking Faulkner's Aesthetics/Politics of Failure') and *Variations* ('Levinas and Blanchot: The Possibilities of a Critical Exposition beyond the Paradigmatic'); edited a monograph titled *Translation Perspectives VIII: Translation: Religion, Ideology, Politics* (Binghamton: Center for Research in Translation, 1995); and has an article forthcoming in *Genre* ('Cosmopolitan Hostility: The Critical Foundations of Derrida's Response to the Global'). In addition to presenting several papers on cultural studies, Dr Kelly has taught courses in popular culture and methodologies of cultural critique.

Stephen A. King is an Associate Professor of Speech Communication at Delta State University, in Cleveland, Mississippi. King served as a Research Fellow at the University of the West Indies during the summer of 1994. King's work on reggae music and the Rastafarian movement has been published in the *Journal of Popular Culture*, *Popular Music and Society*, and the *Howard Journal of Communications*. His book, *Reggae, Rastafari, and the Rhetoric of Society Control*, was published by the University Press of Mississippi in 2002. King is currently working on a book project which examines how the blues is being promoted as part of Mississippi's cultural heritage.

Kathleen McConnell is completing her PhD in Communication and Culture at Indiana University where she is researching the rhetorics of alternative education and private schooling in the 1970s. Her other research projects include a rhetorical genealogy of American playgrounds and a study of the high school underground press. She holds an MA in Popular Culture from Bowling Green State University and a BA from The Evergreen State College. In a former life, she ran the Show-off Gallery, an all-ages punk venue in Bellingham, Washington.

Russell A. Potter earned his PhD in English at Brown University in 1991, and has taught at Rhode Island College since 1995. He is the author of *Spectacular Vernaculars: Hip-Hop and the Politics of Postmodernism*, and has contributed chapters to *The Cambridge Companion to Pop and Rock*; *Key Terms in Popular Music and Culture*; and *Mapping the Beat: Popular Music and Contemporary Theory*. His articles have appeared in *Postmodern Culture*, *Nomad*, *MELUS*, and *Black Sacred Music*.

Jerry Rodnitsky was educated at the University of Chicago and the University of Illinois. He is currently Professor of History at the University of Texas at Arlington. He has authored four books, including *Minstrels of the Dawn: The Folk-Protest Singer as Cultural Hero* and more recently *Jazz-Age Boomtown* and *Feminist Phoenix: The Rise and Fall of a Feminist Counterculture*. He is also the author of 11 articles in various books and 35 articles in journals. Recent journal articles include 'Janis Joplin: The Hippie Blues singer as Feminist Heroine' (*Journal of Texas Music History*, Spring 2002) and 'Back to Branson: Normalcy and Nostalgia in the Ozarks' (*Southern Cultures*, Summer 2002). He is a founding and continuing advisory editor of the journal, *Popular Music and Society*.

James Smethurst teaches in the W.E.B. Du Bois Department of Afro-American Studies at the University of Massachusetts-Amherst. He is the author of *The New Red Negro: The Literary Left and African American Poetry, 1930–1946* and *The Black Arts Movement: Literary Nationalism in the 1960s and 1970s*, and co-editor of *Left of The Color Line: Race, Radicalism, and Twentieth-Century Literature of the United States*.

John Street is Professor of Politics at the University of East Anglia. He is the author of *Rebel Rock: The Politics of Popular Music*, *Politics and Technology*, *Politics and Popular Culture*, and *Mass Media, Politics and Democracy*. He is also co-author of *Deciding Factors in British Politics* and co-editor of *The Cambridge Companion to Pop and Rock*.

Deena Weinstein, a Professor of Sociology at DePaul University in Chicago, has taught a Sociology of Rock class for the past two decades. Her publications include *Postmodern(ized) Simmel* and *Heavy Metal: The Music and Its Culture*. Deena has written numerous essays and reviews, including 'Progressive Rock As Text: The Lyrics of Roger Waters', in *Progressive Rock Reconsidered*, 'Youth', in *Key Terms in Popular Music and Culture*, and 'Net-Game' in *The Cyber-cultures Reader*.

Mark Willhardt is the editor of The *Routledge Who's Who in Twentieth-Century World Poetry* as well as co-editor of *The Routledge Anthology of Cross-Gendered Verse*. In addition to his work in modern and contemporary poetry, Mark has an abiding interest in funk music, including scholarly examinations of authenticity and signification in the work of George Clinton. He is an Associate Professor of English at Monmouth College (Illinois).

Gail Hilson Woldu is Associate Professor of Music at Trinity College in Hartford, Connecticut. Her research and scholarship focus on two areas, hip-hop culture and music in France between 1870 and 1930. Recent scholarship includes 'Debussy, Fauré, and d'Indy and Conceptions of the Artist: The Institutions, the Dialogues, the Conflicts' in *Debussy and his World,* 'Contextualizing Rap' in *American Popular Music: New Approaches to the Twentieth Century,* and 'Women in Rap' in *Women and Music in America Since 1900: An Encyclopedia.* Gail has presented papers on these topics at symposia throughout the United States as well as in Canada, China, France, and Puerto Rico. She is currently working on a translation with critical commentary and notes of French composer Vincent d'Indy's three-volume *Cours de composition musicale.*

General Editor's preface

The upheaval that occurred in musicology during the last two decades of the twentieth century has created a new urgency for the study of popular music alongside the development of new critical and theoretical models. A relativistic outlook has replaced the universal perspective of modernism (the international ambitions of the 12-note style); the grand narrative of the evolution and dissolution of tonality has been challenged, and emphasis has shifted to cultural context, reception and subject position. Together, these have conspired to eat away at the status of canonical composers and categories of high and low in music. A need has arisen, also, to recognize and address the emergence of crossovers, mixed and new genres, to engage in debates concerning the vexed problem of what constitutes authenticity in music and to offer a critique of musical practice as the product of free, individual expression.

Popular musicology is now a vital and exciting area of scholarship, and the *Ashgate Popular and Folk Music Series* aims to present the best research in the field. Authors will be concerned with locating musical practices, values and meanings in cultural context, and may draw upon methodologies and theories developed in cultural studies, semiotics, poststructuralism, psychology and sociology. The series will focus on popular musics of the twentieth and twenty-first centuries. It is designed to embrace the world's popular musics from Acid Jazz to Zydeco, whether high tech or low tech, commercial or non-commercial, contemporary or traditional.

Professor Derek B. Scott
Chair of Music
University of Salford

Acknowledgements

One incurs any number of debts when editing a book. First, my fellow contributors, who completed their insightful and challenging essays in a timely manner, deserve my gratitude. Without their acknowledgement that, in the words of Irvine Welsh, 'music is the ecstasy and the rapture' there would be no book.

My thanks also go to Sarah Charters and Heidi May, Senior Editor in Humanities and Commissioning Editor at Ashgate Publishing respectively. Linda Cayford's help with the manuscript was invaluable. John Attebury's cover design, based on a photograph by Dave Dyet, speaks as eloquently as any amount of words. Brad, Laura, Kim and Sean helped immeasurably during the dark days in the desert and, well, I appreciate that.

Working on a book of this kind, I have also had occasion to reflect on the texts that have enabled this volume, many of which formed a soundtrack to my formative years. As the scope of the book begins in 1975, perhaps it is appropriate to turn to the Sex Pistols, surely that year's most infamous proponents of popular music. Nearly thirty years after it first appeared, then, the Pistols' 'Holidays in the Sun' seems even more resonant than it did first time around. As Johnny Rotten put it, 'I wanna see some history.'

Introduction

Ian Peddie

Music affects a relationship. The myriad assumptions at the heart of this assertion are the foundations upon which the study of popular music is based. Yet, like any other relationship, that which lies at the heart of our experience of music defies easy analysis; it is never quite as palpable as we would wish, never quite as definable as we would want. Even though 'it' – that which defines and coheres our relationship to music – is, to borrow from The Beatles 'here, there and everywhere', our inability to locate easy answers as to what and how that relationship exactly is and works is testimony to the profundity and complexity of music. And it is with one aspect of the complexities of such relationships that this book is concerned: social protest.

For all that, we can and should make some tentative moves towards definition. Few would argue, for instance, that music is anything other than a discursive practice. And as a discursive practice, music 'is situated in particular social relationships and locations that are a product of complex intersections of culture, class, gender etc., in lived experience' (Balliger, 1995, p. 13). In one sense, then, music emerges as always already grounded in the social, as an avenue of cultural contestation or social and political engagement. In piecing together the typical arguments of music and social protest, however, a number of issues tend to surface with regularity. Without running through these arguments, I hope that it is clear that, in terms of popular music and social protest, I have in mind something beyond the all too familiar reductionism of music-as-representative-of-youth-culture ideology. Neither will an 'us and them' argument suffice, simply because popular music was and has always been more sophisticated than that, just as it was always more than a narrative of a running battle between disaffected youth and the establishment. Instead, a much more fruitful way of approaching the issue – one that assumes the fundamental cultural and political importance of popular music and social protest – is to see this relationship as a complex dialectic where musical protest is as fluid as the audiences to which it appeals.

But if the potential uses of popular music have never been in doubt, its uses as a medium of protest critics all too often reproduce in rather limited ways, as the following makes clear:

> Popular music is a contested terrain, where different actors engage in defining the essence of popular music by favoring consumptive escapism or radical disruption and – since the elements of escapism and involvement belong to one structural

relation that can be inverted – also by enhancing a radicalization of consumption
and commercialization of rebellion. (Lahusen, 1996, p. 87)

There are any number of things we might point to here. According to
Lahusen, then, pop music has an 'essence'. Still more intriguing is the apparent
transparent simplicity of pop music, a point that is underscored by the dominant
dichotomies of escapism/involvement and radicalized consumption/
commercialized rebellion. To this we might add that much of Lahusen's account
is built upon the notion that pop music is inherently oppositional. Just as there is
some truth in this implicit claim, there is also a certain logic in the fact that
popular music does, at times, define itself through opposition. Yet what tends to
happen in the minds of critics is that the long dissenting tradition with which
popular music is associated becomes axiomatic, an indubitable truism that fosters
the kind of sweeping generalizations to which popular music criticism seems
particularly prone. Hence articles such as 'Right Rock', intriguingly subtitled
'Rock Music and Reaganism', can begin with the claim that '[d]uring the '60s,
rock and liberal social protest were inseparably associated' (Pasley, 1987, p. 22)
with nary an eyebrow raised, when in fact a more suitable response to such an
assertion may well be 'Yes, but …' A similar conclusion seems the most
appropriate response to Jon Pareles's contention that 'much of the protest
impulse [in music] has migrated into deliberately separatist styles of music …
Politics moved into punk and metal, where it offered reasons for adolescent
frustrations, and into underground hip-hop, where it has surfaced periodically
among rappers' (2003, B3). Why punk and metal and not, say, country? Why hip-
hop and not folk? Moving uneasily behind this account is a desire for order and
classification of the kind which the music of social protest can never fulfil. And
neither should it want to. Popular music and social protests are, in short, too
diffuse, too widespread a dissenting tradition to be confined to a genre, a
category, or a time period. Not surprisingly, even the most tentative of attempts
to define the music of social protest are fraught with problems; the trajectory
along which it travels escapes us, its origins often as elusive as its influence. With
that in mind, perhaps we should conclude that if social protest is made up of
collisions, then it is also formed by fissures and fractures, by the very kind of
resulting ambiguities that make the changing faces of popular music so vexing
and so appealing.

Nowhere are these ambiguities more apparent than when one brings popular
music and social protest together. Even the phrase invokes a compulsion to
dichotomize, to see 'both sides' only, to view an irreducibly complex culture
through the limits imposed by a Manichean vision. An example by analogy may
help. Speaking in 1999 of critical approaches towards popular music, Angela
McRobbie contended that:

> … our critical vocabulary seems sadly lacking. None of the old words, like *collage*,
> *montage*, or *postmodernism*, seem capable of capturing the velocity and scale of

this [musical] output. Likewise, the older ways of making sense of music by placing different styles into different categories, or by posing the commercial against the creative or experimental, or by talking about black or white music as though they were quite distinct are equally inappropriate. Now, in the late nineties, we have to start with an assumption of musical hybridity ... (McRobbie, 1999, p. 38)

These are sentiments that might be usefully applied to popular music and social protest. That they are not commonly held notions is, I think, our loss.

The Resisting Muse: Popular Music and Social Protest is an attempt to come to terms with many of the problems adumbrated above. As such, the volume was conceived with a number of important provisos in mind, one of which was the timescale. Because *Resisting Muse* holds to a post-1975 focus, the volume is not a survey of major twentieth-century musical genres, but a detailed examination of a number of significant genres and issues and their development over the last 25 years or so. Hence many of the essays in the volume will, by necessity, question ideological assumptions implicit in genre – assumptions that can only be challenged via the cultural places, issues, or situations from whence they emerge. This is not, of course, to suggest that the volume will challenge what, for example, 'folk' is or is not. Nonetheless the cultural influences lying behind hitherto apparently easily identifiable popular musical categories have tended to blur the diversity that has always been a feature of social protest and of the audiences to which the music in question speaks. In their attempts to delineate the complexity of popular music and social protest, many of the essays in this volume will tease out these very issues.

During the last 25 years, popular music has, perhaps, come of age. More than anything, it was this belief that suggested that a volume commensurate with the changing face of popular music was required. To this end, one thinks of the rise of issues such as transnationalism, the amalgamation of genres, music and space, music and place as well as the technologies through which pop music reads the social – all of these are now at the forefront of popular music studies. In one way or another, the volume touches on these and other important issues.

Part One, 'Politics and the Parameters of Protest', is an attempt to come to terms with some of the elemental issues that perennially define protest music. The essays in this section examine a number of topics fundamental to social protest and popular music. These include issues such as the prevalence of protest and whether it actually has any discernible effect. Equally important here is how popular music is often constructed as a discourse of protest and how musicians adopt roles within that discourse. All this leads inexorably to questions of authenticity, which are never far away from debates over popular music and social protest.

Deena Weinstein, while touching briefly on the difficulty of agreeing on exactly what a protest song might be, contends that, despite popular opinion to the contrary, there has been remarkably little social protest music. Hence despite the amalgamation of ideology and self-interest, which led early rock critics to canonize 'oppositional' music, and the image/persona of many popular musicians, who often gain kudos from an oppositional stance, the overriding conclusion is that the propensity of protest is something that should not be taken for granted. One of the main reasons for this, Weinstein offers, is that much of mainstream media, particularly in the United States, is now part of a large, conservative conglomerate with ties to the Bush administration. In the face of the cultural and political power of such conglomerates, songs of social protest tend to receive little airplay. Equally, extant protest songs have to be regarded as such, and Weinstein suggests that a simple lack of understanding has worked against their identification. What all this means is that, as Weinstein argues, the dearth of protest songs is commensurate with their relative inefficacy as vehicles of social concern.

From another prospective, Jerry Rodnitsky suggests that because protest music is bound to political activism it is necessarily cyclical. Taking his lead from the heyday of social protest, the 1960s, he suggests that the survival of protest music can be traced to its ability to harness topical issues and particular causes, especially when articulated by the archetypal troubadour of the folk singer/ songwriter. Much of the appeal of early 1970s feminist singers such as Barbara Dane and Holly Neal, for instance, was drawn from their ability to address both feminist and working-class concerns. Yet aside from isolated events such as the various aid projects (Live Aid, Farm Aid and so on) in the 1980s, Rodnitsky suggests that until the appearance of what he calls 'satiric songs', in the guise of political lampooning by The Capitol Steps later in that same decade, only folk music kept the flame of protest burning.

Folk music, surely one of the constitutive genres of social protest music, is the departure point for Mark Willhardt's inquiry into the parameters of authenticity. Through the work of Billy Bragg and Michelle Shocked, along with more than a dash of Woody Guthrie, Willhardt illuminates how false authenticities are read through either the politics of ethics or genre. Instead what he calls the 'authenticity of use', which approximates to moments of agency on behalf of the performer, encourages a new view of authenticity – one that acknowledges and reveals false authenticities. Such an argument removes any lingering notions of transparency that may still be attached to the concept of authenticity while simultaneously encouraging those self-reflexive moments where the artist can address forces such as the market, politics and the like that provide the materials from which their authenticities were carved.

The issue of authenticity is of implicit concern in John Street's essay on the pop star as politician. While attending to the question of why and when musicians engage with politics, Street touches upon a number of important issues, from the nature of political engagement to the concept of moral capital. Beginning with the contention that political pop is the exception rather than the rule, he makes an intriguing case for an analytical focus on the biographical aspects of a musician's life, an approach that allows for political engagement in terms of personal values and commitments. In figures such as John Lennon and Victor Jara, of course, this approach is particularly fruitful. At the same time, however, Street notes that biographical accounts tend to gloss over music or evidence that does not fit the thesis in question, and this leads to a discussion of the extent to which political positions are called into being by movements which require musicians to perform a particular role. Illustrative examples in this respect include Marvin Gaye's political responses to Motown's company policy and Bono's ability to turn musical fame into political communication. All of these and other pertinent examples indicate the difficulty in pinpointing the conditions under which pop stars become politicians.

Part Two, 'Monophony or Polyphony?', emphasizes what we might call the cultural histories or cultural identities through which ideas of protest are negotiated. Given that the voices of protest and resistance are grounded in, or measured against, a discernible history, it is no surprise that one of the pivots of this section is the very real presence of an immediate past. With issues of race very much at the forefront of this section, the complexities of class and gender merge to elucidate, and paradoxically complicate some of the most important vernacular genres of music to appear in the last two decades or so. If hip-hop and rap coalesce as versions of a conscious resistance to society and/or as new forms of organic expression, for all that, their very presence owes its existence to a history that reveals, among other things, the nature and intensity of exploitation.

'Postmodernism in action' is the phrase Russell Potter uses to characterize contemporary hip-hop. Suggesting that hip-hop resistance emerges through music as an event or music as a distinct form of assemblage with no two CDs being the same, Potter suggests that sampling becomes a kind of global vernacular within which categories such as consumer and producer, original utterance and pastiche become blurred. Focusing on the music of DJ Spooky, The Roots and The X-ecutioners, the author asserts that fragments of the past, in samples or influences, emerge as a potential future that is already transnational. As hip-hop has spread around the world, so it has drawn a heterogeneous populace, a 'hip-hop world mix' as Spooky puts it, where discourses become more fluid, signifiers less certain, realities less clear. In this world, the melding of intellectual theories, musical forms, and tropes with an ostensibly infinite number of potential voices and literally any pattern of sounds makes for an extraordinary bricolage that, according to Potter, breaks down divisions between reality, representation and subjectivity.

James Smethurst argues that one of the primary contentious and creative forces of modern Black American music occurs at the intersection between race and class. With a brief nod to the influence of the Popular Front and doo wop on black artists, Smethurst argues that the rap/hip-hop axis has been crucial in maintaining and ironically diluting class-consciousness. From the primitivist fantasies of those white suburban youths who participate in the culture of rap through the idealized presence of the 'thug' rapper as a man who recognizes no legal or moral boundaries, hip-hop offers a model of class identification that is cross-racial. Crucial here is the figure of Marshal Mathers, aka Eminem, doyen of the multiracial American underclass. In his attempts to seek an identity of interests and cultural language between himself and influential representatives of black rap such as Dr Dre, Eminem evokes a common class experience able to acknowledge racial boundaries as a means of asserting membership in a multiracial underclass.

Gail Woldu's 'Gender as Anomaly: Women in Rap' challenges the male hegemony in rap. Through an examination of rhetorical tropes and several other salient themes in women's rap, Woldu suggests that one of the most important issues that repeatedly emerges among female rappers is the desire for independence – whether that is financial, emotional or sexual. Yet if rappers such as Queen Latifah, Foxy Brown, and Salt-n-Pepa continued a tradition that had its roots in the blues women of the 1920s and 1930s, the sexualized images of women rappers made their positions still more complicated. This, in turn, offered a series of marketing opportunities that female rappers were quick to exploit. But Woldu suggests that women were also the exploited. That is, paralleling the way in which female Motown artists were manipulated as purveyors of middle-class black values, female rappers occupy a kind of fantasy world where they can be marketed as 'bitches' and 'hoes'. And this leaves female rappers caught between two stools. On the one hand, their participation in the intensely male world of rap is to be lauded, while, on the other, they remain sexualized and often demeaned in rap's lyrics and its marketing.

Part Three, 'The Problems of Place', takes up a number of themes, not least those of identity, community and place. As a means of forging group identity and community, the value of music is difficult to overstate. And we can, I believe, think of community in terms not only of local or national groups with shared interests or goals, but also in a more postmodern way, as a diasporic community cohered by similar experience and social status. This section, then, moves from the national to the transnational, with traditional ideas of identity and place very much under scrutiny. That is, the very existence of Jamaica's Rastafarians and Australia's Aborigines is contingent upon a sense of group coherence and identity which owes much to place. For these groups, music is a means of assertion, a means of defending a culture and a way of life. And such resistance must, by necessity, be read in terms of place, for such ideas eschew Western music as a reflection upon, or, perhaps more importantly, as a definition of national history and geography. Read in these terms, the hegemony of western pop music begins to decline, its influence perhaps a lingering manifestation of colonial presence, of a world now gone. In this climate, traditional analyses of place become difficult to maintain, and ideas of a transnational music assume considerable significance. This is the domain of music that may not have any apparent geographical location. Such transnational music offers a number of new ways of thinking about community, not least in its fundamental concern of escaping traditional fixed models of community – especially those linked to place.

Stephen A. King addresses how reggae music functions as a rhetorical and ideological branch of Rastafarianism. King suggests that reggae became one of the chief mediums of communication for the Rastafarian movement in Jamaica, and it centred on the redefinition of blackness and the positive promotion of the cultural legacy of Africa. From its origins in the slums of West Kingston, reggae became an important means of identifying the oppression inflicted upon Rastas as well as a medium through which they could organize resistance. Much of the resistance hinges on the group culture that reggae seems to promote, with ideas of brotherhood and camaraderie at the fore. Along with protests against 'Babylon' and the positioning of Rastas as modern-day slaves, it is little surprise that reggae serves as a symbol for group cohesion or the communal sharing of ego well-being. All this effects a rearticulation of self-images through reggae's music of protest, and, more specifically, through critiques of the iniquities of Jamaica, the positive portrayal of Africa, and the consequent favourable images of blackness. In these ways reggae functions as both an expression of dissent and a significant vehicle of self/group enhancement.

Many of these points can, of course, be applied to the issues of Aboriginal cultural reclamation discussed by Peter Dunbar-Hall. Against astonishing domestic levels of ignorance over indigenous culture, Aboriginal music is invariably read in terms of nationalistic protest. And while such music certainly does exist, Dunbar-Hall is at pains to point out that a better way of viewing it is to consider how it works to ensure the survival of Aboriginal cultures. With this in mind, the term 'survival' itself takes on considerable importance, as it reminds us of the spiritual and cultural persistence of a people that successive governments have tried to wipe out. From this perspective, the simple presence of songs about survival or dreamtime effectively announces a sense of protest whether they offer dissent or not. This is one of the principal reasons why so much Aboriginal music addresses issues of cultural custodianship. After all, if survival is contingent upon belief, then the indigenous peoples, as one song puts it, 'better keep on telling those stories'.

Stories of a different kind inform Ian Peddie's essay. With recourse to the Black Country, an area of the West Midlands formerly known for its heavy industry and mining, Peddie tackles the vexing issue of music and place. After touching upon the remarkable success of Black Country musicians, using the work of Robert Plant in the 1970s and post-1990 Goldie, the essay complicates the often simplistic assumptions applied to music from the Black Country, many of which effortlessly connect heavy industry with the music the area has produced. Here the suggestion is that Robert Plant's emphasis on spontaneity and loss of control and more recently Goldie's emphasis upon a diasporic, hybrid community undermines established ideas of place through which the music of many Black Country artists was read. For Plant, 'prefabricated' music was anathema, effectively a synecdoche for what was wrong with post-war Britain. Thus Peddie contends Plant's celebration of fragmentation and loss of control suggested a postmodern politics of multiplicity of the kind taken up by Goldie some 20 years later. By the same token, Goldie's emphasis on the fluidity of identity, his repeated examination of inner-city experience, and his insistence upon commonality of experience among inner-city inhabitants regardless of race, attenuates critical predilections towards place as sites of community and authenticity.

Part Four, 'The Paradox of Anti-Social Protest', might be effectively titled 'protest within protest'. This section addresses a number of related points, from how technology might be manipulated as a means of protest to how the idea of the anti-social is positioned as an axiomatic form of dissent. At issue here are a number of evolving modes of protest, where meaning is once again located in what we might call 'organized' community values. That these values often appear anti-social to outsiders, or at times near legally deviant, is where much of their appeal to members is no doubt located.

Sean Kelly's essay on heavy metal and social technology introduces the possibility of music clearing the ground for new analyses of community. Beginning with technology's potential unveiling of a future without humans, Kelly asserts that the human response was to create alternative conceptions of time and community as a means of resisting a technology that potentially erased the future concept of humanity. Under this rubric, concepts of time, technology and the idea of the human are constantly under negotiation. In this sense, then, through distortion, feedback, and reverberation, hard rock confronts technology at the very site of its production. Here, heavy metal's choice of themes such as Satanism, futurism and various other mythic and archaic icons, places the listener in opposition to linear temporality. Through a reading of aspects of work by Rush, Iron Maiden, and Black Sabbath, Kelly's reading of technology and heavy metal invites readers to consider the extent to which metal can deliver a model of community that offers resistance and universality as harmonious expectations.

The issue of technology is also fundamental to Kathleen McConnell's essay. While focusing on the cassette-tape culture that emerged in America's Pacific Northwest in the early 1980s, McConnell examines how the culture of taping gave rise to the idea of 'alternative authoring'. At issue here is the essential paradox at the heart of authorship, which is something that the independent music scene could never ultimately hope to resolve. The one fact agreed upon was that much of the impetus for the taping scene came from the belief that large music corporations enjoyed too much control over people's listening habits. Consequently, a significant 'scene' emerged around the idea of taping, authorized by journals such as The Lost Music Network's *Op*, as well as *Sound Choice* and *Snipehunt*. In their own ways, each of these publications attempted to valorize tape culture, invariably as some form of resistance. Whether that involved issues of privatization, aesthetics, or the democratization of music depended on the conceptual boundaries with which one approached the scene.

Kimberly Jackson's essay on Gothic or 'Dark,' a genre which enjoyed popularity in Britain, Germany, and parts of the USA from the late 1970s to the late 1980s, asserts that Goth politics was, in fact, an anti-politics. At the heart of this movement was the insistence on a certain antisocialism, in which the music of Bauhaus, Joy Division and The Sisters of Mercy, by way of distortion and disjointed melodies, evokes a kind of anti-community. This feeling is compounded through an examination of Goth dance, where, although Goths were physically close to one another on the dance floor, they actually formed a spectacle of individuals, each writhing in his own pain. From this aspect, Gothicism reflected the dark, ominous rise of individualism in the 1980s, where the individual was not a point of celebration but a wandering lost soul – a point clinched by the 'undead' appearance of Goths.

The problems of community also emerge in Steven Hamelman's essay, 'Straight Edge.' Here the focus is squarely on the failure of post-punk bands to find a means of expressing a sense of protest at all. Implicit in this argument is how little rock music has advanced during the 1980s and 1990s. This sentiment is exemplified through straight edge music, a genre that emerged in the early 1980s. With its mantra of no smoking, no drinking, and no drugs, straight edge becomes a protest against the rebellion apparently endemic to hard rock. In other words, it becomes a protest against a protest. If this incestuous, circular logic tends to escape the committed Straight Edger, then it comes as no surprise to find that straight edge lyrics tend towards negative, cliché-ridden allegories of the evils of quotidian life. Perhaps, then, it was the hard-core, deafening delivery that was the point here; the failure to 'make a difference' might just have inspired the rage that gave rise to the conclusion that 'a difference' cannot be made.

In many ways, then, the departure point for all the essays in this collection is the rich, diverse possibilities offered by popular music. How we negotiate our relationship with popular music owes much to the social, historical and political formations through which we filter cultural narratives; it is at that point where we organize our own relationships to popular music. And, as consumers, producers, readers and critics of popular music we are engaged in a lived social experience with music. Here popular music becomes a discursive element in our worlds, one that offers insight into our lives, one where, as Thoreau put it, 'If a man does not keep pace with his companions, perhaps it is because he hears a different drummer. Let him step to the music which he hears, however measured or far away'.

PART ONE
POLITICS AND THE
PARAMETERS OF PROTEST

Chapter 1

Rock protest songs: so many and so few

Deena Weinstein

As a style of music born out of teenage rebellion and idealistic youth confronting hypocritical authorities, you would think that rock would be jam-packed with protest songs. In light of the spate of protest songs released in the run-up to the 2004 US presidential election, that judgement would be reinforced. And if you do think that rock is replete with political themes, you are not the only one, for that is the prevailing view. Yet it is a view that doesn't hold up to examination. While so many celebrate and enumerate various rock protest songs, I want to account for the myth of their ubiquity and their relative rarity, specifically in the United States. Broadly speaking, the protest in protest songs means an opposition to a policy, an action against the people in power that is grounded in a sense of injustice.[1] But which powers-that-be, or their actions or policies, count? Governments on all levels and their enforcers – military or police forces – certainly qualify. And the preponderance of rock protest songs do focus on what those songs identify as the improper use of force.

For example, there is a vast collection of rock songs that protest police brutality. Among them are: The Buffalo Springfield's 'For What It's Worth (Stop Hey What's that Sound)', Rage Against the Machine's 'Killing in the Name', Bruce Springsteen's 'American Skin (41 shots)', NWA's 'F**k tha Police', KRS-One's 'Black Cop', Body Count's 'Cop Killer', and Vortis' 'The Ballad of Mumia Abu Jamal (F**k the Police)'. Other songs focusing on governmental authority involve civil rights and economic policies. Still others protest corporate power. The few examples of this sort are mainly against record companies (the Sex Pistols' 'EMI', Lynyrd Skynydr's 'Working for MCA', Pink Floyd's 'Have a Cigar', and John Fogerty's 'Vanz Kant Danz'). There is less consensus about what constitutes a protest song when we look at other sources of power like teachers and parents. Are Chuck Berry's and Alice Cooper's complaints about the boredom of school to be included in the category of protest? What about the complaints against parental authority like Suicidal Tendencies' 'Institutionalized'?

Protest songs can be classified on several dimensions. One, just discussed, is the type of authority that is deemed unjust. Another is the specificity of the injustice – whether it is power in general, some particular policy or a specific instance of abuse of power. Songs in this last category are sometimes referred to as 're-ax' or reaction songs. They are 'songs that concentrate their fury upon a single act of injustice'

(Corn, 2001). An example is the Ramones' 'My Brain Is Hanging Upside Down (Bonzo Goes To Bitburg)', which refers to President Reagan's 1985 trip to West Germany where he declared that he wouldn't visit a concentration camp but did lay a wreath at a German military cemetery in Bitburg containing graves of Nazi SS soldiers (Corn, 2001). Crosby, Stills, Nash and Young's 'Ohio', about college students who were shot by the Ohio National Guard while protesting the Vietnam war, is another, better-known, re-ax song.[2] It is arguable that what are classified as protest songs, especially the re-ax type, are best thought of as lamentations.

A third dimension for classifying protest songs is their impact. At one extreme are songs that most listeners fail to perceive as protest songs and thus they have no influence. Argent's 1972 hit 'Hold Your Head Up' was a feminist anthem with no impact, because the word 'woman' that followed the title refrain in the chorus was indiscernible. Most heard the word as 'whoa'. At the other extreme are the few rock songs that inspire action of one kind or another. An example would be a pair of songs by DC hardcore band Minor Threat: 'Straight Edge' and 'Out of Step (With the World)'. These songs exhort people to engage in a lifestyle that renounces addictive drugs and excessive alcohol consumption. The straight edge movement among fans of the genre, who often marked their hands with an X, was strongest at the start of the 1980s when the songs were released, and continues today. There is agreement about the most obvious songs protesting political policies, especially war. However, there is no consensus on what targets of opposition are to be included in the category of 'protest'.

Protest songs are defined as such by virtue of their words, but many make their impact in tandem with their sonic elements, the emotionality of the music, the strength and confidence of the vocals, or their simplicity and repetitive phrases, which allow the audience to sing along. And although lyrics of rock songs are typically used to define them as protest songs, one can also understand music itself to be the locus of the protest. The best example – one of very few – would be Jimi Hendrix's version of 'The Star-Spangled Banner', first heard at Woodstock in 1969. Indie-punk band Vortis goes one better on Hendrix with 'God Won't Bless America Again', hijacking the patriotic anthem both sonically and verbally. Nevertheless, the number of rock protest songs varies by how inclusively we define 'protest' and 'rock'. Even with the most generous definitions of each of these terms, the number of protest songs is dwarfed by the profusion of songs about love'n'lust. Yet we have tended to think otherwise – not only now, but throughout rock's history.

Why do we think that there are so many rock protest songs?

Thanks to the policies and practices of the Bush administration in Iraq and domestically, a raft of rock protest songs has been recorded recently. Artists as varied as John Mellencamp, the Beastie Boys, Lenny Kravitz and hundreds of punk bands have released anti-Bush songs. Metal's protest songs come from all eras of the long-lived genre, starting with the Black Sabbath's counterculture-era 'War Pigs', through thrash (Motorhead's 'Orgasmatron', Megedeth's 'Peace Sells But Who's Buying', and even to death metal (Six Feet Under's 'America the Brutal'), a subgenre not usually given to politics.

Yet rock came into being at a time of high political fervour – the 1960s. This was a time of protest – initially the civil rights struggle, and later demonstrations for free speech by university students and, especially, the anti-Vietnam War movement. Youth were at the forefront of each of these movements and, by the 1960s, rock, as opposed to its 1950s forerunner, rock 'n' roll, was not just greasy kid stuff, but appropriate for an older, college-aged crowd. Youth's involvement in these protests and, simultaneously, their interest in rock music, created the conditions for a proliferation of protest songs. Thus rock's history, which is celebrated more today than ever before, is associated with protest. And those protests, which at the time were vigorously opposed by the powers-that-be and the general public, are now understood, by the establishment, the general public and many of those who were more or less engaged in those struggles at the time, as fully vindicated and successful. (But of course they weren't successful. Indeed, there is much truth in the position held by some leftist political leaders during the 1960s who saw rock as being antithetical to motivating political engagement.)[3]

Nonetheless, the 1960s generation was a generation in the strict sense. Whatever its members's engagement at the time with various protest movements, they tend to feel reflected glory by virtue of having been there, man, and having been fans of the music. Importantly, this was the first generation of young people who continued to listen to the music of their youth long after that youth was gone. They have listened to their old vinyl LPs, bought the songs again when CDs were introduced, listened to the classic rock radio format which plays a canonical set of these songs, bought them again as box sets, and have attended, at increasingly great expense, the concerts given by the artists who recorded their songs. The history of the era as presented by the popular media, especially as TV specials, Hollywood movies and college courses on the 1960s, spotlight the rock protest songs.

Rock's first decade coincided with a time of various social protests, yet, despite newspaper headlines and the newly enlarged TV newscasts, there were only a few protest songs on the Billboard charts. What follows is a list of the top ten records of the 1960s, starting from the highest: 'Hey Jude', 'Theme from A Summer Place', 'Tossin' and Turnin'', 'I Heard It through the Grapevine', 'I Want to Hold Your Hand', 'I'm a Believer', 'Let the Sunshine In', 'Are You Lonesome Tonight', 'In the Year 2525', and 'It's Now or Never' (Weiner, 1998). Are any of these rock protest songs? For all that, the 1960s was the golden age for rock protest songs. Most (if not all) such songs that people can name today come from that era. It was not merely the political situation that encouraged their creation and appreciation. The songwriters, performers and their youth audience were strongly influenced by the infusion of a revivified folk music beginning in the late 1950s. The majority of the rock protest songs of the 1960s can be seen as folk music, or at best, folk-rock.

Another important explanation for the profusion of protest songs in the fabled 1960s is the state of the rock media in its first decade. The established music industry had no interest in the new style, and so it was left to newcomers without established rules or conventional practices. 'When the boomers's explosion of romantic art flared up from London to San Francisco it caught the old music business unprepared,' writes Ronnie Pontiac. 'Most of the old school executives, hating the hippies and their music, saw no opportunity there. That sadly predictable state of affairs became a gold rush for hustlers, young lawyers, agents and accountants' (Pontiac, 2004). These newer record label executives and managers allowed artists to do their own thing, and one of their things was protest songs.

Radio in the late 1960s and early 1970s was also wide open to this new music. Not commercial radio, of course, where the tight Top 40 format ruled. One of that format's rules was to keep off the air anything controversial (although Barry McGuire's 'Eve of Destruction' was a number one record on Top 40 radio in the summer of 1965 [Fong-Torres, 1998, p. 255]). Television, with the exception of The Smothers Brothers Show, avoided protest music even more than radio's Top 40 stations. But, coinciding with the anti-war movement in the latter half of the1960s, the FFC-instigated FM stations embraced controversial songs. The format's name emphasizes its lack of rules: free-form. (It was also called 'underground' and 'progressive'.)

Another reason why rock is seen to have so many protest songs is the role of rock critics. Rock criticism began in the mid-1960s, and early critics shared the views of those who were fighting for civil rights for blacks and struggling against the Vietnam war, and their progressive ideology has permeated rock criticism ever since. As the arbiters of rock tastes in the ensuing decades, they have selected and praised artists with similar views to their own (while ignoring or damning those with anti-progressive sentiments). That is, they underscore the protest songs and highlight the careers of artists with progressive views like Bruce Springsteen and The Clash. The Clash, for instance, was hailed as the 'Only Band that Matters'. That is what Joe Strummer, the band's vocalist, guitarist and sloganeer, told everyone. 'And the press, especially the American critics who've always been patsies for political pop, bought the line hook, line and sinker,' concludes their biographer, David Quantick (2000, p. 9).

Critics are the ones who enshrine their 'greats' in books and halls of fame, and reference them in their reviews of contemporary music. They are the makers of the rock canon – those 'best of' songs that are preserved on lists and comprise classic-rock-format playlists. It is easy to see the ideological current running through the rock press today by noting the spate of articles about protest songs related to the Bush administration. Some bemoan their absence, with articles sporting titles such as: 'Is Protest Music Dead?' (Chang, 2002), 'Where are all the protest songs?' (Young, 2003), 'Few are raising voices for protest music' (Kot, 2002) and 'Sing Now, or Forever Hold Your Peace; Where are the new protest songs?' (Epstein, 2003). Others celebrate the appearance of protest songs: 'Once Again, Anti-war Songs Proliferate in the US' (Bessman, 2003, p. 35) and 'Protest song is back-with a vengeance' (Blagg, 2004). But critics aren't the only ones who call our attention to protest songs. When the powers-that-be are attacked by such songs and react publicly, they manage to promote the very music to which they object. They are far more effective marketers than the rock press. The response to Body Count's 'Cop Killer' by police groups throughout the US is a case in point. They spoke out, refused to work security for the band's shows and marched in front of venues where the band played. The press covered these activities and helped the song become a hit record.

A final important reason for thinking that rock is replete with protest songs is the image provided by rock musicians when they involve themselves with various protest activities in addition to, or instead of, performing protest songs. They proffer political statements during interviews published in magazines and newspapers. They also make comments on stage, such as the embarrassed-to-be-from-the-same-state-as-Bush remark that got Natalie Maine's group, the Dixie Chicks, virtually banned from country radio playlists. By the same token, Springsteen has been telling his audience that 'the Bush administration has run "roughshod over our civil liberties" and cautioning, "It's never served this country well to rush into war". His remarks were greeted with scattered boos' (Kot, 2002). Radiohead's Thom Yorke dedicated 'No Surprises', a song which contends that the government doesn't speak for us and should be brought down, to George W. Bush (Ross, 2001, pp. 117–18). On stage, Pearl Jam went further. 'After making a series of antiwar and anti-Bush remarks ... which were met with a mixture of cheers and boos, Vedder impaled a mask of President George W. Bush on a microphone stand, stabbed it into the floor and began stomping on it. Suddenly the boos were thunderous and dozens of patriotic Pearl Jam fans stormed out of the show' (Berlau, 2003, p. 30). The video clips that played as Black Sabbath did their sixties-era 'War Pigs' at 2004's Ozzfest tour showed a montage of pictures of Bush and Hitler together with the caption 'Same shit different asshole'. Bush was also shown with a clown nose.[4]

Communication breakdown: why are there so few rock protest songs?

Despite the foregrounding of protest songs in rock discourse, there are, then, far fewer of them than one is led to believe. They are but a tiny proportion of all rock songs, even using the most generous definitions of rock and protest. Understanding why there are so few protest songs reveals a great deal about rock music. We can divide a somewhat complex explanation into three categories: (a) there are relatively few protest songs, (b) protest songs that do exist aren't widely heard, and, most significantly, (c) protest songs that are heard aren't understood as protest songs.

The Vietnam era, when the counterculture was in the ascendancy and there was a self-conscious and fairly unified youth culture, has been called the Golden Age of Rock Activism (Pontiac, 2004; Collins, 2003). It was during this time that the best-known, and, for most Americans of all ages, the only known rock protest songs were created.[5] The largest batches of protest songs appear in eras of assertive and highly publicized social movements, especially against wars. One reason for the paucity of rock protest songs is the absence of mass protest movements during most of rock's history. It is easy to understand this feast or famine: if there is no potential audience for protest songs, they are less likely to be written, released or played on the commercial media. A cynical, or perhaps merely realistic, reading is given by David Segal: 'most artists keep at least three bodyguards between themselves and any agenda more complicated than hanging on to fame. Why? Economically speaking, ignoring politics makes sense' (2003, p. 50). We are currently in another era of protest, it would seem. Record industry insider Danny Goldberg, is pleased, stating: 'I can't remember any time, including the 60s, when so many artists were addressing politics' (quoted in Cave, 2004, p. 3).

Protest songs that do exist are not heard on mainstream media

The dearth of protest songs can also be attributed to the mainstream media. The story about the goose that laid the golden egg is mirrored in the history of FM's free-form format. It became so popular, and so profitable that rules were imposed. No longer based on the counterculture's standards, it morphed into a programmed AOR format. Rock record labels also began to achieve financial success in the 1970s. And that era, often called the 'Me Decade', was not friendly to protests. 'By then conditions in the music business had changed radically,' Pontiac laments. 'For obvious reasons the new music business had little use for activism, instead they saw The Beatles in The Knack and punk rock was successfully repackaged as supposedly edgy New Wave acts ideal for ushering in the Reagan years' (Pontiac, 2004). Musicians' careers are not helped, and may be harmed, by any political action. For example, in 2003, New Jersey radio station WCHR banned Jethro Tull after the band's lead singer, Ian Anderson, was quoted in a local paper saying, 'I hate to see the American flag hanging out of every bloody station wagon. It's easy to confuse patriotism with nationalism. Flag-waving ain't gonna do it' (quoted in Cave, 2003).

We now have conglomerates such as Clear Channel – a corporation with strong ties to the Bush administration (Hajdu, 2004, p. 33) – in control of much of the music that gets heard on radio or seen in concert. For these reasons, the majority of protest songs in the past three decades have been released on indie labels – those without the capital clout to get any attention from radio, TV or mainstream print media. Indies currently make up about 14 per cent of releases (Bruno, 2003). Addressing punk in particular, Johnny Temple wrote:

> Today there's only a minimal chance that any music fan – young or old – will encounter through any major media outlet the songs of protest that continue to spring forth from the punk underground; the major record companies have succeeded in erecting a pay-to-play industry that effectively shuts out any band whose label cannot pony up hundreds of thousands of dollars for radio, video, retail and print promotion. (1999, p. 17)

But today more than ever, major media outlets are not the only game in town. And unlike the media conglomerates, which are friendly to the status quo, the underground media – seriously indie labels, innumerable internet sites, rock 'zines, and college radio – do not shy away from protest songs. Protest songs against the Bush administration abound in the underground. Among them are two compilation albums put out by Fat Wreck full of punk fury: Protest-Records.com, a site created by Thurston Moore of Sonic Youth, which collects and makes available free downloading of MP3s of newly minted protest songs from a wide variety of artists, and a website of dozens of anti-Bush parodies, using familiar music to accompany piercing protest lyrics. Major artists, including R.E.M., Lenny Kravitz, the Beastie Boys and Sonic Youth, have posted their protest material in cyberspace too. Yet all of this underground activity is below the radar of the vast majority of rock fans, let alone the general public.

Protest songs aren't heard as protest songs

More important to understanding the dearth of rock protest songs, and more interesting too, is that, often, protest songs that are heard are not heard as protest songs. There are many reasons why a song's intended original political meaning escapes listeners. Those reasons are based on actions of commercial mediators, the limitations of listeners and factors inherent in the music. The classic-rock format that has proven so profitable for rock radio for the past two decades would seem to provide songs of all times with a seemingly indefinite shelf life. But is the song written in one era as a protest song understood as such when heard decades later? Carl Dahlhaus argues that a song's meaning may change over time; it 'is not confined to its moments of origin' (quoted in Mäkelä, 2004, p. 223). At best, as Mäkelä optimistically argues, 'Popular songs may have political potential in terms of content, and they may be used in particular contexts of struggles, but since popular music generally is transitory by nature, songs can be connected to different political agendas in quite specific circumstances' (2004, p. 179). Nostalgia is the preferred mode for classic-rock fans, whether the listener had been around at the song's birth or wished they had been. Hearing a protest song through the filter of nostalgia for the real or imagined past removes its potential political appeal.

Rock's mediators can actively remove the political thrust of any protest song, and not merely by encouraging nostalgia. There are various practices that render protest songs non-toxic. The most incendiary songs are reduced to impotency by reframing them as commercial jingles to aid and abet commercial sales. Whole styles permeated with significant protest have easily been co-opted. One example: 'Advertising and fashion pilfered riot grrrl imagery reducing once powerful symbols to accessories,' Pontiac argues. 'When *Spin* magazine ran a glam photo of Marilyn Monroe version 9.0 Gwen Stefani with the headline "Riot Grrlie," it was easy to understand why many riot grrrls suspected a conspiracy against them' (Pontiac, 2004). Protest songs have also been declawed when they've been used in Hollywood movie soundtracks or accompanied by cute and/or nonsensical MTV videos. Research indicates that viewers take the meaning of songs from the visual, not the lyrical, input.

Misapprehensions

Rock itself is partly to blame for misapprehension of the protest songs, and in rock the music triumphs over the words, or at least wrestles them to a tie. Rock's focus is on the body, not the head. Asked why Spinal Tap, a fictional but true-to-life band whose creation was based on solid research, didn't do more protest songs, even during the 1960s, one of the members replied: 'How can you dance or rock or move your body or shake your fist or your fanny when you're going, "Oh, right, the politician's being bad?" That's not what we're about. Rock 'n roll is sex music, body music'.[7] Contrast rock with a style of music noted for protest songs, folk, where the music clearly backgrounds the lyrics. Even when the vocals are emphasized in rock, it is emotionality rather than clear enunciation that matters. 'The tone of voice is more important ... than the actual articulation of particular lyrics,' maintains Simon Frith. 'We can thus identify with a song whether we understand the words or not, whether we already know the singer or not, because it is the voice – not the lyrics – to which we immediately respond.' Frith argues that the vocals in rock often serve '... as a sign of individual personality rather than as something necessarily mouthing words' (1987b, p. 145).

The intelligibility of lyrics is further reduced because they tend to be heard as phrases, rather than as full texts. Does the phrase that we do hear sum up the song? Does it stand in opposition to the thrust of the lyrics? A nice example of opposition is 'Fortunate Son' by Creedence Clearwater Revival. The first verse, not difficult to comprehend, starts with: 'Some folks are born made to wave the flag / Ooh, they're red white and blue.' The title is a repeated phrase throughout the song, which is about the hypocrisy of wealthy people who avidly support the Vietnam War but make sure that their children do not serve in it. 'Mystifyingly,' writes Don Atapattu (2004) about the song, it 'was often used by American television networks following 9/11 to shore up patriotic sentiment, although the lyrics do not support such a position.'

Lyrics are frequently heard incorrectly. We are all familiar with the experience of learning, sometimes months or years later, that what we thought we heard was not at all what the singer said? People readily admit to these radical errors. Consider the early 1970s hit by Argent, 'Hold Your Head Up'. The song's key line is usually heard as 'Hold your head up, whoa'. The word is not 'whoa' but 'woman'; the song is a feminist anthem. Or it would be if anyone heard it that way. Or focus on Springsteen's 'Born in the USA' which has a line that reads 'I had a brother at Khe Sahn'. Some hear it as 'I had a brother I can't solve', or 'I had a brother in Arkansas', or 'I had a brother, I can't stop'. Is it any wonder that the song isn't understood in the same way as it was written? This is such a common phenomenon that there's even a term for it: mondegreens.[8] Mondegreens are like malapropisms, but instead of saying the wrong words, we hear the wrong words. There are hundreds of websites with collections of them and a book about them; *Scuse Me While I Kiss This Guy,* gets its title from a popular mondegreen from Jimi Hendrix's 'Purple Haze'. Undoubtedly, the context in which people tend to hear songs – on commercial radio surrounded by ads and all the other non-protest songs – also encourages failures in comprehension.

(Mis)understandings/misreadings of songs

But even if the words are heard correctly, they are often, for any number of reasons, completely misunderstood. The point of the song, its message of protest, can be entirely lost. Of all the reasons for the dearth of protest songs, this is probably the most significant one. Songwriters don't help matters. Their lyrics, even if read, are often rather ambiguous or oblique. Consider the popular 1960s song by The Monkees, 'Last Train to Clarksville'. You can't 'get' the anti-war sentiment in the lyrics unless you knew that Clarksville is a city near an army training camp in Tennessee. Or what was the point of Buffalo Springfield's 'For What It's Worth' from the same era? To make any sense of the well-known song, you need extra information, such as interviews with the writers. 'Rock the Casbah', a hit for The Clash, is another song whose message requires more than the lyrics deliver. (It was a response to a ban on rock music by an Islamic cleric. During the Gulf War in 1990 the US military played the song to the troops.)

Read the lyrics to another 1960s era chestnut, John Fogerty's 'Who'll Stop the Rain': 'Long as I remember the rain been comin' down / Clouds of myst'ry pourin' confusion on the ground. / Good men through the ages, tryin' to find the sun / And I wonder, still I wonder, who'll stop the rain.' What is that very well-known song about? I've heard it hundreds of times, when it was popular and ever since, never realizing until recently reading a newspaper feature that it was a protest song. Rock critic Robert Hilburn contends that the song is about 'the helplessness millions felt watching the body count in a war that seemed to them pointless and heartbreaking'. Hilburn praises the song, and the songwriter's new protest song 'Déjà Vu (All Over Again)' adding, with unconscious irony, 'One of Fogerty's strengths as a songwriter has always been his ability to cast tunes in a timeless and universal vein' (2004, p. 3).

Such songwriting is not confined to any era or style. 'U2's Bono says he is attracted to music, like much of Dylan's, that leaves a lot of room for the listener to fill in the blanks: "I didn't grow up in the tradition of pop songwriters who feel it is essential to make everything clear to the listener"' (quoted in Hilburn, 2004, p. 3). Lyricist for the long-respected punk band Bad Religion, Greg Graffin, happily admits in the liner notes to his 2004 release, *The Empire Strikes First*, that although each song is specific to some current issue, 'the songs are universal enough that in ten years time they should still hold up quite well'. David Segal contends that 'Springsteen understands that rock, like most art, doesn't endure when its point is persuasion or propaganda. The vaguer you keep it, the longer it lasts' (2003, p. 50). Radiohead's Thom Yorke embraces the problem, declaring: 'I think that's the nature of good art, it should be interpreted and misinterpreted' (quoted in Burton, 2003). So many protest songs are riddled with ambiguities and vague allusions for both artistic and commercial reasons. In part, lyricists wish to be poetic, creating lyrics replete with metaphors like Fogerty's use of 'rain'. A protest song also has a far longer shelf life if it is oblique, since it can be heard generations later merely as a song relieved of the baggage of a protest that may no longer be relevant or popular. And one can't underestimate the use of 'difficult' lyrics as camouflage to obtain commercial radio airplay.

In this respect, is Springsteen's 'Born in the USA' a patriotic rocker or a critical protest song? Mondegreens aside, if you consider the chorus, vigorously repeating the tune's title, you'd think it is a flag-waver and could understand why the Republican campaign to re-elect Ronald Reagan wanted to use it in their ads. But if you consider the verses, the song's thrust is a rant against the government's treatment of Vietnam veterans. Which interpretation is correct? Well, if you want to privilege the author's intentions, or understand it in the context of Springsteen's other work, clearly it is a protest song. But if you just reference the song itself, its meaning is, as the postmodernists say, indeterminate. At a Springsteen concert in July 1984, I witnessed many in the audience, as a patriotic gesture, waving American flags that they had brought. More recently, Outkast's 'Bombs Over Baghdad' has been given a similar dual reading (Hilburn, 2003, E1).

A similar double-coding appears in Rush's '2112'. The song's narrative, set in a future dystopia, involves the confrontation between the authorities who control the music people hear and a person who discovers a hidden guitar and learns to make his own music. I interviewed scores of the band's fans, all of whom were very familiar with this composition, and many of whom could recite all of the readily discernible lyrics. I asked whose side Rush was on, the single guitarist or the controllers (the Priests of the Temple of Syrinx). Over 70 per cent thought, incorrectly, that the band was on the Priests' side. Their misreading was encouraged by the powerful music that accompanies the Priests (the music for the lone guitarist is soft and weak). In other words, the music is at cross-purposes with the lyrics.

The way in which sarcasm is problematic became clear to me at a 1983 Dead Kennedys concert. As the punk band began their best known song, 'Kill the Poor', a stinging indictment of America's resentfully hard-hearted mistreatment of those in poverty, a tall young man with an impressive blond mohawk who was standing near me shouted out: 'Yeah, kill them. Burn down Cabrini Green.' There was not a hint of sarcasm in his injunction to tear down the infamous Chicago public housing project. In the same vein, East Bay Ray, the band's guitarist relates:

> Someone wrote us from South Africa saying how much they liked 'Kill the Poor' because that's what they needed to do, rather than transport them to their homelands. That was a scary letter. We had problems with that in Germany too, because the licensee for the record over there couldn't be bothered to put the lyric sheet in with the record so we ran across all these guys, 'Ya, ya, kill the poor. I hate Turkish people. Great. Let's do it!' (Quoted in Gregorio, 1985, p. 3)

The age-old tendency to hear what we want or expect to hear is a significant cause of misconstruing lyrics. Our prejudices and resentments towards others, and our own ubiquitous neuroses, have always served to make human communication a dicey proposition.

The astonishing variety of interpretations and uses of John Lennon's 'Imagine' is a case in point. The lyrics are easily discernible to the ear; the vocals are at the front and centre above rather quiet piano-based instrumentation. Nonetheless, the song has been seen as apolitical and utopian by some and as a call to communism by others (Mäkelä, 2004, p. 222). In 1987 'Imagine' was sung as a greeting to Margaret Thatcher by members attending a Conservative Party conference held at Wembley in London. But it was also used in Eastern Europe against the conservative policies of communist governments. And the BBC in 1991, at the time of the Gulf War, restricted broadcasts of the song, because they believed that it, along with some other songs, might distress members of their audience. 'Further, even though "Imagine" has been considered to have an explicitly secular message and even though at the time of its publication many religious listeners apparently were disturbed by its imagery, it has later become a favorite tune at modern-minded religious events' (Mäkelä, 2004, p. 223). High school students in Wisconsin in 1972 were prevented from naming 'Imagine' as their class song; their principal deemed it to be 'anti-religious and anti-American with communist overtones' (quoted in Mäkelä, 2004, p. 223). The various groups recruiting 'Imagine' to their cause may be due to the sheer popularity of the song – that is, the song as sound not as lyrics. As Waldman notes, 'Today a familiar rock hit from the 1950s, 1960s, or 1970s can enliven a rally in California, Maine, and Alabama – Democrat or Republican' (quoted in Segal, 2003).

Effectiveness

The paucity of rock protest songs is even more profound if we define them in terms of their effectiveness. Even when they are understood as intended by their creators, if we address protest songs pragmatically, their impact on political and social change is questionable. Detractors of rock, who tend to be cultural determinists, have constantly assumed that protest songs are powerful recruiting tools. Rock songs have been condemned as causing people to become sexually promiscuous, commit suicide, become Satanists, abuse drugs, become political radicals and the like (Weinstein, 2000). But there is no serious evidence for such power, or even for motivating action to achieve the more noble ends advocated in what are conventionally seen as protest songs. 'There is little, if any, concrete or empirical evidence that songs *do* in fact have an independent impact upon attitudes in the political arena,' wrote R. Serge Denisoff (1970, p. 807) in the midst of the golden age of protest songs.

Some have argued, like Tillman, that 'rock may simply be too sensual and aesthetic and lacks the purposive-rational orientation that is required to realistically engage in political action' (quoted in McDonald, 1988, p. 488). What protest songs do is preach to the choir and, perhaps, to the congregation. Religious leaders have literally been doing just that for millennia, for good reason. Prayers, hymns and sermons bolster our faith and reinforce our knowledge, if not our practice, of what our religion preaches. Singing patriotic hymns or reciting a pledge of allegiance to a nation work in the same way. In a similar fashion, protest songs mainly rally rather than recruit, the troops. Like advertisements, at best they can reinforce our beliefs and perhaps heighten our resolve to act. 'In the context of social movements songs evidence the creation of moral reaffirmation rather than the function of building outside support,' concludes Denisoff (1970, p. 807).

Successful evangelical outreach work through songs probably does not induce conversion, but appeals to an impulse that already consciously exists in a person whose feelings are ambivalent. Yet the impact of protest songs may also work in the opposite direction from their author's intent by evoking 'negative responses from nonbelievers' (Denisoff and Levine, 1971, p. 121) that inspire their active opposition. Some have gone as far as suggesting that protest songs may even work against social movements as a surrogate for activity itself. One critic reminds us of reports by those who attended a major Pete Seeger concert at Carnegie Hall in 1963: 'For a few short hours the audience had the illusion that by singing they, too, were fighting' (quoted in Rosenthal, 2001, p. 14). The songwriter of activist punk band Vortis sees his music as 'providing symbolic and emotional support to activists' (quoted in Weinstein, 2004). That is, he sees the impact of his protest songs as meaningful only to those able to appreciate the sentiments; he knows he's preaching, or in this case, singing, to the choir. 'In the absence of a significant anti-war movement through which the music could be employed, contemporary protest songs have purpose but not function,' writes David Hajdu (2004, p. 33). 'Pete Seeger used to say, "It's not how good a song is that matters, it's how much good a song does." What good is the most impassioned challenge to the Iraq war on its own, in the face of public indifference?' (quoted in Hajdu, 2004, p. 33).

Despite all of the good reasons for questioning the effectiveness of rock protest songs, they do sometimes function to spur political commitment. This result almost always occurs when they are created and performed in the context of 'some supportive organizational form such as a social movement ' (Denisoff, 1970, p. 821). When there is a popular movement for social or political change, protest songs play their major role of reaffirming resolve and firing up the troops, and can even draw outsiders into the movement. When such a movement does not exist, the messages of protest songs are 'intellectualized without any possible social action' (Denisoff, 1970, p. 821). Both defenders and detractors of rock music have overvalorized the effectiveness of protest songs. The truth is far more modest than the myths would have us believe.

Notes

1. Praise of these policies, actions or administrations aren't protests but, because many of the praise songs (most of which are found in country music, a genre which tends towards jingoism in the same way that gospel praises the lord) are conceived when there is opposition in existence, they should be classified as protest songs.
2. Re-ax songs are thus relevant for a very short time. 'Lennon had plans to start releasing 45 rpm singles made of cardboard, a kind of musical newsprint. It was a brilliant idea, in that most topical songs are disposable and best forgotten in time' (Hajdu, 2004, p. 33).
3. 'Disaffection and rebellion that had once led to political commitment were leading instead to the drug culture, the sexual revolution, the cult of Eastern religions, rock, music, and the world of "hippies" and "dropouts" ... But the new culture and the new politics did not reinforce each other; they clashed. The heart of the counterculture was not commitment but withdrawal; it was the search for what Norman O. Brown called the "Dionysian ego," personal fulfilment through "narcissism and erotic exuberance' (Brinkley, 1987, p. 16).
4. As a result of the complaints from various sources, the video was altered after a few

concerts, eliminating the image of Bush.

5. For the past few years I've asked students in my Sociology of Rock class to name protest songs, and, except for the contributions of two or three students, all of them came from this 'golden age'.

6. The end of the protest era came a few years earlier. Greil Marcus states that 'after Jackson State and Kent State, people got really scared. They found out that you could really get killed by doing this stuff at any time. They began to back off and they began to shut up' (quoted in Hargus, 1997, np).

7. The Spinal Tap script can be found at http://spinaltapfan.com/atozed/TAP00414.htm.

8. The term 'mondegreen' comes from a 1954 article by Sylvia Wright in the *Atlantic Magazine* in which she describes how she (mis)heard an old folk song about the death of the Earl of Moray. The line 'And laid him on the green' was heard as 'And Lady Mondegreen'. People are so enamoured of their own and others' mondegreens that thousands of websites are devoted to misread of lyrics.

Chapter 2

The decline and rebirth of folk-protest music

Jerry Rodnitsky

On a 2004 NPR radio show that featured singer Judy Collins, a caller asked Collins when she would start singing protest songs again. Collins replied that some of her current songs were protest songs, but that they did not necessarily protest what was in current vogue. She also noted that she 'was never a protest singer', she simply sang about things that mattered to her. Many current singer-songwriters would echo Collins's approach. They would insist that their songs do protest aspects of modern life, but they are not protest singers. It sounds somewhat like the famous feminist disclaimer: 'I am not a feminist, but I believe in equal pay and a woman's right to choose'. Indeed, American folk songs had traditionally vented individual emotions and problems, but were seldom connected to any political or social protest movements.

However in the 1960s Judy Collins had been a protest singer. She pointedly gave up protest music back in 1969, because she no longer wanted to be 'a political agitator' with her music, constantly facing an audience she recognized from the last rally. She suddenly decided that protest songs were 'like hitting people over the head' and 'finger pointing' and that the end result was 'not a statement of emotional depth, but of unity in the face of an … enemy or idea which does not agree with you' (Anonymous, 1969, pp. 45–46). As Arlo Guthrie noted at that time: 'You don't accomplish very much singing protest songs to people who agree with you. Everybody just has a good time thinking they're right' (Anonymous, 1966, p. 110).

Even earlier, in 1965, Bob Dylan made the first important move against protest music. He suddenly stopped writing protest songs of any kind and, at about the same time, switched from acoustic to electric guitar. Indeed, Dylan declared his artistic independence from movements and national issues. He made it crystal clear in a remarkable song, 'My Back Pages'. Here Dylan proclaimed that he had oversimplified right and wrong in his earlier songs and had become what he hated most – a preacher. One line noted that he had convinced himself that liberty only meant 'equality in school'. However, at the end at each scathing verse, denouncing social protest movements he had participated in, Dylan explained that while he was older back then, he was a lot younger now.

Thus, like so many folk music trends, the movement away from specific, topical protest songs was initiated by Bob Dylan, the most creative and influential American performer of the 1960s. In 1965 he also combined folk music and rock 'n' roll, which the music industry labelled folk-rock. This not only allowed record companies to merge college and high school markets, but also brought hazy message songs to teenagers and the best-selling singles chart. Good examples would be Dylan's 'Mr Tambourine Man' and Paul Simon's 'Sounds of Silence'. These were really do-it-yourself protest songs, since you could read many different problems into them. Throughout the 1960s and 1970s folk-rock became heavier and more electric, and those who supported it as teens remained faithful as collegians. Starting in 1965 there was a sudden media hunger for thoughtful songs such as 'Universal Soldier,' a pacifist song, written by Sioux Indian Buffy Sainte-Marie and recorded by Glen Campbell, and idiotic songs such as 'Eve of Destruction,' a thermonuclear warning song recorded by Barry McGuire. However, there was often a wide gulf between the message song and its commercial value. Thus Glen Campbell, who made a lot of money by recording the pacifist 'Universal Soldier', later argued that if a man was not willing to die for his country, he was no real man. Moreover, teenagers were now dancing the latest steps to the newest folk-rock, topical songs and often paid no attention to the lyrics.

Folk music led the way towards relevant 1960s music and continues to play that role today. Protest songs were always a part of American folk music and showcasing them within the folk spectrum gave them a wholesome image. In this all-American guise, folk singers invaded the musical vacuum on college campuses during the late 1950s. While jazz had become increasingly complex and abstract, rock 'n' roll had become more nonsensical and meaningless. For example, rock hits such as 'Shboom' and rock lyrics such as 'splish splash, I was taking a bath' were senseless. In contrast, folk songs were usually filled with meaning and integrity, and protest songs are still often hidden in contemporary folk and topical music. However, after 1975 there were few well-defined, mass social movements to tie them to.

The 1960s had brought events and mass movements that called folk guitarists to arms, and the civil rights movement was the catalyst. Martin Luther King's movement was clearly a sing-in, as well as a sit-in, campaign. While black Southern activists wrote new songs, and 'We Shall Overcome' became the civil rights anthem, Northern folk singers developed leaders and anthems of their own. Performer-composers such as Bob Dylan and Phil Ochs recorded both general and specific songs against discrimination, the arms race and the military–industrial establishment. Song titles such as Ochs' 'I Ain't Marching Anymore' and Dylan's 'Talking World War Three Blues' suggested common mass concerns. Young, gifted singers, such as Judy Collins and Joan Baez, reached out for an even wider audience. Pleasant melodic groups such as The Kingston Trio and The Brothers Four popularized folk-protest even more. As commercial success increased, protest characteristics were diluted, but they remained vivid elements of popular music. The syrupy, apolitical Kingston Trio was challenged by the more cynical and irreverent Chad Mitchell Trio, and by 1966 both groups were surpassed in popularity by the aggressively liberal trio, Peter, Paul and Mary.

Although pacifist and anti-war music wound down with the Vietnam War after 1970, feminist and ecology music began to hit their stride in 1972, even though a backlash against the 1960s counterculture accelerated until the 1973 Watergate hearings. Throughout every decade since the 1960s, however, music continued to hold its mesmerizing grip on American youth. Frank Zappa put it best in 1967 when he noted that many youths were loyal to neither 'flag, country, nor doctrine, but only to music' (quoted in Kofsky, 1969, p. 256). Increasingly, however, the folk-rock protest song radiated general discontent and a vague, anti-establishment mood, as opposed to focusing on specific issues or evils. The protest flavour was still there and, if anything, the fervour had increased, yet the lyrics were now less important and often could not be heard clearly over the music anyway. This new psychedelic music registered a protest of form rather than substance. It often featured sexually explicit lyrics, high creativity and non-conformist delivery. It presented a hazy, but direct protest to white, middle-class America. Protest songs had increasingly been diluted by their success. By 1969 the most popular folk-rock songs of Dylan, Simon and Garfunkel, The Byrds and others had largely evaporated into an existential haze. By trying to be all things to all people, these popular songs became universal protest ballads. One could read whatever one wanted into the lines. By saying everything, they in effect said nothing.

Of all the 1960s activist movements, the one with the most staying power, and perhaps the most important, was the Women's Liberation Movement. This feminist movement was also the most divisive, since it largely excluded males. Topical music was particularly useful to young feminists, who followed the New Left maxim of organizing around your own oppression. Furthermore, since feminism pioneered consciousness-raising, what better device to accomplish this than topical songs? Women's liberation music was very diverse, ranging from workers' songs to ballads of cultural pride and psychological independence. Compared to the previous women's movement – the Suffrage Movement – the new mood was much more strident and the goals much more fundamental. Early 1960s feminist songs such as 'The Modern Union Maid' (a parody of Guthrie's 1936 ballad about wives of union men), 'Stand and Be Counted'(a marching song), 'The Freedom Ladies' (a firm, but humorous declaration of independence), and 'Papa' (a put-down of sexist male rock musicians) were all adept at capturing the verve and complexity of the early feminist movement The first feminist singers were usually obscure groups of rather amateur musicians, but they often made up for their musical weaknesses with their spirit and sisterly solidarity. More polished individual feminist singers such as Holly Near would emerge in the late 1970s.

In fact, women folk singers who did not explicitly identify with feminism, such as Joan Baez, Judy Collins and Malvina Reynolds, were excellent feminist role models throughout their careers. They often sang songs about independent, aggressive women and they ably competed with the best male topical singers. They pre-dated Women's Liberation – a term first used in 1968. Although there was a women's movement in the early 1960s, dating either from John Kennedy's Federal Commission on the Status of Women in 1960 or from Betty Friedan's 1963 publication of *The Feminine Mystique*, the Women's Liberation Movement originated in 1966 when young 'New Left' activist college women split from male-dominated radical groups such as the SNCC (Student Nonviolent Coordinating Committee) and SDS (Students for a Democratic Society).

These younger feminists completely transformed the early 1960s women's movement, with its stress on equal rights, into a diverse countercultural movement that concentrated on capturing and changing the next generation of men and women. Increasingly, it found more talented feminist songwriters and musicians who had themselves grown up with the movement. These feminists had also grown up with protest songs, but since they had separated from the New Left just as topical music declined, they escaped the malaise. Feminist songwriters felt that everything they wrote broke new ground. Whether they performed traditional songs, wrote topical ballads or wrote about their own experiences, they felt that they were speaking to the conditions of all women. Women's Liberation greatly encouraged women songwriters. In 1976 the introduction to *All Our Lives: A Woman's Songbook* summed up the fruits of the past decade: 'As women and as feminists who love folk music and who love to sing, we have produced this book as a reflection of our own struggles in a society which still has so little room for a woman with a mind of her own—even less for a woman with a song of her own' (Cheney, 1976, p. 3). By the early 1970s the second wave of feminist singers was producing diverse music that reflected the wide world of feminism. For example, *Hazel and Alice*, a 1973 recording, featured Hazel Dickens and Alice Gerard – two middle aged bluegrass musicians with roots deep into traditional rural music. The best of their original songs were two feminist tunes, Gerard's 'Custom Made Woman Blues' and Hazel Dickens' 'Don't Put Her Down, You Helped Put Her There'. The first song covered the problems of a rural wife trying to follow *Cosmopolitan* magazine advice on how to hold her man and the second put the blame for the female bar floozy squarely on her male companions. Hazel and Alice, with their rural, family working-class orientation, neatly bridged the gap between the consciousness-raising, countercultural feminist records and those of the more overtly political, socialist Left. The remnants of America's young Left had increasingly come to recognize the threat that women's liberation posed to their already declining ranks. After 1972 they began to highlight women as a uniquely oppressed victim of the capitalist state.

Two good musical examples of this socialist–feminist relationship were Barbara Dane's 1973 album, *I Hate the Capitalist System*, and the Red Star Singers 1974 album, *The Force of Life*. Dane's recording proceeded from 1930s union songs, such as the title song, to a ballad about the 1970 Kent State Massacre. Yet the album ended with one of Dane's songs, 'Working Class Woman', which was filled with socialist women's liberation themes. The song's heroine works in a factory and, although her kids are in high school, the boss still calls her 'girl'. Despite her many problems, the song heroine always sees a brighter future for women. One verse ends with the triumphant declaration that she's 'a hard working woman' and the future is hers.

The Force of Life by the Red Star Singers was a much livelier album, with a contemporary 1960s anger. The group appeared as a cross between the Yippies and the Stanford SDS with a few socialist and Third World women thrown in for good measure. The songs were all upbeat and hit hard at the image of an oppressive national state. Songs such as 'Pig Nixon' and 'Vietnam Will Win' quickly told you where the Red Star Singers stood politically. However, each album side also featured a militant women's liberation song – 'I Still Ain't Satisfied' and 'The Women's Health Song'. These songs mocked the progress of women's liberation as 'co-optation'. One line, for example, declared that women weren't asking for crumbs; they wanted the whole deal. The most talented, and hardest to characterize, early feminist singer was Holly Near. Her first two albums, *Hang in There* (1973) and *Holly Near: A Live Album* (1974) showed steady growth and brilliant singer-songwriter talents. *Hang In There* stressed songs against the Vietnam War, but also included two sensitive feminist songs – 'It's More Important to Me' (about how competition for men drives women apart) and 'Strong' (a beautiful ballad about women's social conditioning). On her live album, 'Feeling Better' (a satire on high school sex-role expectations) was the best showcase for her feminist ideas.

On balance, early women's liberation music was far better than one would expect. Art and politics are often joined, but seldom compatible; and women's liberation music was necessarily political. Yet political mission often fuels the imagination, while audience enthusiasm can provide creative incentives. Considering the political pressures, the most surprising thing about the feminist movement and its music was its diversity. Feminist critics sometimes patronized women who made music in traditional ways – with acoustic guitars or piano accompaniment. The big challenge was proving that women could play rock and that hard rock need not be sexist to be good. But the best feminist music largely followed women's traditional musical forms, and, in practice, the traditional feminist singers were not put down. For one thing, the women's movement stressed the need to support *all* women artists. For another, feminists realized the potential that quality feminist music offered for making new recruits think seriously about the women's movement. The traditional women whom the movement hoped to attract were more likely to seriously consider a subtle, sensitive, well-crafted ballad than a second-rate, derivative rock number. The woman rock musician (Bonnie Raitt or Joan Jett, for example) would later get more attention, but they often drew attention to themselves at the expense of their music. Feminism had quickly concluded that the real power of music was its ability to communicate rather than its ability to shock or cross male boundaries. A host of effective feminist singer-songwriters, such as, Willie Tyson, Meg Christian and Kristin Lems, would follow the example of the pioneer feminist singers.

Most attacks against protest music came from the Right; however, music can also have conservative sentiments. The preponderance of left-wing music has perpetuated the idea that political music always involves humanitarian attacks against the status quo. Historically, this has not always been true. The Ku Klux Klan, for example, used songs to further its movement, and throughout the 1950s and 1960s conservative and patriotic country and western songs made popular music an ideological battleground. The conservative songs were few in number, but ballads such as Merle Haggard's 'The Fightin Side of Me' (attacking pacifist sentiments) and 'Okie From Muskogee' (attacking hippie protestors) as well as Charlie Drake's 'Welfare Cadillac' (ridiculing welfare recipients) were clearly protest songs.

In the 1970s and 1980s political songs were a much smaller part of popular music than in the 1960–1973 period, but they were far from obsolete. In the 1960s and early 1970s political songs such as 'Blowin' in the Wind' were on the top ten chart, and anti-war songs were featured in best-selling rock albums by bands such as Country Joe and the Fish. The more recent political songs remain a powerful American art form and played a role in America's contemporary social struggles. Yet, as good as they often were, they attracted a much smaller audience, being usually heard only by left-wing activists. For example, in the 1960s Charlie King's songs might have attracted a mass audience, but in the late 1970s and 1980s he was known only by seasoned left-wing activists who heard him at fund-raising concerts or political rallies. His songs of social protest were reminiscent of the best protest songs by Bob Dylan and Tom Paxton, while his wry humour recalled comedian Mort Sahl and Jerry Rubin, a leader of the Youth International Party, both of whom were known for their rather offbeat humour. However, the always fickle youthful audience kept moving on to new types of stylish rock music, from disco to punk to Metallica to grunge. Suddenly the music and style meant everything, and the message was in the music and not the lyrics.

Not only protest music, but folk music as well, had lost its identity. This had happened gradually since the late 1960s when folk-rock first devoured folk music. Rock had assimilated the whole of American music, from ragtime to gospel and it now added folk music. Here and there, record stores began filing folk-protest albums in with those of the rock superstars. There was surely no other place for Bob Dylan, but it somehow seemed sacrilegious to find Joan Baez albums stacked in front of those of the theatrical transvestite, David Bowie, or to see Phil Ochs albums sandwiched between Procul Harum records and those of Nico and the Velvet Underground. Rock often overpowered meaning by highlighting the music. As rock music and concerts introduced stage theatrics and fancy lighting, as well as generally increasing the sound volume, it became more difficult to centre on the lyrics. Rock concerts provided musical performances to see and hear but hardly to think about. Thus, the strength of folk music – strong solid lyrics – has largely been the weakness of rock. Whereas Woody Guthrie and Pete Seeger played below their guitar skills to highlight their lyrics, rock groups who try to be masters of sound often become prisoners of noise and theatrics. From folk-rock to acid-rock to country-rock, the music moved on but in no particular direction. Rock lacked any tangible reason for being except commercial success. True, folk-protest music had its commercial side, but it left an important social legacy.

Nonetheless, a few popular singers who had been affected by folk-protest in the 1960s when they were growing up continued to write a message song or two along with their more popular songs. These artists became known as singer-songwriters by the 1980s. Good examples would be John Prine in the 1970s, Mary Chapin Carpenter in the 1980s and Iris Dement in the 1990s. All three of these became known largely as country singers, because nobody knew what else to call people who often played acoustic guitar with electronic back-up bands. The generic singer-songwriter label was also pinned on those whose lyrics sometimes carried a social or philosophical message or appeared to border on poetry. In a subtler and unstated way singer-songwriter also meant that the songwriter was the only one who recorded the song and thus the song was personal and seldom recorded by another singer.

On a simpler level the singer-songwriter was seen as a storyteller. The stories sometimes had a social message that commented on American society; however, more often the story related the problems of the singer. But some very popular singer-songwriters of the 1970s and 1980s such as Bruce Springsteen, Jackson Browne and Billy Joel, sang a few story songs with social messages about groups of oppressed Americans. Billy Joel sang about victimized troops in Vietnam in his song,' Goodnight Saigon' and displaced Ohio factory workers in his ballad 'Allentown'. Springsteen wrote songs that highlighted the problems of lower-middle-class Americans (the group from which he emerged) and even one about Tom Joad – John Steinbeck's fictional proletarian hero in *The Grapes of Wrath*. Rap music, too, often focused on the social problems of African-Americans, although the goal was almost always commercial success rather than solving social problems.

Most popular rock music was oblivious to social concerns, although some notable exceptions stand out. In the 1980s rock superstars U2 and their lead singer, Bono, led the way in rediscovering social conscience. The No Nukes, Live Aid and Farm Aid benefit concerts and the 'We Are the World' benefit record showed even clearer connections between politics and music. The 1979 No Nukes concert at Madison Square Gardens in New York brought together Carly Simon, James Taylor, The Doobie Brothers, Jackson Browne, Bruce Springsteen,

Tom Petty, Bonnie Raitt and Crosby, Stills and Nash. Yet the concert featured only one obvious protest song – Bob Dylan's 1960s anthem, 'The Times They Are A-Changin'. The Farm Aid concerts at several locations during the 1980s and 1990s were organized primarily with the aid of Willie Nelson who brought in Nashville Country stars such as Waylon Jennings and even enlisted Bob Dylan to help needy farmers. Yet here, too, the relationship between the music and the cause was hazy at best. The aid concerts established that the superstar singers who donated their time had a social conscience. But most fans attending the concerts came primarily to hear performers sing their hit songs. The singers were usually not even part-time activists or protestors and neither were the vast majority of the audience.

The 1985 Live Aid Concert in Philadelphia perhaps made the clearest connection between music, protest and activism. Joan Baez's six minutes on stage were a good example. She opened with two verses of 'Amazing Grace' for the older people and followed with several verses of 'We Are the World', so that the young kids could sing along with a chorus they knew. But, before singing, Baez opened the US section of the worldwide show with a call to arms:

> Good morning children of the Eighties! This is your Woodstock and it's long overdue. And it's nice to know the money out of your pockets will go to feed hungry children. I can think of no more glorious way of starting our part of the day than by saying grace together which means that we thank each of us… for the many blessings that we have in a world in which so many people have nothing. And when we say this grace, we also reach deep in our hearts and say that we will move a little from the comfort of our lives to understand their hurt and their discomfort. And that will make their lives richer and it will make our lives real. Amazing Grace, how sweet the sound. (1987, pp. 357–58)

Baez had suddenly taken us back to the 1960s and used songs to cement old and young in a proactive group.

Unfortunately the various aid concerts existed in a musical vacuum. There was no ongoing stream of topical and protest music or performers that had mass audiences. Here and there, various annual folk festivals and concerts temporarily brought mostly older people together to enjoy new topical music and wax nostalgic about old performers and their songs. However, the 1960s generation which supported the nostalgic folk revival concerts had generally become affluent and uninterested in protest. This led to some ironic juxtapositions. I recall a 1982 concert in Fort Worth, Texas that headlined Peter, Paul and Mary and included Tom Paxton. Paxton sang his recent song, a parody of 'Ghost Riders in the Sky' entitled 'Yuppies in the Sky'. It ridiculed the young urban professionals of the 'me generation' and their penchant for $200 boots and BMW cars. The baby boom audience, mostly 40-something yuppies themselves laughed and applauded the song and, afterwards, many marched out to the parking lot in their $200 boots to find their BMWs. It reminded me of protest singer Julius

Lester's complaint in 1967. Lester said that he had heard that Woody Guthrie had carved 'This Machine Kills Fascists' on his guitar. Lester added, 'Maybe his did. Mine didn't. The fascists just applauded me.'

Some hoped Bob Dylan's Rolling Thunder tour in 1975 signalled the start of another era of protest music led by the great man. On the surface it looked promising. The tour was an attempt to aid a supposedly wronged and imprisoned boxer, Rubin Hurricane Carter. Dylan recruited many famous protest singers, notably Joan Baez, Jack Elliot and, for a few concerts, an ailing Phil Ochs. The tour visited almost every major American city and introduced some local singers such as Texan Kinky Friedman to the nation, but it hardly rejuvenated protest songs. It also created sympathy for Hurricane Carter about whom Dylan had written a long topical song. However, Dylan was uninterested in reviving protest music; he was just having a temporary fling with outlaw heroes, which also brought forth his songs about a martyred Lenny Bruce killed by a drug overdose and a cheap Mafia gangster, Joey Gallo, shot down in a restaurant. The songs, 'Joey' and 'Lenny Bruce' appeared on the same album (*Desire*) as 'The Hurricane'.

Without famous singers to consistently champion them, protest songs floundered in the shadowy, fringe folk revival that has been nurtured by folk festivals and the coffee house circuit since the mid-1970s. If there was a starting point for this movement it was the Kerrville Folk Festival in Kerrville, Texas, close to San Antonio. The first Kerrville Folk Festival was held in June 1972 in the 1200-seat Kerrville municipal auditorium. It attracted 2800 fans from Texas and around the US. The most famous performers included Jerry Jeff Walker, Townes Van Zandt, Mance Lipscomb and Peter Yarrow (of Peter, Paul and Mary). The following year Kerrville expanded to five concerts and attracted 5600 patrons. The most important performer additions were Willie Nelson and B.W. Stevenson.

The increasing attendance led to a larger nearby concert site on a 60-acre tract of land, nine miles from Kerrville, and an outdoor festival on a new stage. The 1974 festival added performers such as Asleep At the Wheel and Willis Alan Ramsey and attracted 6000 people. Lucinda Williams was among the finalists for the New Folk Performer Award that year. In 1975 a Kerrville Music Foundation was organized to help novice songwriters and promote folk music forms such as yodelling, mandolin and instrumental bluegrass music in general. Camaraderie grew steadily among campers at the site and it became known as the Quiet Valley Ranch. Campfire singing became a concert staple and by 1980 the attendance numbered 13000. At the tenth anniversary concert in 1981 the programme extended over 11 days. The 1986 concert added a documentary album of that year's singers and a tour through nine states by performers. In 1987 Kerrville expanded to 18 days, including three weekends, and it has retained that format.

In 1990, attendance reached 25000. There were now folk Mass events and 40 new artists performing at 'New Folk Concerts,' as well as six children's concerts and an American Indian Festival. In the 1990s Kerrville, clearly the largest and best-known folk festival in the world, attracted a worldwide audience. By the mid-1990s over two dozen of its previously undiscovered performers had national recording contracts and were becoming household names. Among these Kerrville alumni were Nanci Griffith, Tish Hinojosa, Lucinda Williams, Lyle Lovett, Steve Earle, James McMurtry, John Gorka and the Flatlanders (Joe Ely, Butch Hancock and Jimmie Dale Gilmore).

What was left of protest music after 1972 existed largely within the folk music movement – itself a very small segment of the burgeoning popular music industry. Although, increasingly, most of the songs described as folk music were very personal, a few touched on social problems such as poverty, race and gender discrimination, civil rights and thermonuclear war. Once every decade there was a song produced that was so 'protesty' that it was a catalogue of America's faults. Such a song was Iris Dement's 'Wasteland of the Free' on her 1996 album, *The Way I Should*. This flashback to the 1960s criticized commercial religion, education of the young, the pay of CEOs relative to workers, job outsourcing and the Gulf War. It concluded that America now blamed its 'troubles on the poor,' which was a 'Hitler remedy' and thus had become 'The Wasteland of the Free'.

Vaguely defined folk music largely flourished only on the coffee house circuit and small-label record companies such as Philo, Rounder and, later, Red House. The top-name folk artists such as Mary Chapin Carpenter, Emmylou Harris and Kathy Mattea recorded on major labels and performed in huge auditoriums rather than in small coffee houses, but they were usually seen as country artists. Coffee houses were a throwback to the small 1960s folk clubs which sprang up near college campuses in coffee shops, taverns and sometimes churches. Then and now, folk coffee houses often rearranged the worship area of a church into a coffee house for Friday and Saturday concerts and reconverted it for Sunday church services. Often part of the admission price was donated to a charity, and coffee and sweets were also sold. The performer generally received only a few hundred dollars a night and the right to sell their own recordings at the show.

By touring nationwide and signing up people on their personal mailing lists or websites, performers were able to develop small, but devoted, fan clubs. One cannot judge their social effect by the mere numbers of recordings they sold or audiences they attracted. Their songs often influenced more famous performers who covered their songs and spread their fame. An example would be Lucinda Williams's song 'Passionate Kisses' which was covered by Mary Chapin Carpenter and became a top-ten crossover. Even when the songs were not covered they may have subtly influenced socially conscious singers such as Bruce Springsteen or Willie Nelson, just as Bob Dylan had been influenced by largely unknown folk singers in the early 1960s.

Another musical genre which has subtly replaced protest songs is satiric songs. Satire in general, whether on talk shows, in cartoons, or songs, has become more politically effective than editorials or speeches in changing mass political opinion. Since 1980 perhaps the best example of musical political satire is the path-breaking Washington DC group, The Capitol Steps. This satiric group originally included 16 male and female, younger Washington staffers. They included both Republicans and Democrats, and starting in 1981, they poked fun at everything political (but especially presidents) with clever, wicked satire. They usually used popular rock music and standard tunes for political parody. Thus Dolly Parton's hit, 'Workin' 9 to 5', became a song satirizing President Reagan's poor work habits, titled 'Workin' 9 to 10.' And 'Puff the Magic Dragon' became 'Dutch the Magic Reagan' (about Reagan's personal political magic).

The Capitol Steps were soon releasing a record each year and taunted George Bush Sr with songs such as 'If I Weren't a Rich Man', 'Georgie's Kind and Gentle Land' and a 1990 album, *Georgie on My Mind*. President Bill Clinton got special attention, with songs about his inconsistent politics, such as 'I've Taken Stands on Both Sides Now' and 'Return to Center'. His long speeches were mocked with 'Don't Stop Talkin' Until Tomorrow'. His rich White House guests were roasted with 'White House Hotel' to the tune of 'Heartbreak Hotel', while The Capitol Steps took special delight in satirizing President Clinton's sexual affairs from 'Sneakin Flowers through the Wall', about his pre-presidential mistress, Jennifer Flowers, to 'Happy Monica', 'The Bimbo Collection' and 'You'd Better Sleep Around', about the Monica Lewinsky affair. George W. Bush is getting the same rough treatment. Most of The Capitol Steps satire centres on Bush's trading on his father's name and ex-staff. Typical are such songs as 'Son of a Bush' and 'My Staff Belongs to Daddy'. Other songs, such as 'Don't Go Faking You're Smart', question Bush's knowledge and intelligence. His decision to invade Iraq, his problems in stabilizing Iraq and his general foreign policies were mercilessly satirized as too aggressive and unintelligent in a 2003 album, *Between Iraq and a Hard Place* and a 2004 album, *Papa's Got a Brand New Baghdad*.

The Capitol Steps also led the way in using satire for general protest on a variety of issues. A good example is their 2003 song, 'God Bless My SUV', sung to the tune of 'God Bless the USA'. The song subtly protests American excess in car and petrol consumption. These general protest songs are just a small part of The Capitol Steps's largely political oeuvre. However, most of the songs of the new topical singers are cultural protests against American trends and ways of doing things that affect them personally. Most topical singers and, more importantly, their audiences find blatantly political protest songs stiff, outdated or both. Politics and politicians have become so generally distrusted and identified with corruption that political protest has become largely meaningless. People do, however, still identify with personal problems that also affect the masses. Examples would be problems of working mothers such as Mary Chapin Carpenter's, 'He Thinks He'll Keep Her', unemployed workers, in Billy Joel's 'Allentown', and immigrants in Neil Diamond's 'America'. The songs might be about abused waitresses, children, parents or any unfortunate Americans that you read about daily. These are a throwback to Guthrie's songs about individuals devastated by the Depression and some of Bob Dylan's early songs, such as 'The Lonesome Death of Hattie Carroll' and 'The Ballad of Hollis Brown' about victims of race prejudice or poverty.

In the 1960s few people would have identified these personal complaint songs as protest songs. In that era protest songs were almost always about big national issues such as civil rights, war and poverty. But a slogan of 1960s New Left radicalism was 'The Personal is Political', and reformers were urged to 'liberate the ground you stand on'. Also, America's new subtle, personal songs are a throwback to the protest songs of the distant American past. Personal folk-protest songs permeate America's past, although there is a natural tendency to overlook them. Past trials are quickly forgotten, and yesterday's protest song usually became increasingly ludicrous and irrelevant. Since topical songs are, by definition, custom-made for a particular time and place, they tend to remain rigid period pieces. Thus there have been no real classics of American folk-protest. Diverse, local and elusive, the protest songs of the past are now nowhere simply because they were everywhere and sprang from a multitude of now irrelevant social settings.

Topical songs held an obvious appeal for pragmatic pioneers. Unlike sophisticated European symphonies and operas, they told a simple story and vented simple emotions. From the beginning, Americans sang about politics, wars, heroes, bad men and misery, but their style was overwhelmingly personal. In contrast to most 1960s protest songs, the earlier ballads lacked positive social goals. We have now come full-circle and what is loosely called folk music and what are often personal protest songs are part of a slowly emerging movement of serious singer-songwriters. Nobody knows what to call this music. The term 'folk music' has had many different meanings. Perhaps Pete Seeger defined folk songs best in a concert, when he whimsically noted that 'if folks sing them they are folksongs'.

Nevertheless, contemporary folk performers on the coffee house circuit are generally more polished and innovative then their 1960s predecessors, since they had a strong foundation to build on. However, so far they lack a mass national audience, not only for their protest songs but for their music in general. Yet those who mourn the collapse of protest music may take solace from that perennial optimist, Pete Seeger. In 1965 Seeger celebrated the miraculous revival of social concern among youth in contrast to declining worker and union reform activity and noted:

> History shows that there is a hidden heritage of militancy which comes and goes, but never completely dies . . . but the lessons learned by one generation, even though in defeat are passed on to the next. Right now, many of the song traditions of the 1930s are seeing new life as never before — in the freedom songs of the South and in the topical singers of many a campus. (1965, p. 31)

The eternal cycle that Seeger suggested may soon be ready for another round.

The 'rock the vote' tour (unsuccessfully) aimed at defeating George Bush's presidential re-election in 2004 was led by blue-collar rockers such as Bruce Springsteen and John Mellencamp. And it brought out a bevy of conservative country singers such as Ricky Skaggs and Toby Keith to defend Bush. Some see it as a return to political and protest music. But it may well turn out to be just another brief flashback to the 1960s.

Chapter 3

Available rebels and folk authenticities: Michelle Shocked and Billy Bragg

Mark Willhardt

Showing the cockatrice its own face: authenticity

Ask two fans what 'real' rock and roll is and you'll have an argument; ask three and you'll have a fight. Ask two critics what 'authentic' popular music is and you'll have a contradiction; ask three and you'll have a mess. The truth is that 'authenticity' has become such a fabulous creature that a casual glance in its direction might freeze us in our path, killing sense along the way. If we are intent on pursuing it – as I am here – perhaps an oblique but lengthy look might reveal its face best and, with such a look, make apparent 'authenticity's' elements, arguments, criteria and uses.

To talk of any 'authentic' popular music is to invoke a plethora of histories, biographies, autobiographies and theories, and to enter into one of the most universally contested areas of popular culture, with a concomitant overwhelming embarrassment of discourse on the subject. It's enough to make a music-lover simply close the book and turn up the volume. Withdrawal in the face of the cockatrice, however, is a dangerous proposition: uninformed, we are forced exclusively to react in a game controlled by the creature and thus risk being surprised into stupefaction. Instead, we need a mirror to show the cockatrice its own face and, in so doing, perhaps disempower it. My mirror is to offer three authenticities within the folk/blues/rock nexus – authenticity of genre, of ethos, and of use – and to explore their relation both to the literature on the subject and to the lived examples of Michelle Shocked and Billy Bragg.[1] Admittedly, this mirror is founded on the convenient illusion that the three authenticities are discrete when, in fact and practice, they often overlap. However, by examining them individually, we might be able to see what the whole cockatrice otherwise obscures and assail what appears unassailable.

Authenticity of genre is as much a social ache as a musical quality. That is, authenticity of genre is cast as history, the tale of lost roots recovered. Such roots are musical only insofar as they are indicative of a greater recovery. The rise of 'folk' (originally an umbrella term for both folk and blues) is exemplary in this regard. Certainly, the musics that became known as 'folk' existed well before the term was popularized and disseminated. Yet the establishment of an authentic folk genre came about not only because of a musical experience, but also because of a cultural need. If folk is our example, then Alan Lomax will be our symptomatic authenticator. Although others such as Harry Smith and John Jacob Niles also collected folk music, as folklorist and musicologist, Lomax's combination as preserver and proselytizer has been potent.[2] He recorded Leadbelly and Muddy Waters first; his tireless dedication to folk created the seminal Newport Folk Festival – and his passion for it and its authentic folk music led him to at least one famous fistfight, when the folk musicians, including Dylan, plugged in at the 1965 Festival (Shelton, 1986, p. 301).

> Yet no matter how central the music was to his project, there was always more at stake: The first function of music, especially of folk music, is to produce a feeling of security for the listener by voicing the particular quality of a land and the life of its people. To a traveler, a line from a familiar song may bring back all the familiar emotions of home, for music is a magical summing-up of the patterns of family, of love, of conflict, and of work which give a community its special feel and which shape the personalities of its members. Folk song calls the native back to his roots and prepares him emotionally to dance, worship, work, fight or make love in ways normal to his place. (Lomax, 1960 p. xv)

And here is our 'social ache' writ large: the folk enterprise was, in fact, an attempt to document, if not regulate, normalizing practices in America. It was to discover what gives a 'community its special feel' and 'magical[ly] sum-up' 'the quality of a land and the life of its people'. It was to return to that 'magical' place where all is whole and normal; there is, after all, only one unified and authentic 'people' to feel 'secure' about.

Such a narrative gets to the heart of the authenticity of genre: fixing genre serves an essentially conservative agenda of attempting to recapture an absent past, a '"purer" moment in the mythic history of the music' (Auslander, 1998, p. 4). Or, put another way, 'traditional musical forms are part of that lost world, and a longing for them is a utopian impulse' (Pratt, 1990, p. 101). In the face of Depression and a work-starved transient population, alongside New Deal ideals and against the 'slick' urban, urbane and fleeting Tin Pan Alley popular musics, such a utopian project makes perfect sense. To unearth and valorize authentic folk music – naïve, mimetic, traditional, timeless – was to unearth and valorize the real American folk, those dispossessed people themselves. What ought to be apparent in this explanation is its basis on an unstable tautology: something is folk music because it comes from the folk who are defined as such because they generate folk music. Moreover, Lomax's vision of 'the folk' is extremely limited; it elides, for instance, other possible native communities – 'forms of [American] life' – such as urban populations living in neighbourhoods no more prosperous nor privileged than the rural South from which he drew his music.

Likewise, this narrative of authenticity elides an alternate history of the 'folk' genre, one which acknowledges studio as well as field recordings. Perpetuating an inaccessible utopian past via a 'pure' folk music as Lomax did obscures the hybrid roots of the folk music itself in order to publicize and popularize only one of its forms. Thus, as Sean Chadwell has recently shown, even the 'old-timey' music which was in vogue in the 1920s and 1930s on the nascent medium of radio (and which has recently undergone a resurgence on the heels of the *O Brother Where Art Thou?* soundtrack) was really an invention – an amalgam of several previous sorts of music brought together in order to sell, amongst other things, the newly formed Grand Ol' Opry (Chadwell, 2004, p. 5). In a related context, it is likewise clear that 'the folk blues was a highly mediated phenomenon as soon as the phonograph developed' (Pratt, 1990, p. 103) because records were portable and repeatable; a regional 'purity' was no longer impregnable, if it ever had been. The move to establish an 'authentic' 'folk' music, then, entailed cordoning off those traditions and technologies which had little to do with *music* per se. Instead, they had much to do with who controlled the definition of 'authentic folk' itself. What we get when we expose the authenticity of genre in this instance is a telling reminder that 'folk music is a kissing cousin of what anthropologists call ethnography – an attempt to define a people's way of being' (Weisbard, 1998, p. 72). Alan Lomax's ethnographic/ musicologist methodologies – used to establish an authentic genre, 'folk music' – in the end amount to nothing more than an instance of 'the cycle of authenticity and recuperation' (Davies, 1996, p. 3) where that which was never really lost must be found and advanced as real. Moreover, that which is 'lost' is always more than musical. The authenticity of genre seeks to recuperate history itself. The extra-musical is no less central to the authenticity of ethos than it is to the authenticity of genre. Here, however, it is personal history and personal affect which combine to authenticate music. The authenticity of ethos, then, is cast in biographical terms, most often as a narrative of struggle over time – struggle overcome through the redemptive power of personal talent.[3] And just as early folk music provided an embodiment of the authenticity of genre in Alan Lomax, so the authenticity of ethos is perhaps best embodied by one of Lomax's discoveries, Woody Guthrie.[4]

What is it about Guthrie that demands comment? Put simply, Guthrie is legend.[5] There is, first and foremost, the very overwhelming presence of the singer in any lineage of contemporary folk music. *Everyone* who has ever held an acoustic guitar sees him as a progenitor; if Pete Seeger has proven more long-lived and Dylan more influential, it is only because the former started his career by touring with Guthrie and the latter acknowledged early and repeatedly in his storied career that Guthrie was the better and more important songwriter. Indeed, the early 'Song to Woody' (Dylan, 1962) perhaps expresses it best: 'Hey, hey, Woody Guthrie, but I know that you know / All the things I'm a-sayin' an' many a-times more. / I'm a-singin' you this song, but I can't sing enough, /

'Cause there's not many men who done the things that you done.' There is the usual sort of anxiety of influence here – Woody already knows 'all the things' that Dylan is singing, though Dylan sings them anyway – but there is also a key admission that Guthrie is distinctive, if not unique. 'There's not many men who done the things that you done' to be sure. Contemporary singer-songwriter Steve Earle echoes this notion:

> We all tried, every one of us who came along later and tried to follow in his footsteps only to find that no amount of study, no apprenticeship, no regimen of self-induced hard travelin' will ever produce another Woody. Not in a million years. (Earle, 2003, p. 30)

I would argue that Guthrie becomes a template for what an authentic folk performer has to be, even if few can match his experiences and achievements. Instead, Guthrie's 'cunningly fabricated public persona' (Christgau, 2000, p. 67) sets a standard of biography which legitimizes the lyrical content of the folk songs themselves. That is, to be a folk singer, one must have met the folk and understand their lives, just as Guthrie did, singing not only at concerts but also on the picket lines and in the street, travelling the US from one hard-bitten area to the next. In fact, Dylan ends his tribute by saying that he will go 'hard travelin' just as Guthrie had done. Moreover, the pose within those travels was a balance between anger and whimsy; although Guthrie's guitar famously proclaimed 'This Machine Kills Fascists', he was as likely to perform one of his many children's songs as any protest piece. Taking up the struggles of the areas in which he found himself, or moving on to areas where he knew the struggle was, Guthrie established his authenticity by giving their own lives back to his audiences, whom he famously projected as his peers, in his own articulate and pointed – and self-deprecatingly funny – voice.

Likewise, Guthrie established the precedent of activism which now seems self-evident in folk music.[6] Cowboy songs, folk-blues, and folk 'hollers' were largely apolitical. Guthrie, however, crafted sharp anti-government, pro-union and pro-communist lyrics which foregrounded his humanist, radical politics. This he combined with community activism so that it is now obvious that 'he deliberately constructed the celebrated wise-hayseed persona, all the while expanding his role as a savvy grass-roots organizer' (Light, 1991, p. 50). He established the image of the folkie who sings a social truth engagingly enough to make it seem a personal confidence, even as a large measure of his fame rested on the uniqueness of his own personality and not the music itself. This is particularly true in the face of 'singing [that was] famously unassertive' or recordings that lack 'a warm clarity' (Christgau, 2000, p. 67). The ethos of the performer carries the authenticity which the performance itself might lack.[7]

Guthrie's music, then, is authenticated not only because of its position as part of a tradition established by other singers (and, let us not forget, folklorists), nor by his acoustic-powered songwriting alone. Instead, the authenticity of ethos helps establish Guthrie as a real folk performer. Biography carries the weight of authority, so that, from his moment onwards, authentic music will hinge on the alignment of ethos and content. Interestingly, with the past 25 years of biographical work (particularly fertile now that Guthrie's daughter Nora has opened the archives to scholarly pursuit) the legend of Guthrie has changed from hayseed everyman to savvy autodidactic strategist. Yet this only underscores the fact that biography authenticates the music: to be folk, one must appear folk and live folk, and Woody Guthrie became the first template of that appearance and life.[8] Thus, to unpack the authenticities of genre and ethos is to reveal the discourses of history and biography when they masquerade as public myths. Unpacking the authenticity of use is more difficult because its driving forces are both conscious and hidden, stated and obfuscated. This is because the authenticity of use really marks the intersection of the political and the marketplace.

All the artists in the purview of this essay are thus political singers. As such, we might chart their desire to use music to espouse social views, either by preaching to the converted or trying to convert the preached-to. In the former case there is an act of communicative assent so that solidarity between performer and audience occurs – something that communications theory highlights as common in protest music (Knupp, 1981, p. 382). In the latter case, the performer imagines an unformed, but needed, constituency and performs in order to try to engender this community.[9] Again, communications theory suggests that this might be an effective strategy since:

> ... when listening to a message couched in music, one is less prepared to argue in opposition to the projected message. Listeners do not ordinarily anticipate persuasion and, as a result, they are ready recipients of the rhetorical statement without being aware of its complete implications. (Irvine and Kirkpatrick, 1972, p. 273)

Still, there is one further explicit desire on the part of performers which opens up perhaps the most telling aspect of the authenticity of use: performers want to use music to make a living. What is most authentic is what sustains the performer materially. For this to happen, however, there must be a market for performance, both live and recorded, and the singer's output must be reconceived not only – or not *even* – as desire/politics but instead as product to be consumed.[10]

This viewpoint is the predominant critical take on the whole debate over authenticity. Less monster and more Muppet, the cockatrice of authenticity is perceived as a mechanism for perpetuating sales: 'in the last thirty years folk-derived notions of roots have functioned to authorize successive modes of commercial product' (Coyle and Dolan, 1999, p. 29). In light of the relative absence of protest music post-9/11, this viewpoint has only been amplified:[11]

The effects of consolidation and deregulation in the music industry are invisible to many, but that's the point. Without our consent, choice – at the megastore, on the air, in the concert hall – is being dictated by the big companies that manage music. (Feingold, 2003, p. 4)

or

When it is not possible to find an expression of realpolitik anywhere on the music charts or on the radio, then popular music has become nothing more than a mindless commodity to further distract the public from any sort of citizen involvement in the world they inhabit. (Puterbaugh, 2004, p. H1)

or

... the lack of politically motivated music on mainstream radio is due to the rigidity of the corporate structure behind the business. (Orris, 2003, p. 10)

Authenticity of use in these contexts is a pejorative, cynical thing; indeed, it serves only those forces which profit, quite literally, from its discourse.

Recent thinking, however, has opened up a new avenue by which to access the authenticity of use. Rather than seeing business interest as a closed and hegemonic system which co-opts authenticity as yet another marketing tool, critics such as Jude Davies have proposed the possibility of subject formation, with its attendant political connections to like subjects, as an alternative (Davies, 1996, p. 4ff). That is, this authenticity of use acknowledges not only the false authenticities of genre and ethos, but recognizes the force of capital as well. In the face of these things, artists may authenticate their music through small, lived moments of agency. (In this they eschew the mythic status of the authenticity of ethos.) Repeated over time, over performances and recordings, these agentive moments may not only provide artists with a way of being authentic, but also provides us with a way of discussing authenticity, this renewed authenticity of use, as something other than a capitalist endgame or a cockatrice waiting to turn another listener's ears to stone.

'Hard travelin'': Michelle Shocked

If one of the strategies for an authentic use of music is to encourage making inroads against the larger corporate culture of music, Michelle Shocked is perhaps the poster child for the authenticity of use – or the authenticity of ethos. And in that battleground between individual effect and mythic proportion lies one of the most self-possessed folk singers of the past two decades.

In a pattern echoing Guthrie's autobiographical tale-spinning, as well as his globetrotting, Shocked made little bones about talking openly to the press about her life when she broke in 1986. And, like Woody, the stories have become legend: how she left her strictly Christian mother's home as a teenager and travelled the US and abroad as an itinerant/squatter; how her mother committed her to a mental institution until the insurance coverage ran out; how she hitchhiked in Italy and was raped, an experience which took her to a separatist women's community for a period; how her first album was recorded at a Texas folk festival (where Shocked was working as a volunteer) on a Walkman by a British producer for Cooking Vinyl records who subsequently released the tape without Shocked's knowledge as *The Texas Campfire Tapes* and how it climbed the British charts; how, within a year, Mercury courted her and offered her a six-figure advance, most of which she refused so that they could use the money to support other artists; how, in return for a lesser advance, she managed to negotiate for complete ownership of, and rights to, her catalogue on Mercury; how she recorded a roots burner, *Short Sharp Shocked*, which earned Grammy nominations; how Mercury refused to promote her subsequent albums because, essentially, her rights deal allowed them no profit margin; how she sued to be released from her contract on the basis of the Thirteenth Amendment; how she won her freedom from Mercury, retaining her whole major label catalogue while also freeing herself to make the albums she wanted to make on her own Mighty Sound label.[12] Whew. What mortal could steer clear of becoming myth with this sort of biography?

How, then, to avoid a false authenticity of ethos which this tumble of narrative might generate? In Shocked's case, she has managed it by musical 'hard travelin'' as well as the physical hard travelin' she obviously did earlier in her life. In other words, her roots – as her time in San Francisco shows – are as much punk as they are Texas singer-songwriter. Visually, her mildly punk look and oppositional stance are cemented on the front cover photo of *Short Sharp Shocked*, which shows her being manhandled by the police during a protest at the 1984 Democratic National Convention. Inside there is scant musical evidence of this anger and energy. The first single of the album, 'Anchorage', does have a friend ask her 'What's it like to be a skateboard punk rocker?', but the music of the song belies the lyric, with its lilting chorus and whimsical tone. The remainder of the songs show more of the East Texas strain of songwriting (Townes Van Zant, Guy Clarke, Nanci Griffith) than the West Coast thrash that we saw unplugged with Spot. A Jean Ritchie cover ('The L & M Don't Stop Here Anymore') provides a highlight of the album, while 'Black Widow' draws on hammered dulcimer to attach the album even more fully to the folk tradition. Yet, at the end of the album there is the hidden track, 'Fogtown', an out-of-the-blue thrash performed with MDC (Millions of Dead Cops), one of the hardcore bands she befriended while on the West Coast. Literally buried in the unannounced of the album, then, are Shocked's punk roots and past. Such a surprise move presages the musical restlessness which carries her through the rest of her catalogue.

Lyrically, *Short Sharp Shocked* shows more fire than the (generally) folksy arrangements would indicate. In addition to the rural desolation of 'L & M', Shocked crafts her own straight-up protest song, 'Graffiti Limbo' which, in a spoken break, she dedicates to a teenage tagger who was murdered by the New York police in 1985. Interestingly, she has since disavowed some of the power of the song by saying that it was really written about herself, out of her own sense of powerlessness as a homeless squatter and artist being manipulated by a system she didn't quite understand yet. In any case, *Short Sharp Shocked* establishes a linkage to previous folk models, even as it acknowledges the individual roots of the artist herself. That is, Shocked manages to avoid being 'the next Baez' (or Joni, or Laura Nyro or ...) by reminding us that there is authentic punk as well as authentic folk in her: 'Punk in spirit, punk in culture. But always the music was this very naïve roots music' (Soghomonian, 2002).

Sort of. Her follow-up to *Short Sharp Shocked*, *Captain Swing*, was a brassy album filled with much more than 'naïve' songs and arrangements. Mercury was puzzled by her switch to the big band sound – as were audiences (Guzman, 2001, p. 44). Politics still figured in the work – the title is the name of a mythical English organizer brought to her attention by friend and touring partner Billy Bragg, and much of the album deals with homelessness, but not in the intimate singer-songwriter pattern established on *Short Sharp Shocked*. This had the effect of driving a wedge between performer and label, which wanted her to continue in the confessional/folkie vein. Essentially, *Captain Swing* was an attempt to assert an authenticity of use against the perpetuation of an authenticity of ethos. Mercury wanted a mythic product that they could peddle; Shocked wanted the ability to use her music to build an audience, a constituency, unique to her particular muse. This tension would increase with what Guzman calls 'her masterwork' and her most successful album to date, *Arkansas Traveler* (Guzman, 2001, p. 44). Taking the title seriously – and again, I would argue, acknowledging the model of Guthrie's travels – Shocked hopped the globe, performing with various roots musicians, from Doc Watson and Taj Mahal to Uncle Tupelo and Ireland's Hothouse Flowers. The songs are her own but smack loudly of a folk tradition of the Lomaxian sort, something emphasized both in the musical collaborations and the instrumentations. Indeed, in her liner notes she includes a mini-essay on the importance of the blackface tradition to folk music, which is entirely problematic. At face value, it advances a sort of authenticity of genre which, though it attempts to establish a lineage, is not supported by the album it is attached to – only the song 'Jump Jim Crow' actively engages the tradition of cakewalk minstrelsy. Thus the note comes off as misleading, at best. At worst, 'aside from being obvious and simplistic, it's just plain unnecessary' (Kemp, 1992, p. 105). In this regard, her attempts to carve her own musical career on *Arkansas Traveler* engage the most basic sort of authenticity of genre, trying to achieve an impossible straightforward and straight-faced revival of past musics.

Likewise, her liner statement that her 'early intention was to present this record with a cover photo of myself wearing blackface' indicates an intentional politics but it is hard to read how such a statement should be received. The gesture could be seen as shocking since, no doubt, it was intended to be. Shocked, however, invests in ethos more than authentic political use, since tying her own figure to the blackface builds her image as contestatory without fully articulating a position which allows us to read the image clearly. We might see it, but we won't know what to do with it. It could be sincere protest, as her liner notes seem to indicate, reminding us of a forgotten chapter in popular music history. However, such an image could also be read parodically, so that the artist's proposal that *Arkansas Traveler*'s dated folk music is actually contemporary would metonymically suggest that blackface itself could be similarly contemporary. In short, though the music of *Arkansas Traveler* is often moving and the performances stirring, they are so primarily because they are quoting earlier music. Even updated versions of folk standards such as 'Prodigal Son', which is refigured as 'Prodigal Daughter (Cotton Eyed Joe)', don't shift musically, though the lyrics certainly introduce a feminist vision of country/religious politics. Even the single 'Come a Long Way' echoes a previous source, 'American Pie', in its references to various other songs – 'Gone 500 Miles', 'MacArthur Park', 'All Along the Watchtower', 'Great Balls of Fire' and so on. In general, then, instrumentation, arrangement and idiom of lyric do not shift Shocked's oeuvre, and the politics advanced are most often politics in retreat to that earlier moment of folk (or folk-rock) purity. Her hard travelin' took her around the globe physically but returned her to an unrecoverable and ambiguous place musically. By playing into the authenticity/recuperation vision, *Arkansas Traveler* might have been a boon for Mercury, since it gave them something to hang promotional copy upon. However, as Shocked was later to claim, Rand Hoffman, senior vice president of business affairs at PolyGram (owner of Mercury), found the album less than satisfactory: he allegedly said that *Arkansas Traveler* was a 'shitty' album (Rosen, 1995, p. 11). Consequently, Mercury refused to promote the album and refused to fund Shocked's next album (Rosen, 1995, p. 10).

And so Shocked sued to be released from her contract – based on the 'involuntary servitude' clause of the Thirteenth Amendment. Here is where the renewed authenticity of use returns to our discussion. If, as she has said, 'the truth is you are selling a product, you are like a name brand and it's not such a problem … except you are then expected to be the product you are selling' (Freeman-Greene, 1991, p. 13), then her move to extricate herself from her contract is that small, lived moment of agency discussed earlier. Rather than be content with operating within a business structure which often obscures its methods, she took action – admittedly in a hyperbolic fashion – and, in an out-of-court settlement, made Mercury enforce the contract they had originally arranged with her, essentially releasing her whole catalogue back to her after ten years. As she puts it now, 'the fact that I won my own masters means that fifteen years into my career, I'm in control of my destiny' (Wielenga, 2002, p. 15). I would argue that this attempt to wrest her music from a corporate structure which didn't support her and which, in fact, actively worked against her, is an authenticity of use: protest linked to action, creating agency, resulting in change. The music is used as the tool and occasion to help the musician determine her own course.

Shocked's career was kick-started in 1996 with her release from Mercury. She has continued to tour relentlessly, even though her recorded solo output has been confined to a greatest hits collection from the Mercury years, *Mercury Poise* (released as part of her separation deal) and two studio albums, *Kind Hearted Woman* (1996) and *Deep Natural* (2002, released with *Natural Dub*, a mostly instrumental disc), plus assorted individual songs contributed to various compilations and causes. Musically, Shocked has tended to 'travel' less than earlier in her career. Partially this is due to her finding midlife stability in marriage (though she recently separated from husband and manager Bart Bull), home-owning and her born-again Christian faith, a stability she neatly sums up: 'I have a fairly middle-class lifestyle. We have mortgages on two homes. When you consider the level of working class I was raised in, God is good' (Getlen). Her faith certainly suffuses the spirit of her music since *Arkansas Traveler*, if only occasionally its form. Though her support for women's issues and human rights causes has been unflagging,[13] in this sense it is perhaps a new authenticity of use that infuses her music as well that desire to spread the joy of religion which she has found central to her life. *Deep Natural* opens with 'Can't Take My Joy' and its enthusiastic chorus, 'Joy, Joy, Joy, Hallelujah / Joy, Joy, Joy Hallelujah', highlights this new use. Without shifting to 'Christian music,' a term she hates (Wielenga, 2002, p. 14), what we can see as a new authenticity of use as social commitment continues to align with spiritual belief and musical stability. How Shocked's career will develop in future will probably depend on what hard travelin' – physical, personal, spiritual and musical – she undergoes next.

Walking the dog with the available rebel: Billy Bragg

The career of Billy Bragg – 'Britain's outraged and tender, brainy and fun-loving, left-wing, punky folk rocker' (Epstein, 1992, p. 31) – offers some interesting parallels with his 1980s touring partner Shocked. Both find their roots in punk as well as folk, again exhibiting that punk-absent-the-feedback connection; both had ties to Cooking Vinyl (though Bragg's major distribution deal is now through Elektra); both are passionate, vocal and public in their support of social causes; both have been touted as the 'authentic' folk voice of their generation. However, whereas Shocked foregrounded biography and has had to live through the legacy of an early authenticity of ethos, Bragg's life has been much less fabled. In contrast, his career has involved a certain flirtation with the authenticity of genre which, I will argue, turns into an efficacious authenticity of use as his concerns and lyrics turn from socialist politics to identity formation.

Bragg was raised in Barking, England with a 'very straightforward suburban working class upbringing ... we were educated to go and work in the line at Ford's, and if we were lucky, technical skilled labor' (Talvi, 2001). Leaving school at 16 in the hopes of escaping this destiny, Bragg did a very brief stint in the army before turning his efforts wholly to music. He released the musically and thematically diverse *Life's a Riot with Spy vs. Spy* in 1983, a volume that included an assortment of the whimsical love songs for which Bragg is almost as well known as his political oeuvre. However, he began to hit his political stride with B*rewing Up with Billy Bragg* the following year.[14] (These two albums were released with the *Between the Wars* EP as *Back to Basics* in 1987.)

Bragg's sound on these albums was not acoustic, but it echoed acoustic music in its spare solo electric guitar work. Likewise, its lyrical content was conscious of its folk predecessors – 'I was quite inspired as a songwriter by Bob Dylan' (Talvi, 2001) – without the unquestioning replication of an *Arkansas Traveler*. *Brewing Up* opens with 'It Says Here' an indictment of the media's complicity in spreading a conservative agenda and in distracting the public with 'politics mix[ed] with bingo and tits'. It name-checks unions, 'the right of the House', 'this year's prince', 'a large dose of Law and Order / and a touch of the short sharp shock' (this released four years before Shocked's album), and 'the fact that your paper is Tory'. In so doing, it aligns itself with the protest songs of the folk tradition – Guthrie's and Dylan's songs.

But it does not align with the immediate tradition, English folk song. Though it could be argued that 'much of what has passed for folk music in North America is nothing other than the popular music of the past imported from the British Isles two centuries or more before' (Pratt, 1990, p. 101), the undoubted originality and inventiveness of figures such as Guthrie and Dylan cast doubt on this assertion's truth post-1960. English folk song, however, almost never appears in discussions of Bragg's career: over and over, he is cast as the inheritor of the legacy of Guthrie and Dylan, not Harry Cox or Bob Copper, seminal twentieth-century English folk figures. The reason for this is clear, and becomes clearer as Bragg's career wears on: his political concerns and expressions align more with his American counterparts than his British ones. Whereas the Americans pushed for a politics of opposition, most of the British work tended towards the Lomaxian authenticity of genre, conveying generations-old song. Although Bragg's concerns and political context are English, his musical antecedents are found in North America. As he puts it, like Guthrie he's 'writing songs about unions too, and there's not many of us about' (quoted in Collins, 1998, p. 32). Yet this doesn't quite get at the truth of his work, either. As he has repeatedly said, he came to political consciousness in the late 1970s and early 1980s as Margaret Thatcher's policies alienated more and more of the working class. Thus Bragg's *real* immediate musical context was punk. Despite his winsomeness about his own punk credibility – 'that was more of a T-shirt than a developed idea' (Frey, 2002, p. 35), 'I was an anarchist. Which kind of meant that I was just grumpy' (Talvi, 2001) – the influence of The Clash in particular can be felt throughout Bragg's work. Their political songs and forthright support of social causes, including international issues, converged with the Thatcher government's clampdown policies to focus Bragg's energies.

This litany of influences could certainly be used to build either an authenticity of genre-canonical British punk combining with canonical American folk or an authenticity of ethos – an English biography as informed by North American (musical) history as by English, a hero for two continents. However, there are four movements in Bragg's career, which allow us to understand his music as enacting an authenticity of use. The first of these comes early in his career:

> Then, the 1984 Miners' Strike was the real politicization for me. I started doing gigs outside of London in the coal fields and found that I was able to articulate what I believed in so that these people who we were doing the benefits for – the miners – didn't think I was just some pop star from London trying to enhance my career by doing a few fashionable benefits. (Quoted in Frey, 2002, p. 35)

There are a number of things which we might point to here. The first is that Bragg's attempt to legitimize playing these shows moves beyond a self-aggrandizing authenticity of ethos. Instead, the music allows him the opportunity to define and articulate a political vision on which he can act. Rather than attempt to centre the events on himself and his music, he uses the music as an occasion to develop agency, much as we saw Shocked do when she fought Mercury.

Second, this moment of articulation is an opportunity for Bragg to exceed the punk culture that first inspired him. If punk's 'practices never went far beyond the rhetorical [if] punk was about protest, not change' (Simonelli 2002, p. 128), then this was a chance to enact change, create agency, through music. Bragg realized that the punk model was not sufficient in and of itself: 'you're naïve to believe that bands can change the world. Bands are very naïve to think that just if their audience thinks that they can change the world, that they can' (quoted in Talvi, 2001). To quote Bragg further, this naïveté needs to be answered because 'political rock 'n' roll can only really be effective against a backdrop of social pressure, rather than just working on its own' (quoted in Epstein, 1992, p. 33). Taking the music to the site of the struggle, the coal fields themselves, was thus an opportunity to build that social pressure, develop an audience and a political constituency at the same moment, to authenticate the use of the music with action.

Thus Bragg became known as a socialist singer-songwriter and activist,[15] the 'seasoned pinko storyteller' that *New Musical Express* recently christened him (Johns, 2002). With the return of the Labour Party to government in the 1990s, however, the change in political climate allowed for a change in musical direction as well. This change came in the form of *Mermaid Avenue* (1998) and *Mermaid*

Avenue Volume II (2000). Like Shocked's *Arkansas Traveler*, these albums gave Bragg the opportunity to connect with an earlier musical tradition, specifically the hundreds of previously unseen lyrics written by Woody Guthrie while living on Mermaid Avenue in New York City during the last 25 failing years of his life. Never set to music, these lyrics afforded Bragg an opportunity that Shocked missed, the opportunity to eschew backward-looking longing in favour of modern partnership:[16] 'This is not really a Woody Guthrie record, it's a true collaboration' (Molenda, 1998, p. 64). In this sense, Bragg made an attempt to match Guthrie's spirit with his own musical sensibilities, which are coloured not solely by the roots music that surrounded (or pre-dated) Guthrie himself:

> The point of reference for me was to stand back from the Woody Guthrie legend and look at where he was coming from, which was Anglo-American folk music. But, in making this record, we could not undo the fact that we had also heard *Highway 61 Revisited* and the first Clash album and whatever else. (Quoted in Molenda, 1998, p. 64)

The *Mermaid Avenue* projects served a dual authenticity of use, then. On the one hand, they served to connect Bragg to his musical forefather. This could happen in the realm of the political: 'I'm gonna tell all you fascists you may be surprised / The people in this world are getting organized / You're bound to lose, you fascists are bound to lose' ('All You Fascists'). It could happen in the realm of the romantic: 'Ingrid Bergman, you're so perty, / you'd make any mountain quiver / You'd make fire fly from the crater' ('Ingrid Bergman'). In neither case did the connection serve to establish a particular history of legitimacy, an authenticity of genre; the words were Woody Guthrie's to be sure, but the voice, arrangement and ludic sensibility were Bragg's (and Tweedy's) own. On the other hand, the projects served to recuperate Guthrie himself from that authenticity of ethos we saw earlier. By highlighting his lyrical range, the two albums helped break Guthrie out of the mytho-poetical, mytho-political status he had achieved. In both cases, the *Mermaid Avenue* albums establish an authenticity of use, giving both collaborators an opportunity to craft music touched by their respective histories but not beholden to either. In doing so, they made what Robert Christgau calls 'the finest Guthrie albums there are' (Christgau, 2000, p. 67).[17] The third moment at which we might chart an authenticity of use in Bragg's work actually began before the *Mermaid Avenue* albums appeared. The album that gave Bragg his biggest United States success, *Don't Try This At Home* (1991), opened with 'Sexuality', a paean to sexual frankness and openness. In this song, we can mark a shift from a social politics figured around groups such as unions to a politics figured (literally) on the bodies of individuals. This interest in identity formation marked something new in Bragg's work and we can see it resurfacing after the Guthrie albums, in *England, Half English* (2002).

Overt politics are certainly not absent from this album – the first single was

'NPWA' ('No Power Without Accountability') – but the majority of the songs are concerned with more personal issues, and more intimately national ones, as the work's title suggests. In the eponymous title song, Bragg tells us that he is a 'great big bundle of culture tied up in the red white and blue' and proceeds to tell us about all the other half-English people in his world, including his mother, his neighbours, and 'those three lions on your shirt, / They never sprang from England's dirt'. The idea here, carried off in the jokey but only half-joking wordplay, is that English identity is hopelessly bound up with other cultures. There is an implicit cultural argument inherent in these sentiments against 'England for the English' arguments. This anti-essentialist position is one which Bragg has espoused both in song, such as *England, Half English*'s 'Take Down the Union Jack' (where we are asked 'what it really means / to be an Anglo hyphen Saxon in England.co.uk'), and in print:

> In their campaigns for the elections, the BNP [British National Party] and the UK Independence Party (Ukip) used the British flag to represent everything that they stand for: an inward-looking, white society, angry at the present, fearful of the future, clinging to the past. There is an ugly xenophobia out there, but it's waving the Union Jack. (Bragg, 2002)

'England, Half-English' attempts to break this xenophobia in a number of ways. The first is to set its chorus, which catalogues a set of 'very English' things, from Morris dancing to Morrisey, to 'this very English melody' itself, over a very *Eastern* melody. The instrumentation here, as elsewhere on the album, includes darabouka, resozouki, bender and curdo drum, as well as guitar, bass and a Hammond organ.[18] That is, from the ground up, 'England, Half English' wants to show that identity, particularly national identity, is no simple proposition. This is perhaps no more apparent than on the joyous, uplifting 'Baby Faroukh', a welcoming song for a child. The baby's name marks it as other-than-English, but the song's placement on this album just before 'Take Down the Union Jack' makes us check our own preconceptions and realize that name doesn't necessarily mark national difference, or fix identity, at all.

I highlight *England, Half English* here because it demonstrates another authenticity of use in its lyrical and musical content. Though nowhere does Bragg forego a socialism-informed, union-proud politics, this album acknowledges that 'it's very easy to get marginalized as a political singer-songwriter' (Talvi, 2001) but that it's 'the job of the singer/songwriter [...] to try to reflect the world around him' (Frey, 2002, p. 36). By the time *England, Half English* was recorded, the political grounds had shifted from those pertaining in 1984 when Bragg emerged as a political artist. The shift in emphasis from workers' causes to issues of identity and nationality might be understood as an attempt to shift the grounds on which his music might authentically be used, from expressing government opposition to wariness about the identity politics floating in the English air.

Like any use authenticity of use, the reception to *England, Half English* remains ambivalent. *New Musical Express* complains that 'we're now faced with the ludicrous predicament of receiving our radical infotainment via a middle-aged people's crooner laying good intentions on thick … while the music is a symptom of deep-rooted passion outstripping relevance' (Johns, 2002). *Rolling Stone* concurs, calling the political songs of the album 'dippy fake Guthrie' (Wolk, 2002, p. 71). Yet *The New Statesmen*'s Books of the Year list for 2002 suggests that 'if a booklet accompanying a CD can pass as a book, the lyrics of Billy Bragg's *England, Half English* (Cooking Vinyl) propose more stimulating and varied ideas about who we, in these islands, are or might become than most heavyweight political texts have ever done' (Howe, 2002, p. 44). Given our discussion throughout this essay, it ought to be clear that the first two arguments are making recourse to an authenticity of genre dependent on denigrating Bragg's performances as both outdated politically and inauthentic musically. The second recuperates the album by ignoring the music (no surprise since the list is literary not musical) and concentrating on the identity politics which I argue Bragg himself foregrounds. Further, I would argue that the two music reviewers miss Bragg's attempts to authenticate his arguments via the instrumentation and arrangement of the songs themselves, particularly those dealing with national identity directly. I read *England, Half English* not as a tub-thumping failure, then, but as an attempt to authenticate the music through its use as a medium for inquiry into identity.

Finally, I want to argue briefly that Bragg's savvy about his place on the political landscape allows him to use music for one final authentication. Besides his role as musician/activist at benefits and other concerts, since the mid-1990s Bragg has been a regular contributor to *The New Statesman*, a national (English) political magazine. In his 'Diary' column, Bragg is able to amplify issues which crop up in his songs, such as national identity. Moreover, he has used it as a forum for making substantial political proposals, such as the plan for constitutional reform in the House of Lords which he advanced earlier this year (Bragg, 2004, p. 8). This idea was taken seriously enough to result in meetings with high-ranking members of the government, as well as wide coverage in the popular press (Anonymous, 2004, p. 38). Without exploring this particular issue further, it ought to be apparent that the music that Bragg has performed, and the activism that has accompanied it, has given him a regular entrée into widely disseminated 'legitimate' (that is, non music industry) magazines which other pop musicians simply do not have. In this final way, we might see how Bragg establishes an authentic, political use for his art, even if music itself is absent in this particular instance.

Andrew Collins characterizes Billy Bragg as 'very much the available rebel' (1998, p. 34). By this I think he means to indicate Bragg's affability in the face of people hostile to his beliefs; to a music industry which doesn't quite know what to do with political artists yet makes good money from Bragg's solid sales; to his presence in at least the British political landscape. Whether forcefully political or whimsically romantic or somewhere in between, Bragg's music certainly invites us in. Yet my reading of his various career facets also suggests that Bragg is 'available' in a more precise sense, as the person who is 'capable of producing a desired result' (*OED* I.1.). Skirting those false authenticities we have explored, Bragg has consistently found ways of engaging authenticities of use, even as the world around him has changed, and of producing results. In this way we might see his music as a unifying force for action, a critical voice in the discourse of national and personal identity, and a window through which to see the world. In the end, though, perhaps one reason why he seems such an available rebel, so authentic in the uses to which he puts his music, is because he balances politics against living itself:

> I don't mind being called a political singer/songwriter, but I really object to being dismissed as a political singer/songwriter. I write about the way the world is. Politics isn't everything. Sometimes it does feel like it, but that's when you've got to look out the window, take the dog for a walk. (Quoted in Hutcheon, 2004, p. 83)

'There ain't nobody who can sing like me': some conclusions

I draw my epigram for this section from one of the Guthrie lyrics, 'Way Over Yonder in the Minor Key', which Bragg put to music for *Mermaid Avenue*. After all the places we have been here, I want to return to the one thing that has threaded through this whole discussion: the power of someone singing. No one can sing like Alan Lomax; no one can sing like Lead Belly; no one can sing like Woody Guthrie; no one can sing like Bob Dylan; no one can sing like Michelle Shocked; no one can sing like Billy Bragg. Yet what their various individual singings mean, and what their singing means when taken together, is open to contestation on every front, and most frequently that contestation involves some notion of what is authentic, or not, in their singing. From the outset my argument has been that the criteria by which we judge authenticity is always multiple and most often not transparent. No matter how open-minded we are about music, when we are trying to gauge how 'folk' something is when the instrumentation is electric or how 'folk' someone is when she plays swing music or how 'folk' someone is when he keeps naming The Clash as his early ideal, we employ standards of authenticity, comparing what we hear with what we already know. These internalized standards are no more escapable than breathing.

But, like breathing, they can be controlled, broken down and understood. By first looking at how false authenticities were figured in generic and ethical terms early in the twentieth century – a cockatrice meant to freeze the listener in discourses of unrecoverable history and mythic personality – I have attempted to discuss authenticity in the contemporary moment by positing an authenticity of use. Both Michelle Shocked and Billy Bragg are open to assault on the grounds of those false authenticities; both history and biography might be engaged to lessen the lived political effect of their art. However, if we understand elements of their musics and musical careers as moments at which they consciously addressed the forces that circumscribed them – market, government and lack of solidarity – we might see how they crafted an authenticity of use for, and from, their work. Both are authentic insofar as they use their music not only to proselytize change, but also to effect it: Shocked's business sense allowed her to maintain her cultural product as her own and set an example for others to follow; Bragg started by building social protest in the mining fields to supplement his musical message and has ended by employing the national press to profess his ideas. Their authenticity, then, inheres not solely in the lineage they follow, nor the experiences of their lives; it is established every time they assert 'ain't nobody who can sing like me' and use that individual song for social ends.

Notes

1. This means that one of the most careful thinkers on the topic of musical authenticity, Peter Kivy, will largely be ignored here. However, I recommend his study of classical music, *Authenticities: Philosophical Reflections on Musical Performance* (1995), to anyone truly interested in this field. His parsing of 'authenticity' into authenticities of intention, sound, practice and personal authenticity, though not directly applicable here, shows a delightful lucidity and depth of insight.

2. Lomax's career is not without controversy or detractors, however. Often at issue are Lomax's own preconceptions about what constituted 'real' folk music. As David Hajdu succinctly puts it, Lomax 'was really a nineteenth-century figure – a domestic colonialist who mistook "discovery" for creation and advocacy for ownership' (2003, p. 41). Rock critic Dave Marsh's reaction to Jon Pareles's *New York Times* obituary also points out many of the contradictions, if not small-mindedness, of Lomax's work (Marsh, 2002). Likewise, Weisbard points out a number of the limitations on Lomax's method, including the ways in which extant commercial recordings of folk music and some of Smith's work provided superior examples (Weisbard, 1998, pp. 73–74).

3. And here we have the familiar blueprint for most telebiographies, from A & E's *Biography* to VH1's more lurid *Behind the Music*.

4. The relationship intimated in this phrase is not strictly true, since Guthrie was an established singer in the West and Dustbowl by the time he met Lomax in 1940. Guthrie and Lomax both played the same show in New York in March of that year; folk singer Will Geer arranged the concert and was the force who brought Guthrie east. See Klein (1980, pp. 146 ff).

5. A legend he certainly helped craft in the autobiographical *Bound for Glory*. Joe Klein's 1980 biography still portrayed Guthrie as a wandering troubadour, profligate lyricist and, mostly, the authentic embodiment of American folk culture in all its glories and contradictions. Granted access to the Guthrie archives which Klein didn't have, Ed Cray presents a more balanced and human vision of Guthrie in his *Ramblin' Man: The Life and Times of Woody Guthrie* (2004).

6. Guthrie's activities for communist causes, even though he never joined the party, are well documented. One of the most interesting studies of the intentional political uses

of Guthrie's music comes in John Gold's 'Roll on Columbia' (1998), an examination of the songs Guthrie wrote for the Bonneville Power Administration in 1941. The study highlights Guthrie's self-conscious progressivism as well as his interest in itinerant populations.

7. For more on the ethical qualities as they relate to rhetorical effectiveness, see Irvine and Kirkpatrick (1972, pp. 274, ff).

8. He would be the first template, but not the last. Dylan's shape-shifting career has been more influential for the rock world in this respect.

9. For a more fully developed example of this community-formation (in the context of George Clinton's funk music), see Willhardt and Stein (1999).

10. Audiences, of course, have their own authenticities of use. They want to identify with the performer, to find their own experiences reflected in the singer's wordplay, to be entertained. What may be quotidian for performers is generally distinct for the audience – unless they are Deadheads, Phishheads and Parrotheads who will sometimes 'tour' almost as much as the bands themselves because they want the authenticity of the live performance.

11. Although it is true that protest music has not been as visible recently as might be expected in a time of war, this doesn't mean that it doesn't exist. The website Protest-Records.com, founded by Sonic Youth's Thurston Moore, has gathered and disseminated many examples in the past months. Likewise, *The Nation* (**276** [2], January, 2003, 13–20) ran a special issue highlighting various forms of protest musics.

12. Because Shocked has related these stories in such similar forms throughout her career, the number of places these events could be verified is legion. Her own narrative version, found complete on www.michelleshocked.com/bio.htm largely matches the version authenticated by interviews in *The Washington Post* (Harrington, 1989), *Rolling Stone* (Gleason, 1988) and elsewhere.

13. She has, for instance, appeared at Washington DC rallies for Codepink, a part of International Women's Day, as well as performing at the Image: Art, Faith, Mystery conference in 2003 in Seattle, at benefits for the Green Party, at the 2004 Coalition for Peace Action benefit in Princeton, and at many other socially active concerts/causes.

14. In this assessment I differ somewhat from Ian Peddie, who sees the album's two Falkland War legacies, 'Island of No Return' and 'Like Soldiers Do' as its primary and mild political content. Peddie's analysis of the *Between the Wars* EP, however, is the best commentary on Bragg's shift to more direct and anthemic political song in light of his commitment to the 1984–85 miner's strike. See Peddie (2000).

15. Amongst his mid-1980s activisms was the founding of Red Wedge, a musicians' get-out-and-vote organization.

16. Though my concern is Bragg's work here, the *Mermaid Avenue* projects were also carried out by Jeff Tweedy and his band Wilco, who are as important to the American music scene as Bragg is to the British. Like Bragg, Tweedy wrote songs to match Guthrie's lyrics; both Bragg and Tweedy sang, backed by Wilco.

17. Perhaps no one has a finer take on the line of influence which this project entails than Bragg's official biographer Andrew Collins: 'Writer Mick Farren once said that Bob Dylan wanted to be Elvis but there was a vacancy for Woody Guthrie, so he took the gig. Billy Bragg started out as Bob Dylan with a dash of The Clash, but now there's another vacancy for Woody Guthrie, and he's got the job' (Collins, 1998, p. 30).

18. It is significant that Bragg is working with a band, The Blokes, on this album,

following upon the collaborative experience he had with Wilco on *Mermaid Avenue*.
The band not only allows Bragg to broaden his musical approach – here into eastern
instrumentation – but also connect to his punk/rock roots, since members of the
Blokes come from the Faces, The Damned and Shriekback.

Chapter 4

The pop star as politician: from Belafonte to Bono, from creativity to conscience

John Street

In 2002, a *Time* cover asked, 'Can Bono save the world?': The answer to this question was not a dismissive 'no'. Instead, Bono was treated seriously, as a potential saviour of a world in which conventional forms of political leadership and public policy had failed. After all, it wasn't just *Time* that took the lead singer of U2 seriously; so did world leaders. Bono was pictured at the White House with George W. Bush, at the Elysée Palace with President Jacques Chirac, at 10 Downing Street with Prime Minister Tony Blair, and in the Vatican with Pope John-Paul. While these meetings might be seen simply as tempting photo-opportunities, they were not just exercises in image-making. There was a political price being extracted, a recognition of the cause for which Bono was lobbying: the relief of Third World debt.

Although Bono's political involvement may be unusual to the extent that he directly engages with political and other leaders, in other ways it is almost commonplace. Pop stars have featured prominently in campaigns about nuclear weapons, civil, gay and women's rights, famine, environmental issues and so on. Protests against the war in Iraq are just one recent example of pop stars assuming the guise of political activists. In the UK, George Michael sang Don McLean's 'The Grave' on *Top of the Pops*; Chris Martin of Coldplay used his appearance at the Brits Awards to protest at the war; Elton John, Damon Albarn, Billy Bragg and countless others signed public petitions against the war; Ms Dynamite rapped with the Reverend Jesse Jackson at a Hyde Park rally. And, perhaps most famously of all, the Dixie Chicks disassociated themselves, albeit briefly, from their fellow Texan, George W. Bush, from the stage of their Shepherds Bush concert and incurred a dramatic fall in sales and a ban from many US radio stations. Meanwhile, elsewhere the Web was alive with sound of protest songs from Nanci Griffith, REM, the Beastie Boys, Lenny Kravitz, John Mellencamp and countless others.

What I want to ask in this chapter is how are we to make sense of this kind of political engagement? Why and when do pop stars come to see themselves as political activists? The point is that, while we can list any number of examples of pop stars engaging with politics, they will always be in a minority. Most pop stars, most of the time, are not making political statements or gestures. And, even if they were, we might still be curious about why professional entertainers, who make their living from selling records (among other things), feel able or obliged to pronounce on the serious business of politics. This essay is, therefore, an attempt to establish the conditions and reasons for pop's political role. But before doing this, it helps to make a couple of general distinctions. First, the examples mentioned above can be separated into two categories. One might be called political activism and the other political argument or polemic. The first describes the case of people who happen to be musicians, and as such have acquired a public presence or status which they use to support causes or candidates. The second captures the case of those who use their music to give expression to their political views. The two may be linked – Sting and Bruce Springsteen, for example, perform both roles – but not necessarily. Elton John is not noted for his politically conscious repertoire, but he became actively involved in the campaign against the 2003 Iraqi War. By contrast, Morrissey writes songs with explicitly political messages, but does not actively engage with politics. The point of making this distinction is that the explanation of each may be different: why musicians stand on platforms may differ from the reasons why they deliver polemics. As Coldplay's Chris Martin commented, 'My songs have nothing to do with war, they're all about the sad insecurities of a balding rock star' (*The Guardian*, 17 March 2003). The explanation we give for why musicians write political songs need not be the same as the explanation that we give for their political participation; equally, the fact that they write political songs does not tell us whether they will be politically active (and vice versa).

The second distinction is between intention and interpretation. It is important, at least for the discussion here, to separate examples of music that are intended to be political and those in which the politics derive from the interpretation of that music. In the first volume of the *Continuum Encyclopedia of Popular Music of the World*, Dave Laing (2003, p. 345) captures this distinction in the contrast between 'protest music' and 'music of resistance'. The former he describes as 'explicit statements of opposition' and the latter as 'coded or opaque'. With the first type the politics are a product of an explicit intention of the performer. This is to be contrasted with examples where, irrespective of the intentions of the performer, the music is interpreted as being political. State censorship can operate like this (songs become 'political' because they are seen as 'threatening', even where this was not their intention (see Cloonan and Garofalo, 2003). Equally, audiences and fans can turn otherwise politically innocent music into political statements. Thomas Cushman (1995) provides examples of this in his discussion of youth dissent within Soviet Russia. The music of T. Rex, seen in the West as 'glam rock', became symbolic of the dissatisfaction felt by Russian youth. Such reversals or twists of meaning and significance can also be a product of state policy (the act of censorship gives political value to the illicit item and turns it into a potential symbol of protest). The point is that this process of politicization takes place independently of the performer's intentions. In the same way, analysis of music by academics can reveal its politics. Close reading of songs can reveal 'hidden transcripts'. Although such readings are valuable tools of analysis, and although anyone interested in the politics of music needs to be aware of them, my concern here is primarily with *intended politics*. I want to reflect on why musicians choose to become politically engaged. What follows are a series of suggestions and ideas about how we might account for the political engagement of pop stars. The essay reviews different arguments that might be deployed to explain political involvement. My suggestion is that we need a multifaceted account – one that is sensitive to both musical and political dimensions. To begin, though, it is important to reiterate and develop a point already made: that pop's political engagement is less common than can sometimes appear.

Political pop: the exception rather than the rule?

There is a danger of exaggerating the degree of political engagement. The reaction to the Iraq War is, in many ways, the exception, rather than rule. Most pop stars spend most of their time *not* engaged in politics. The same is true of musical content. A survey, conducted by Laing (1985, p. 27) of the debut albums of the top five punk groups released in 1976–77, found that 25 per cent of the songs involved direct social and political comment. But 25 per cent were also about 'first person feelings' and 21 per cent were about 'romantic and sexual relationships'. While such statistics compared favourably with the content of the Top 50 at the same time (60 per cent were about sex and romance and 18 per cent about music and dancing), it does indicate that (a) punk was not as politically obsessed as it is sometimes portrayed; and (b) that pop is not typically about politics.

Looking through a list of UK number one records between 1952 and 2001,[1] it is striking to see how few have any explicit political content. Typically, the politics comes in the form of social-comment songs like The Specials' 'Ghost Town' (1981). Protest is largely confined to Pink Floyd's 'Another Brick in the Wall' (1979). The year of Woodstock (1969) did see several hits – relative to almost every other year – which displayed some element of explicit political or social awareness: 'The Ballad of John and Yoko', 'Something in the Air', 'Bad Mood Rising'. Two 1983 hits voiced anti-war sentiments: 'Two Tribes', '99 Red Balloons'. Bands whose music and pronouncements have linked them to politics have occasionally enjoyed number one records: The Jam, The Specials, Manic Street Preachers and U2. Only rarely, though, have their number ones been their most political songs. A crude generalization might be that the more explicitly political the song, the lower the chart placing (cf. Public Enemy, The Clash, Bob

Marley). Were charity records to be included as songs of protest, then the number increases marginally. Nonetheless, were chart hits to be a measure of pop's character, we would be forced to conclude that explicit political content is rare. As Dave Harker (1992) once pointed out, the soundtrack of *The Sound of Music* dominated the album charts in the era of political radicalism – the 1960s. Even more systematic studies of musical content reveal similar results. Richard Cole (1971, p. 390) noted that his laborious exercises in content analysis had found that 'love' was the predominant theme in popular songs, and that the only variation was to be found in the form and character of courtship and love. Other topics hardly got a look in.

In contrast to this impression of the marginalization of politics, a recent survey of music censorship (Bastian and Laing, 2003) has shown that, of the music censored worldwide over the last 20 years, 75 per cent of the cases were for political reasons. Two qualifications need to be added. The first is that very few of these instances involved British or US artists; the second qualification is that such censorship may owe much more to the interpretation of the state than the intention of the artists (for example, the recent ban by the Chinese authorities of particular Stones' songs). But even when we include the history of censorship, we are still left to conclude that, at the very least, politically engaged popular music is not the norm. What could be some of the possible explanations of the exceptions to the general rule? One argument used to explain the political content of popular music is that it reflects or responds to reality. This is an argument that is made all the more plausible by the suggestion that, relative to other cultural forms of expression, music is by far the most accessible. Consider the words of Gordon Friesen, one of the founders of *Broadside*, the publisher of the early protest songs of Bob Dylan and Phil Ochs:

> The question was frequently asked as to why so many *Broadside* writers concerned themselves with topics like wars; why didn't they write more often about love, flowers, winds upon the hills? Well, the magazine did print such songs. But topical-song writers, as distinct from other creators of music (which is often commercialized escapism), have always tended to deal with reality. (Quoted in Cohen, 2000, p. 15)

Friesen's suggestion is a straightforward one: music, especially folk music, chronicles contemporary reality. It is a form of news reporting, and news reporters, musicians are political because of their sensitivity to the times they live through.

Certainly the standard histories of pop and rock tend to mark the passage of time through the rise and decline of pop's political awareness and to link this to social and political change more generally. Reebee Garofalo argues that '[b]ecause popular music always interacts with its social environment, it often serves as a lightning rod for the political controversies that invariably accompany change. ... popular music has been connected quite explicitly with social change and political controversy' (1997, pp. 14–15). Later, in commenting on the rise of the civil rights movement in the 1960s, Garofalo contends that 'it is possible to analyze the impact of the movement on national consciousness by charting the trajectory of popular music during the period' (1997, p. 184). Paul Friedlander writes of how rock's turn to humanitarian causes (Live Aid and so on) was a product of 'a Western political environment dominated by Thatcher-Reagan conservatism' (1996, p. 14). Explaining the Stones' adoption of a political stance in an earlier era, Friedlander writes: 'Students took to the streets on the continent, and Mick and Keith spent time in America, enveloped as it was by the political and cultural maelstrom … These experiences seeped into their new material' (1996, p. 113). Punk's engagement with anti-racism is seen as a direct product of the rise of racist politics (Friedlander, 1996, p. 257). In short, the argument is that pop's politics is a product of the politics of its context. Even more sophisticated accounts of African-American musical history rest upon an implicit assumption that social change is translated into musical expression, and that, in particular, political change takes musical form. So it is that Mark Anthony Neal writes: 'As the political terrain for blacks began to change after the Brown vs the Board of Education of Topeka, Kansas trial in 1954, so did the style and content of the dominant forms of black popular music '(1999, p. 28).

The problem with these accounts is captured in the distinction between correlation and causation. While it is possible to correlate the rise and fall of political pop with social and political change, this connection depends on privileging political pop over other types of (apolitical) pop (which, as we have seen, may be more prevalent). It also depends on generating some kind of causal connection between the two – a way of showing how particular times and experiences become incorporated into the music. The examples cited above imply such a causal chain, but do not tend to show how it operates and why it affects only certain artists or types of music.

Becoming political: a biographical approach

An alternative approach is to focus less on the general patterns of cultural and social change and more on the individuals. This, at least, has the advantage of not assuming grand cultural–political shifts. Biographies of the politically engaged musician tell the story of that engagement in terms of personal values and commitments. The songs emerge because of what the performer sees and thinks. Hence, Jon Wiener (1984, p. 523) describes how John Lennon's 'political interests continued to develop' during the time he was meditating with the Maharishi and how Lennon's awareness of sexual politics was learned from Yoko. The writing of 'Revolution' for the *The Beatles* (a.k.a. 'The White Album'), according to Wiener, 'marked John's decision that he had political responsibilities, and that he ought to fulfil them in his music' (1984, p. 61).

Lennon's observation of, and involvement in, political change, the argument runs, transformed his music. His political music was the product of his personal history. In a similar way, Dave Marsh maps Bruce Springsteen's political engagement by tracing the star's involvement with community initiatives. Marsh explains it in terms of the information that Springsteen received from the workers he met: these encounters were 'integrated into the bedrock of his performances' (1987, p. 271).

Joan Jara (1983) tells a similar story in her biography of her husband, the Chilean singer Victor Jara, who was murdered by the Pinochet regime. She writes of his growing political awareness, of family traditions and encounters with different forms of musical expression (much of Jara's formative years were spent in the theatre). All of these combined to trace his emergence as a singer of what he chose to call 'revolutionary songs'. In the same way, Robert Cantwell (1996, pp. 34–43) explains Joan Baez's political commitments by reference to her family background. Such explanations do not just apply to those in the folk tradition. A fascinating example of a biographical explanation of political engagement is provided by Gerald Meyer's story of Frank Sinatra's politics: 'The political part of Sinatra's life-activities, associations and avowed beliefs – grew out of his early experiences and reverberated throughout his life, in ways large and small' (2002, p. 312). Sinatra himself attributed his politics to his mother's own political commitments (Meyer, 2002, p. 314).

Such accounts are, it might be supposed, the direct product of the generic conventions of (auto)biography. Biographies may contain important elements of the story of how musicians become political but, in reconstructing the rational logic of individual awareness, they reduce the artist to an isolated political actor, one removed from their role as an artist. In other words, we learn about how individuals become 'political', but this is a story that might be told of anyone, whether or not they are musicians. We are left to wonder why *as musicians* they became politically engaged.

Should we think of singing about politics as the equivalent of a fashion? It goes in and out of favour, and this is what explains why at certain points musicians engage with politics. It is certainly possible to see the history of popular music in terms of its more or less political phases (from flower power to glitter rock, from punk to new romantics). Protest becomes fashionable just as does a style of clothes or choices of children's first names. In a fascinating study, the sociologist Stanley Lieberson (2000) explores changes in the fashion for different children's names and asks whether the changing taste in names can be explained extrinsically. He notes that some social commentators argue that 'cultural events reflect the social order', but argues: 'Although broad social developments do affect fashion and taste, their influence is neither as common nor as overwhelming as these commentators would have us believe' (Lieberson, 2000, p. 273). He is critical of the habit of associating cultural change with social change on the grounds that, however plausible the explanation, it rests upon very weak evidence (2000, p. 274). Instead, he contends that 'internal mechanisms' are more often the source of change.

Many of the claims made in pop histories are vulnerable to Lieberson's complaint about 'reflective theories' of culture. As we have noted, they provide very little evidence of the causal connections they are claiming and they are very selective in the examples they cite. Little attention is given to the music that does not fit the thesis. Alternatively, in a determination to see everything as a reflection of the politics of the times, the 'political' becomes a catch-all category which deprives the term of any substance. In questioning the 'reflection theory' of cultural change, Lieberson is not suggesting that such accounts are necessarily wrong, but that they are rarely supported by more than observation of an (interpreted) coincidence.

One of the few attempts to provide systematic evidence of cultural–social effects, of Lieberson's type, is Michael Haralambos's (1974) account of the decline of the blues. Ironically, in direct contrast to those who claimed that musical content was a product of material conditions, Haralambos argues that, in fact, economic circumstances do not provide an explanation. The blues *declined* even as unemployment among African-Americans rose. What we might conclude from this is that, whatever the connection between social conditions and musical form, it is much more complex than has traditionally been allowed for.

There is a second line of criticism that may also apply, concerning whether or not historically plausible connections may be drawn between social and political events and musical sounds. The argument is that music cannot, and should not, be reduced to a blank screen on to which events are inscribed. Music does not function as a noticeboard or a newspaper. This point is made forcefully by Robin Kelley (1997) in his critique of the way in which African-American cultural history is written. It tends, he says, to treat the music (and other cultural forms) as simply responses to ghetto conditions and, in doing so, it eliminates the creativity and pleasure that are inextricably bound up with cultural experience – and, indeed, without which that experience does not exist. Kelley rejects the suggestion that culture provides a 'set of coping mechanisms that grew out of the struggle for material and psychic survival' (1997, p. 19) and argues against a tendency to 'reduce expressive culture to a political text to be read like a less sophisticated version of *The Nation* or *Radical America*' (1997, p. 37). In other words, any attempt to connect musical expression to political conditions must place the pleasure derived from the culture at the centre of the explanation.

Just as it is necessary to pay attention to the pleasures of music in explaining its political content, so we need to have a more refined and sensitive account of how politics is experienced. The general accounts of music's history paint politics onto a broad canvas. But in seeking to make the connections between the two we need to look at the ways in which 'politics' exists for people – as rules and regulations, as laws and constraints. In his account of blues and soul, Haralambos points to the particular relationship between Jim Crow and musical change. The suggestion here is that it is state policy that determines cultural change. This is an argument that is explicit in many recent analyses of the political role of music in the Soviet bloc. What the analysts suggest is that, under conditions where the state monopolizes the conventional forms of political communication and seeks to regulate all forms of artistic expression, it becomes possible for musicians (in particular) to assume a leadership role, legitimated by their success as performers and artists. The state, in its regulatory role, politicizes musical expression, and music's aesthetics in turn makes possible an alternative form of political expression. Peter Wicke (1992), for instance, argues that East German rock musicians were instrumental in uniting the opposition to the Honneker regime that led to the collapse of the Berlin Wall. Anna Szemere (2001) highlights the role of popular musicians in the management of the transition from communism to capitalism within Hungary. Thomas Cushman (1995) and Peter Sheeran (2001) document the ways in which the rock underground articulated political opposition to the Soviet authorities. Sheeran claims that 'it was the dissident content of coded Soviet lyrics that caused most damage to the longevity of the Soviet system' (2001, p. 8). Even allowing for the hyperbolic character of such remarks, these studies make a powerful case for seeing how musicians become political as a result of the state's political strategy, and that understanding the latter is crucial to understanding the former. But states are, of course, not the only political actors that may be involved in the process.

Where the state is a key actor in particular, authoritarian political structures, political parties and social movements can be important agencies in connecting music to politics within liberal democratic regimes. This is the argument that emerges from accounts of the rise or revival of folk music, where writers such as Robert Cantwell (1996) and Michael Denning (1997) trace the impact of organizations such as the Popular Front on music's political role. In one sense, these organizations become, in the language of political science, 'political entrepreneurs' – equivalent to rock entrepreneurs like Bill Graham – in the way in which they create a political focus for a cause or a movement and then provide a context within which alliances are formed. CND performed this function in relation to traditional jazz in the 1950s (McKay, 2003); the Socialist Workers' Party did it for Rock Against Racism in the 1980s (Frith and Street, 1992). The Progressive Party was intimately linked with People's Songs (Cantwell, 1996, p. 165), just as the Popular Front was instrumental in the framing of Sinatra's politics (Meyer, 2002).

Ron Eyerman and Andrew Jamison (1998) make the most systematic case for this relationship. They argue that social movements create a context within which music assumes a political role, while at the same time those social movements depend on the performers to act as 'truth-bearers' for the movement. What is being suggested here is that musicians become political as a result of a political process. Their political commitments are, as it were, called into being by the movements which need people to perform a particular function. In other words, while personal biography and history may have something to do with the politicization of musicians, so too do the political processes and agents acting on the performer.

Music into politics, politics into music

The entrepreneurial role of a party or a social movement is itself dependent on the networks that connect the realms of culture and politics. These pathways establish the links between musicians and causes; they translate a functional need into a practice. These networks are marked by the way in which different types of 'capital' are traded on them. This is the argument of Christian Lahusen (1996) who has documented the ways in which the use of pop musicians to promote causes like Amnesty depends on the distribution of capital available to the actors. Such capital extends from the basic economic capital necessary to organize rallies and the like, through to the social capital that forges the links between cultural performers to political organizers (a matter of knowing Peter Gabriel's phone number or that of his manager). The argument here, as elsewhere, is that the political engagement of musicians is not simply a product of their personal commitments or their biographies, or indeed of their times, but of the networks that organize them into (or exclude them from) political activity.

One network that deserves particular attention in this context is the music industry. We are familiar with stories of the ways in which the political content of popular music has been ruthlessly excised by commercial 'imperatives' (see Denisoff, 1975; Harker, 1980). Sinatra and Belafonte suffered because of their association with left-wing causes (Meyer, 2002, p. 324; Ward, 1998, p. 323). Although such processes are sometimes portrayed by some as crude forms of 'gatekeeping', others have argued that they are more the product of the complex interactions of large organizations (Negus, 1999). The outcome, it might be said, is the same: the 'right' to be political can be granted and taken away by the organizations that produce popular music. The treatment of the Dixie Chicks by Clear Channel in the US and Madonna's decision to withdraw her video for her 'American Life' because of its politically contentious images might suggest that the industry plays a significant part in creating the opportunity structure for political engagement.

It is important, though, not just to see the industry as acting negatively to prevent political participation. It can also promote it. Suzanne Smith's (1999) study of the cultural politics of Motown reveals, for example, how the political engagement of performers like Marvin Gaye was dependent on the shifts in company policy (and the interests associated with it). Initially, the company confined its support for black power politics to a subsidiary, and only gradually did it allow its mainstream artists to make explicit their political concerns. In a similar vein, Negus notes that rap, one of the most overtly political of musical genres, is 'a self-conscious business activity as well as a cultural form and aesthetic practice' (Negus, 1999, p. 84). Rap's claim to be on/about 'the street' is a discursive device that enables the record industry to manage its forms of production. The explicitly political content of rap is partly conditional on its production through independent labels, at one remove from the corporations that subsequently license or distribute the music. The sense that rap is on and about the streets is part of a marketing strategy – selling/promoting it on the streets. Such corporate strategies intersect with aesthetic ones. The representation of rap feeds off, and legitimates, a rhetoric of 'telling it like it is' which tends to politicize the content.

The fact that musicians can perform as politicians is also a product of the way in which politics has been transformed. The particular role of the artist as champion or advocate of political causes, their endorsement of candidates and the like, has much to do with the ways in which politics has been 'personalized'. Elections are increasingly about 'personality', and election campaigns are organized around displays of personal style (captured in photo-opportunities, among other things). At one level this explains why a politician like Tony Blair chooses to pose with a Fender Stratocaster or Bill Clinton with a saxophone; at another, it explains why musicians, as experts in style, can easily transmute into politicians who represent political ideas and constituencies.

These phenomena are the product of the generic and technological conditions of the mass media, especially television (Meyrowitz, 1986), and the larger changes in the form of political communication in the modern era (Mancini and Swanson, 1996). Individuals become the focus of politics. John Keane (2002) describes the contemporary order as one of 'communicative abundance' in which celebrities and stars assume the decisive function in representing contemporary identities and sensibilities (British tabloid newspapers regularly feature front pages whose sole concern is the activities of a soap star or sportsperson). In a similar vein, Thomas Meyer (2002, p. 65) traces a media logic that leads, he says, to politainment: politics as a branch of show business. It is this that helps to account for the political role adopted by Bono and Bob Geldof. Their capacity to speak for 'us' is a product of their capacity to turn fandom into citizenship through the universal medium of political communication. Meyer, who is no fan of this process, writes:

> If democracy is nothing but legitimation by the most successful form of communication, then the communication artist is the best democrat, with no effort whatsoever. And if the authentic play of body politics is the most efficacious form of entertaining communication, then 'briefcase politics' with its institutionalised procedures and long-winded arguments might as well bow out now. (Meyer, 2002, p. 79)

The musician as politician might, therefore, be seen as the product of this larger trend. But in focusing on the transformation of political communication that may account for the rise of political pop star, we need to remind ourselves of the basis of the legitimacy they claim for their views. That for each of them, their capacity to act politically is dependent – at least in so far as they are taken seriously – on their careers as artists. Or put another way, the seriousness with which they are taken is not simply a product of the cause they support or the earnestness with which they support it. When the boy band Blue announced it was to set up a Live Aid 2 to support victims of the Iraq War, they were derided. Much the same happened to George Michael when he released his single 'Shoot the Dog' (a satire on the Bush–Blair relationship) in 2002, or when, before that, Geri Halliwell, the ex-Spice Girl, became an honorary UN ambassador. Their claim to political authority was threatened by their perceived lack of artistic credibility. The implication is that genre is an important determinant of the credibility and possibility of political engagement.

In her study of R&B, Mary Ellison suggests that the political engagement of music is prescribed by a law of nature: 'The coupling of black music with protest is a natural alliance' (1989, p. 1). Rather than personal biographies or political histories providing an account of political engagement, it is the generic conventions that explain the political character. They establish the rules and norms which apply to lyrical content and other elements of musical expression. They rule out certain topics and modes, and rule in others. Thus, political content may be organized into or out of musical forms. Folk provides a home for political sentiments in ways in which dance music does not; and those genres that accommodate politics may differ in the type of politics they sustain. (For the changing forms of the protest song, for example, see Denisoff, 1972a). But there are limits to this explanation. The historian Brian Ward, for example, writes of the support for the civil rights movement in the 1960s:

> While it may appear heresy to some, the fact remains that in certain respects Joan Baez was more important and conspicuously committed to the early Movement than James Brown, while Harry Belafonte did more to assist the struggle for black freedom in practical terms than all the soul icons of the 1960s combined. (Ward, 1998, p. 303)

Not only does genre not determine political engagement but, as we have already noted, the politics of a given genre are a product of its relationship to, and the influence of, political parties and movements.

But whether or not their chosen genre provides a platform for their political role, musicians' capacity to act politically also depends on factors that may be particular to them as individual performers. Not everyone within a genre will adopt the same political stance or will be accorded the same respect. Their claim to 'represent' their audience or a cause has to be legitimated and authorized. This is not achieved through the standard political procedures of election and accountability, but instead depends on some other basis. This can be a very traditional one: they have the money and fame which buys them access to the inner courts of the political establishment. Their claim may also derive from a sense of their affinity with their fans who give money for causes they represent and who identify with them in ways that resemble the representative-represented relationship.

One way of understanding this bond is in terms of what John Kane (2001) calls 'moral capital', a source of power that derives from the way in which individuals are judged as moral beings (Nelson Mandela is a paradigm case). Although Kane doesn't discuss the case of musicians, his argument suggests that his notion of moral capital may be of value in accounting for how pop stars operate as political actors. But it begs the question of how this moral capital is created. The answer, I would suggest, lies in the way in which they perform their role as musicians, the way they convey their politics in their art and in the other activities which connect to it (the interviews, public appearances and so on). This is a matter of style. Style, in this case, is the key to the politics. The study of popular music has paid woefully little attention to the business of creativity, but it has spent even less time on how it connects to political expression, to the link between creativity and conscience. Jason Toynbee is a notable exception. Toynbee invokes the image of a 'radius of creativity' within which various creative possibilities exist, mediating between 'subjective experience and objective social relations' (2000, pp. 41–42). Political music, by this account, emerges as a product of a particular combination of possibilities within the 'radius of creativity'. Being successful as a political representative depends on success as an artist, even if the conditions and criteria of both are different.

Writing about traditional forms of political representation, F.R. Ankersmit (1996) has argued that, contrary to convention, representation is matter of style and taste – a matter of the connection between politics and aesthetics. He writes:

> When asking him or herself how best to represent the represented, the representative should ask what political style would best suit the electorate. And this question really requires an essentially creative answer on the part of the representative, in the sense that there exists no style in the electorate that is quietly waiting to be copied. (Ankersmith, 1996, p. 54)

Politics, suggests Ankersmit, is a form of aesthetics, and aesthetics a form of politics. Such neat symmetries are not adequate (we need to look more closely at how particular aesthetics and particular politics are linked), but for the moment they serve to indicate how we might begin to make sense of the conditions under which pop stars become politicians. This essay began by asking why and when musicians engage with politics (given that this was not what most musicians do). No pretence has been made to giving a definitive answer; it is not clear that such a thing is possible. Instead, the essay has explored a range of possible factors – some more significant than others – that play a part in the process. The argument has been that general social trends and political events, though relevant, are not decisive. We need, instead, to look at the detailed political, creative and commercial processes that make possible political engagement.

Acknowledgements

An earlier version of this chapter was presented to the Experience Music Project Conference, Skip the Beat, in Seattle, 2003. My thanks are due to Eric Weisbard and to the other participants for their help in formulating my rough ideas.

Note

1. See http://www.britishsingles.com.

PART TWO
MONOPHONY OR
POLYPHONY?

Chapter 5

The future is history: hip-hop in the aftermath of (post)modernity

Russell A. Potter

When hip-hop first broke in on the (academic) scene, it was widely hailed as a boldly irreverent embodiment of the postmodern aesthetics of pastiche, a cut-up method which would slice and dice all those old humanistic truisms which, for some reason, seemed to be gathering strength again as the end of the millennium approached. Today, over a decade after the first academic treatments of hip-hop, both the intellectual sheen of postmodernism and the countercultural patina of hip-hop seem a bit tarnished, their glimmerings of resistance swallowed whole by the same ubiquitous culture industry which took the rebellion out of rock 'n' roll and locked it away in an I.M. Pei pyramid. There are hazards in being a young art form, always striving for recognition even while rejecting it – Ice Cube's famous phrase 'Fuck the Grammys' comes to mind – but there are still deeper perils in becoming the single most popular form of music in the world, with a media profile that would make even Rupert Murdoch jealous.

In an era when pioneers such as KRS-One, Ice-T, and Chuck D are well over 40 and hip-hop ditties about thongs and bling bling dominate the malls and airwaves, it's noticeably harder to locate any points of friction between the microphone commandos and the bourgeois masses they once seemed to terrorize with sonic booms pumping out of speaker-loaded jeeps. Indeed, in an age marked by a far more material presence of 'terror', perhaps the oddest development is the way in which so much mainstream hip-hop has fled the scene of social issues, embracing the comfort zone with all the abandon of Huey P. Newton leaping into a Barcalounger. The dominant hip-hop artists of the first few years of the twenty-first century are tense but restrained, their lyrical forays recontained within the persistent metaphorical landscape of guns and sexual innuendo, and they boast familiar rhymes and familiar subjects. At the same time, hip-hop's audience has grown in every direction, and many elements that once made it distinct – spoken rhymes, sampled beats, drum 'n' bass – have become part of the broader spectrum of musical conventions.

All this is not to say that there is no longer such a thing as political hip-hop, or that the music has lost its edge. As one reviewer of my 1995 book, *Spectacular Vernaculars*, aptly observed, 'there is more to the hip-hop story than the self-consciously political, and there is more to the political itself than can be consciously thought' (Wood, 1996). This is a crucial point which is even more important today: the most vital and substantial dimension of the politics of hip-hop has always been *underground*, in its collective verbal, vernacular political sensibility. What has been counted as 'political' rapping in the past was only one *part* of the double historical movement of black culture, which has, from its earliest days, alternated between an outward-looking progressive stridency and a no less powerful interior, reflective force.

The crucial hip-hop artists of this new millennium are aligned along the interior arc of that pendulum: introspective, local and idiosyncratic. The sometimes obscure, free-ranging lyrical disquisitions of The Roots' Black Thought are characteristic of this new movement, as are the evanescent, free-verse lyrical rambles of UK rapper, The Streets. Even the names of such rappers as these are at once abstract and personal, absolutely idiosyncratic and just barely tangible, questions for answers that are blown away in the wind or lost in the sounds of traffic. It's not just rappers who are seeking the truth in a more vernacular and yet more abstract form; the resurgence of DJ culture at the beginning of the new century is still going strong, featuring artists such as Rob Swift, the X-ecutioners, DJ Shine, and DJ Spooky. Spooky, aka Paul D. Miller, has been one of the most profound innovators of this new school, moving seamlessly from scratching discs to live multimedia re-edits of videos and music. Among his projects has been 'Errata Erratum', an online, user-modifiable remix of the cut-ups of Marcel Duchamp, as well as *Rebirth of a Nation* (2004b), an hour-long live digital re-edit of D.W. Griffith's *Birth of a Nation* which takes the film's racist visual tropes and stands them on their heads.

At the same moment, the fundamental landscapes of race and class in America have shifted in profound ways. Latinos – 'Hispanics' to the Bureau of the Census – are now a numerically larger minority in the US than African-Americans. Even being black ain't what it used to be, as illustrated by recent tension on college campuses between Africans of American descent versus Africans from Africa and other formerly colonized nations around the world. This is no longer than age, it would seem, of Malcolm X or Jesse Jackson; it's the new multiracial, multicultural era of Barack Obama and Tiger Woods. Of course, it's never really been news that racism in the United States has never been completely understandable in simple terms of 'black' and 'white', but it's fast becoming a tangible reality that no one can ignore.

Hip-hop has enjoyed a second adolescence in this shifting landscape, first by spreading around the globe in the manner of earlier American cultural exports and, second, by absorbing, as audiences and tastes developed, performers and listeners from an increasingly varied and heterogeneous populace. Eminem was never the first white guy to rap – who could forget MC Serch, Vanilla Ice or the mostly white Young Black Teenagers? – but he may well be the first rapper whom we could *honestly* say 'just happened' to be white. Back in the day, there was cause for celebration when hip-hop beats made their way from the park to the clubs to the stadiums. But, just as importantly, they've moved on further, thumping lightly into supermarket aisles, lifts, and dentists' offices. Hip-hop has gone from being invisible to visible to ubiquitous, and in the rearguard of that ubiquity new forces of combination and resistance yet lurk, declaring that upon these fragments they will shore new ruins, new modalities, new possibilities.

Yet this is not simply a revolution in style. It's an age of unprecedented flux, with forces within new media and its nascent models of file-sharing, streaming, downloading and home mixing increasingly blurring the boundaries between consumption and production. Once upon a time, hip-hop turned these tables by taking the LP, hitherto an end-user product, blowing the dust off it, and re-producing it as the source of new beats and loops. Now it's rare for a rap or a rhyme or a beat or a riff to remain in any fixed form long enough for dust to settle; every act of consumption opens up potentially endless acts of sharing, editing, remixing and resharing, almost all of which fall outside of the traditional music markets so beloved of an increasingly out-of-touch recording industry. The response of that industry – locking up music downloads in protected formats, suing its own consumers, inventing self-destructing DVDs and encrypted formats – fails to recognize that the cat is out of the bag, the horse is out of the barn and no amount of relocking the doors will do the least bit of good.

It seems to me that there are two key modes of hip-hop resistance enabled by new media technologies and culture. The first of these operates on a kind of retro rocket, eschewing the notion of music as an object and recovering it as an irreproducible event. The Roots chose this model for their recent album, *The Tipping Point*. The Roots had always been a live band, even back in the days when unpacking a drum kit on stage at a hip-hop club brought laughs of derision from some in the audience. But with *The Tipping Point*, they built a new bridge between the live, jam-session feel they sought and the more 'produced' aesthetic of contemporary hip-hop. In a series of jams that took place over weeks and months, they worked out new musical ideas with a wide variety of guest artists; when the jams seemed ripe they were 'plucked' and thrown down on tape. Then it was time for Black Thought to have a listen, picking out the bits and pieces he wanted to rap over. Finally, studio versions of the tracks were compiled, and the final vocals were ladled over them like syrup over a stack of pancakes: 'Some cats that play dirty didn't live, to regret it / But move to the music he can live through the record / I'm a Philly boss player, a dope rhyme sayer / *It's Black Ink back gettin cake by the layer* / by the stack, comin at us, get your weight right yeah / If not, you makin a mistake right there, f'real' ('I Don't Care', The Roots, 2004).

The second mode reaches back to the old days of DJing, when the mix was a fundamentally live occurrence, produced 'on the fly' with no two performances the same. The 'mix tape' of the old school days was the embodiment of this freestyle cut 'n' paste, with the reputation of the tape depending as much on the component tracks as on the skills of the DJ. Circulating primarily on a trade basis among hip-hop headz and other DJs, such tapes weren't initially intended for a commercial audience; their underground exchange was a kind of fermenting pot for talent and exposure, something like the club scene, but more portable. Eventually, however, the artistry of the DJs became an end in itself, and a market developed for the mix tapes based increasingly on the skills of the turntablist, whose sonic palette combines an increasingly wide range of raw sonic materials.

similar to/same as cultural exchange amongst blues musicians in juke joints of the early 1900's

[It might have seemed that the copyright scare of the early 1990s, which forced artists such as Biz Markie to pay large fees in order to declare 'all samples cleared', would have had a dampening effect on such recordings, but it didn't. For one, many of the materials sampled were from derived other rappers and DJs – people who were less likely to file lawsuits against their own medium of cultural exchange. For two, since the mix tapes – and later mix CDs – were more often given away than sold, the lack of monetary compensation made mixes a far less clear-cut violation of copyright law. In a recent instance of this evolution, digital download centres such as Apple's iTunes are now offering their own mix tracks, many running to 25 or 30 minutes, and which, unlike other single tracks of far shorter duration, can be downloaded free of charge. This is not, however, your father's – or your grandma's – turntable. In the post-Victrola age, crates full of vintage vinyl are only one ingredient of many in the latter-day mixmaster's stew. A hodge-podge of old and often copyright-free audio recordings-instructional records, promotional films, unidentifiable snippets from television commercials and self-help tapes is folded in with beats, rhymes and musical riffs from every kind of music under the sun. Like the street sound-men of Kingston, Jamaica in the early 1960s, this new generation of DJ artists scrubs the names off the labels to keep audiences guessing – but, like the hip-hop producers of more recent years, they don't hesitate to use a full range of digital editing, voice manipulation, synthesized sounds and pop-cultural detritus. New technologies, among them digital CD 'turntables' such as Pioneer's CDJ-1000, which mimic vinyl scratching with uncanny precision, have made it possible to do many things live that used to require studio preproduction.

At a recent appearance in Providence, Rhode Island, DJ Spooky handed everyone in the audience free mix CDs (*Public Talk* (2004a)) containing hour-plus mixes that brought together everything from Aerosmith guitar chops, Slick Rick vocal snips, an educational tape on the origins of written language, a remix of George W. Bush's most recent State of the Union speech and traditional vinyl scratches. Every disc was slightly different – itself a defeat to the uniformity of conventional production – and the disc itself was the means, not the end, to musical dissemination. At that same appearance, DJ Spooky played a track he had assembled entirely from 'elements' sent to him via e-mail and the Web, including vocals from Chuck D and beats from the drummer for Slayer, all of them sent with the artists' blessing and no strings attached. This kind of assemblage, done without the aid of studios, labels, sound engineers or overhead, and involving people and performances who only meet in the DJ's hands, is a harbinger of things to come. As Spooky notes in his book, *Rhythm*

Science, 'in the future, the voice you speak with may not be your own' (Miller, 2004).

Spooky has extended the same radical aesthetic of cut-n-paste resistance to visual media, most notably in his *Rebirth of a Nation* remix of D.W. Griffith's *Birth of a Nation*. Armed with a bank of computers and turntables on to which digital sound, film and computer elements are loaded at the ready, Miller puts Griffith through a digital grinder, shredding the racist imagery of the original into its constituent bits, then re-assembling these shreds and shards into something completely different. The replicated images – framed by the title cards with the looping name of Griffith – are refracted by repetition, looping and digital effects, then renamed and reframed by cards with 'Paul D. Miller' and 'PDM' the place of 'DWG' and his celluloid trademark. The entire pastiche, projected on to three giant screens in a move reminiscent of Gance's Napoleon, is mixed *live* from elements stored in a series of computers arrayed along with CD decks and digital mixers in an illuminated sound station on the left of the stage.

In his very person Miller, with degrees in French and philosophy, confounds the academic/DJ split, practising and mixing with a kind of self-reflexivity hardly possible in the past. Recently in Paris, he dedicated a concert to the late Jacques Derrida, who had just died a few weeks previously, surely a first in the annals of DJing. But, more importantly, he's a mixer who knows his intellectual roots as well as his musical ones, explicitly invoking the work of Marcel Mauss, Michel de Certeau, Guy Debord and Marcel Duchamp, claiming his video/aural ready-mades as the embodiment of *detournement*, sonic *bricolages* with critical theory in bold print on the list of ingredients. In *Rhythm Science* (2004c), Miller extends these connections, shifting between his own theoretical freestyle and textual 'samples' of everyone from Emerson to Sun Ra. It's a *tour de force* and possibly the first book to comment on the cut 'n' paste culture which truly embodies what it preaches.

Some may dismiss Miller as a kind of anomaly; after all, how many other DJs have or could follow in his footsteps? But it's equally justifiable to see in his work the kind of synergy between intellectual theories and musical forms and tropes that has fermented in previous African-American cultural moments; one thinks of the 1950s, when many a serious bop fan's shelves bent heavy not only with Bird and Dizzy, but with Sartre and Camus, or the Black Arts movement as it drummed out philosophical musings over congas and cowbells. Evoking those movements, Miller situates himself equally in the 'Afrological' and contemporary theory, a postmodern griot who doesn't have to 'change keys to play these'. And he's not alone; as Rob Swift, of the legendary turntable crew the X-ecutioners, put it like this on a recent recording: Turntablists enable this culture's continuation / With collaboration of mics to lay the foundation / Peep the instrumentation while others be fakin' / Jacks not acknowledging elements and we be takin' 'em back with a swiftness ... / We come to transform the forms in modern day music / Recognize true artful collaboration-we can't lose it! ('Modern Day Music', Swift, 1999). The X-ecutioners themselves are an example of what Swift calls for; as an all-DJ crew they broke the mould of the rapper/DJ just at the point where many DJs were being eclipsed by producers whose fingers were more at home on the sliders of a mixing board than on the edge of a vinyl disc. Originally known as the X-men, a moniker they had to abandon, ironically, after pressure from Marvel Comics who regarded it as a trademark violation, they have been at the forefront of what DJ Prime Cuts calls the 'turntablist revolution'. Along with artists such as DJ Skribble, DJ Q-Bert, Mix Master Mike and DJ Infamous, the X-ecutioners have redrawn a map of hip-hop with the DJ in the middle in the place of the rapper.

All this has rich and varied implications for those at the crossroads of hip-hop and critical theory. Specifically, within the theories of radical everyday practice set forth by the Situationist International, as well as in the models of quotidian or vernacular resistance articulated by Michel de Certeau, contemporary hip-hop practice forms one of the most potent enactments of such resistance. *Retournement* – in the classic sense, a turning aside, reappropriation and/or reversal of the hegemonic signified – was, in the past, always somewhat stronger in theory than in practice. Pasting random words over a newspaper advertisement, wandering the streets by making random choices at intersections, or creating absurdist apothegms out of mix 'n' match clichés – however radical their conception – had little or no effect on society; such acts, inscrutable as they were pure, had all the clatter of the proverbial feather dropped into the Grand Canyon. Similarly, de Certeau's examples of *bricolage* and 'la perruque' – workplace interventions, doodles, making little people out of office paperclips – appear so small, so quiet that they pose little threat to the larger power structures of the workplace. Conceptual art based on such ideas – such as the art exhibition, 'La Perruque' presented in 2001 at the office/gallery in San Francisco[1] – tended to remain just that, conceptual. It was never quite clear what impact tiny words on ceiling tiles, soundproof wall boxes, or flowers made of steno pads would ultimately have, either on those for who the artplace was a workplace, or vice versa. Translated into the mixmasters' medium, in contrast, these same principles move instantly from the potential to the kinetic. The beats themselves, punctuating the air and propelling the body into movement, are woven within found sounds, sampled speeches and aural fragments; as Psychic TV's Genesis P. Orridge put it, music can be 'absolutely any pattern ov sounds – you can even dance to (or *on*) people you hate (Orridge, 1990). DJ Spooky, for one, has pioneered this kind of kinetic resistance, having remixed not only George W. Bush but even an old interview recorded with Nazi propaganda minister Joseph Goebbels, which was aired on German radio in 2004. Material created with all kinds of intentions – to sell, to convince, to educate, to indoctrinate – is both neutralized and re-assembled into absurd aural doppelgangers who deform and overwhelm their contexts.

The re-assembly of the familiar jumbles and fuses the auras of the original, creating a new kind of narrative sequence that plays out at the level of the mythic signified. Paul Miller has spoken of this kind of tactical sampling as forming a powerful 'global vernacular', within which every consumer is potentially a producer, every utterance transferable, and pastiche supplants the old ideologies of 'pure' originality (Miller, quoted from a personal interview). In this sense, a sample is merely a vocabulary item in a potentially new utterance; it is no more 'owned' or 'used' than a word in a natural language can be said to be. The major music labels and others who claim control over this lexicon suddenly appear as absurd at the letter-vendors in the town square of Dictionopolis, blithely unaware that what they purvey as a limited commodity can actually be minted by anyone.

Miller, as Spooky, plays on this metaphor in his *Hip-Hop World Mix CD*, where a woman's voice clearly appropriated from a language learning tape inquires,

'Can you speak [DJ]?'
'What about that other language we talked about? The language of [DJ]?'
'Now, to begin with, here are some expressions you will use most often'.

This is followed by a series of densely articulated vinyl scratches, to each of which a different voice replies, 'I just don't understand'. Then, another voice of authority – this one evidently explaining the invention of writing – remarks:

Well, poor Mr. [Disk Jockey] had a hard time making himself understood. How much easier it would have been if he had used a name for [scratches]. So, people began to agree on names for things, and they found they could talk to each other … and when you're using [scratches] to stand for the things you say and see, that's the language of [DJs] – let's find out some more about them. (Miller, 2004d)

It's a pedagogical *tour de force*, quite literally appropriating a discourse on the nature of written language and making it over as a lecture on DJ tropology. The scratches here are, in a sense, just place-holders; the full power inherent in the substitution of signifiers only appears when elements with a strong affective or mythic significance are placed, as it were, inside these blanks. A clip from Slick Rick brings back the days of his predominance, memories of his time in jail, 'Free Slick Rick' T-shirts, and anything else that happened from 1990 to 1996. A KRS-One sample from 'Return of the Boom-Bap', itself a deliberate echo of an earlier line from 'Criminal Minded', brings back all the affective and memorial cards indexed under 'BDP'; the Aerosmith chop from 'Walk This Way' transports the listener back to 1983 and Run-DMC's breakthrough single. Or, of course, it doesn't – new affective lines, new memorial traces, are constantly being layered over the old ones, such that plenty of people who weren't even born in 1967 will get a memory flash out of The Beatles' 'Sergeant Pepper', and listeners who only know James Brown from samples will see a far different aura from those who rocked the house with the original JBs.

In a different way, The Roots play with the same deck, taking Sly and the

Family Stone's 'Star', lopping it, looping it and even adding what sounds like digitally-mimicked groove, hiss and rumble in their single 'Star/Pointro'. It's not just sampling in the limited sense that it used to be used, as a kind of spice, some salt 'n' pepper for the sonic stew; it's sampling as a point of sustained reference, the uncanny return of the familiar in an unfamiliar, even distorted, form. No one has quite matched the audacity of Negativland – who once sampled an entire album by U2 and released it as an ironic clone of itself – but it's getting closer. Larger and larger song 'elements' are being employed; if, as Public Enemy's Chuck D used to say, hip-hoppers used to throw away the turkey and take the bones, there's a lot more 'meat' – and a lot more 'juice' – on the sonic shopping list of today's DJs and producers (Chuck D, 1994).

All of this takes place, of course, as mainstream hip-hop has risen to the summit of the pop-cultural pyramid, replacing rock 'n' roll as the biggest selling kid on the global block. For those cultural critics and musicians alike who had come to regard hip-hop as the essence of resistance, it's been a frustrating time, living in the shadow of one's own shadow, with many political rappers consigned to the same musical graveyard that Whodini and Kurtis Blow were buried in two decades ago. In defence of the change, industry types shake their heads and say, 'well, it's just a youth culture', much as they did when rock sank slowly into the sunset of catalogue sales and reunion tours. Yet the same 'youth' who seem so clear and easily defined when viewed through the cross-hairs of media marketing may also, like their rock peers, know a thing or two about their history, along with more about their future than the popcorn prognosticators of pop culture ever dreamt of. Hip-hop, just as it always has, discovers its future in the fragments of its own past, cannibalizing its own parts in the ancient backyard tradition of vernacular recycling, and it's just here – at the crossroads of the already known and the not yet complete – that the new schools of turntablism and stream of consciousness rapping intersect.

So just where is cultural theory in all this? Back in the day – in the early 1990s – it seemed that postmodern theorists needed hip-hop far more than hip-hop needed them. There was something missing from the po-mo celebrations of pastiche and countervalence, a material allegory gone wanting and unfilled. Hip-hop seemed to fit a number of bills, and Houston A. Baker, Tricia Rose, Michael Eric Dyson and many others, myself amongst them, welcomed the political hip-hop of the day. Of course, the welcome was not quite universal, as some critics – Henry Louis Gates among them – tried to have their pie while eating only a slice. The highly overdetermined and conflicted political valences of the rappers of the day made some people nervous; if you wanted resentment, you had to take it straight, downing that revolutionary bottle complete with its chasers of anti-Semitism and misogyny. Who can forget Professor Griff or Eazy-E? And yet the dissonance was a reminder – a reminder that the academic dreams of an unsullied resistance were as much fantasies as the threatening black minions who populated white suburbia's night of the living Willie Hortons.

[margin handwriting: reference this paragraph to Zion I's: "There's A Stranger in my House"]

The present tense – and 'tense' may well be the operative word – is far more heteroglot, impure and jumbled, and yet within its multimedia palimpsests there remain words, there for the scraping, which may well be more true to the 'complex and contradictory' forces of postmodernism than intellectual 'postmodernists' ever expected. The serpent bites its tail, and the sound and fury of cultural commentary sounds a bit hollow in post-terrorist America. And still there are those who cross over the cultural chalk marks, whether it be Cornell West cutting a hip-hop CD (much to the consternation of mortar-boarded heads at Harvard), or DJ Spooky, transfusing the weft and weave of his family cloth business into the rumblings of new French criticism while an undergraduate amongst the pine trees of Maine. It might almost be a face, a collection of singing, bearded professors waving their hands in unison to the Wagstaffs of cultural convenience. And yet, at the end of it all, here we are, facing the empty room where the old opposition between the chalkboard and the turntable may at last be starting to collapse.

And in the midst of this unexpected *detournement*, the landscape continues to shift. African-American traditions of music, dance and verbal signifying, so crucial to the twentieth century, are beginning to be eclipsed by an indigenous alliance of forces which are altering the landscape, deterritorializing the territory before it can even be mapped. Hip-hop can no longer be conceived of as just a black thang, a New York thang, a West Coast versus East Coast dust-up or even as a primarily American artform. International artists of the 1990's, such as France's MC Solaar and Britain's Apache Indian, turned out to be just the tip of the iceberg; today a vast roster of global hip-hoppers have extended the slanguage in every direction. Italy's Articulo 31 has sliced and diced Dylan; the Senegalese crew Blaw has picked up where MC Solaar left off; Chile's Sonido Acido has merged Latin beats with high-hat and bass; and the Sona Family has dropped mad rhymes in Urdu at the centre of a booming Asian/British scene. Although it's true that there is a technology lag, many artists from the *pre*-industrial world have leapt over it, telegraphing their blows to the *post*-industrial world via the Internet; every one of the acts I've mentioned has distributed its work over the Internet or can be tracked down on file-sharing servers by the diligent searcher.

If there's one postmodern theoretical prophecy that best accounts for the state of hip-hop and other musics which have jacked into the Net to the fullest extent, it is Deleuze and Guattari's concept of the *rhizomatic*:

> There is no longer a tripartite division between a field of reality (the world) and a field of representation (the book) and a field of subjectivity (the author). Rather, an assemblage establishes connections between certain multiplicities drawn from each of these orders, so that a book has no sequel nor the world as its object nor one or several authors as its subject. (1988, p. 23)

One has only to replace 'the book' with 'the recording' to see that, in the age of post-mechanical reproduction, the aura is in the eye of the beholder. Not only have recordings no single author and no single sequence, but the old orders of 'production' and 'consumption' have been rendered practically indistinguishable – we are all consumer/producers, and the object has been supplanted by the process. This is postmodernism in action, not a theory on a hill but a thoroughly vernacular practice, 'in full effect' without the intervention, support or even the knowledge of the theoretical *cognoscenti.*

Note

1. Art exhibition, 'La Perrugue', 13 August–November 2001 (curators Amy Balkin and Sean Fletcher). Arts included Peter E.V. Allen, Amy Balkin, Amy Francheschini, Lissa Ivy, Josh On, Timothy Hutchings, Fallout and Indigo Sam.

Chapter 6

Everyday people: popular music, race and the articulation and formation of class identity in the United States

James Smethurst

It should go without saying, but I'll say it anyway, that the formation of class-consciousness is complicated. But even if we don't precisely adhere to Marxist definitions of class, there is still a widely held Marxist or post-Marxist sense of class as an objective fact or condition that can be revealed with various degrees of accuracy. Thus the forming of class-consciousness is basically a question of recognizing one's true identity. In this view, one famous problem that can arise is that the subject might get it wrong, especially under the influence of those who benefit from the misapprehension of class identity. In short, we have the notion of false consciousness as it has been variously named and conceived.

Nonetheless, as much as we might subscribe to something like traditional Marxist notions of class, we obviously understand that, say, a carpenter, a teacher, and an assembly line worker are quite different in many respects, even if we consider them all to be working-class. Other factors, such as race, ethnicity, language, region, historical period, religion and so on, also obviously inflect a subject's sense of class identification. At the same time, we recognize that, despite these differences, people can also, though not inevitably, find a sense of shared identity as members of something like the working class, at least symbolically. The point here is that class-consciousness is an imagined community based on a variable process of distinction and commonalty that is not simply a given. This may seem incredibly banal, but the point that people don't come with class-consciousness imprinted in their DNA and consequently can construe it in a variety of ways is worth remembering since it is apparently easy to forget.

One thing that I continue to find strange is the still persistent notion that class and class conflict is something occluded in the public discourses of the United States since the Second World War – that it is a dirty little secret buried beneath the false consciousness of 'identity politics' and rhetoric about a 'middle class' that encompasses all but the richest and poorest in the United States. On a certain level it is true that the term 'class warfare' has gained a certain currency as a Republican Party tool for shutting down discussions of class in national politics. The term 'middle class' has been, and is still, widely used in education, mainstream politics, the mass media and scholarly discussions of popular culture with the intentional or unintentional effect of blurring class divisions and class identification. And, the nationalist (and often Left nationalist) liberation movements (for example, Black Power, the Chicano Movement, the Asian American Movement, the Women's Movement and Gay Liberation) of the 1960s and 1970s foreclosed any simple notion of class identity uninflected by race, ethnicity, gender or sexuality – though I don't believe that there was ever a time in the United States when such a notion existed or could have possibly come into being in a broad and deeply-felt public sense.

Nonetheless, it seems strange because popular culture, particularly popular music, is now and has long been saturated with quite overt, generally masculinist representations of class and class conflict – class warfare, really. For example, when I started listening to the radio as a child in the 1960s, such representations filled the airwaves, in songs like the McCoys' 'Hang On Sloopy', the Four Seasons' 'Rag Doll' and 'Dawn', Johnny Rivers's 'Poor Side of Town', Paul Revere and the Raiders' 'Hungry', the Vogues' 'Five O'Clock World' and, a little later, Sly and the Family Stone's 'Everyday People'. Sometimes these songs portrayed a difficult crossing of class (and sometimes racial or ethnic) boundaries (as in 'Hang On Sloopy' and 'Rag Doll', and 'Everyday People', for that matter). Sometimes they imagined resistance to class oppression through class solidarity (as in 'Poor Side of Town' and 'Five O'Clock World'). Sometimes they pictured class lines as insurmountable (as in 'Dawn'). Still the feeling of class conflict and even class hatred was palpable in them, with the figure of the working-class woman serving as an icon of class solidarity, class betrayal and even salvation from class domination.

Such visions of class identity projected by, with and through popular music in the United States are diverse and often contradictory. Though I will briefly sketch out some different ways in which class has inflected US popular music since the Second World War, my primary interest here is not to create a broad taxonomy of the direct invocation and figuration of class and class community – a subject far beyond the scope of this essay. What I want to take up here is a subset of that subject: the existence and persistence of important, but somewhat understudied imaginings of convergences of interests and identity across ethnic and racial lines, often in ways that strangely depend on notions of ethnicity and race in various sorts of popular music in the United States.

Class identification and the creation of a feeling of class community are often created indirectly by a cultural form that has gained a sort of class association. Opera infrequently refers directly to bourgeois life in the United States and, in fact, sometimes tells the stories of people we might consider poor: bohemians, fruit vendors and even miners (as in Puccini's *La Fanciulla del West*).

Nonetheless, from its very beginning, opera has been associated with the bourgeoisie in Europe *and* in the United States. Similarly, heavy metal music relatively rarely refers directly to class oppression, but its sounds, performance styles and tropes have been prominently linked to a working-class audience.

Sometimes, as in rap and country and western, the genre is significantly defined by the thematization of a class experience as well as the associative sounding of it. Country and rap are notable because their framings of class identity and class conflict are so often linked to race in the mass media, presidential candidate-nominating conventions and so on – with country and western framed, in the United States, as the music of the white working class and rap as that of a black urban 'underclass'. Of course, such castings of these musical genres present some obvious problems. Country has long had a significant black audience, especially in the South, and black musicians and musical forms associated with African-Americans have exerted a profound effect on country, including the personal mentoring of individual country artists – as musicians from Jimmie Rogers to Hank Williams, Jr have publicly acknowledged. And rap and hip-hop have had a large number of non-African–American and suburban and even rural participants for decades.

Ironically, critical discussions of the supposed migration of rap and hip-hop from their original mean urban streets to the suburban shopping mall have in some ways strengthened notions of hip-hop as black through the familiar language of racial authenticity and racial appropriation that has often been applied to popular music. Critical discussions of the intersection of popular music and race in the United States have been (and still are) couched in terms of primitivist appropriations of African–American music by white artists and audiences for fun and profit while reinforcing racial hierarchies and stereotypes. Elvis Presley is, of course, the classic icon of this view.

Another approach to this intersection between race and popular culture can be found in the work of such historians and cultural critics as David Roediger, Eric Lott, Jeffrey Melnick, W.T. Lhamon and Matthew Jacobson. Though often coming from differing ideological viewpoints, these scholars examine how racialized and ethnicized notions of whiteness and blackness, often articulated through various ventriloquisms of African–American subjects and expressive culture by white artists, were crucial in adjudicating who was 'American' and in creating a sense of class identity and solidarity among white workers. As Jeffrey Melnick notes, one example of this is the so-called doo wop revival of the late 1960s and early 1970s, which used vocal R 'n' B largely performed and significantly consumed by African–Americans during the 1950s and early 1960s to figure or sound a vision of a sort of all-white working-class (or 'white ethnic') urban utopia.[1]

Here I have to confess that I attended quite a few 1950s rock 'n' roll/R 'n' B revival shows in New York City and northern New Jersey in the early 1970s. Perhaps because my friends and I were considerably younger than the average member of the audience at these shows, people there frequently took it upon themselves to explain at greater or lesser length what the music meant to them. What I took away from these discussions was that this utopia was not one of a simpler, more 'innocent' America of *Ozzie and Harriet*, or even of the *Patty Duke Show* and 'the sights that a girl can see from Brooklyn Heights' (where the upper-middle-class or, if you will, the petty bourgeois Lane family of the *Patty Duke Show* lived) as it is often framed – or the racial utopia posited by Greil Marcus (1995, pp. 225–26) and Philip Groia (1983, p. 10). Rather it was a dream of stable urban working-class neighbourhoods, union jobs and working-class connected-ness or solidarity often linked to a sense of being ethnic (especially Italian–American and Jewish–American) outsiders.[2] In this vision, the Ozzies and Harriets, and their children, are frequently portrayed as the class enemy. This dream was, in many respects, inflected by racism, with African–Americans and Puerto Ricans (in the north-east) seen as prime culprits in the dissolution or decay of the mythic 'old neighbourhood' to which they often looked back from blue-collar suburbs or newer (for them) urban neighbourhoods in the north-east Bronx, southern Brooklyn, Queens and Staten Island. And yet the hard-core doo wop revivalist generally considered (and still apparently consider) African–American groups as the only true purveyors of authentic doo wop and hold dear the memory (or sometimes the fantasized image) of integrated audiences at the Apollo Theatre in Harlem or the Paramount Theatre in Brooklyn.[3]

In short, one could find within the doo wop revival a strong sense of class identification, and often class warfare with obvious lingering Popular Front sentiments of what Michael Denning calls 'laborist social democracy' as well as a vision of society that, like much of the post-CIO labor movement, alternates between racially exclusionary and multiracial notions of class, even among so-called 'Reagan Democrats' (Dennis, 1996, pp. 151–59). And, while this utopian vision was both promoted and parodied to a national audience in the musical play and movie *Grease*, the television show *Happy Days*, and the rise to stardom of the singing group *Sha Na Na*, many of the older doo wop fans to whom I spoke did not like Sha Na Na *et al.* because they felt, with considerable justification, that they, their music and their dream of class community were being ridiculed – hence one reason for wanting to set the record straight to a teenager like me.

Alongside models of class articulation and identification that depend on notions of whiteness (and sometimes ethnicity) and blackness, of racial theft and authenticity, there have long existed broadly popular multiracial and multi-ethnic models of class and class-consciousness that can be traced, at least from the Knights of Labor (and perhaps from the religious movements of the Second Great Awakening in the South) to the present. However, it was with the rise of the Popular Front period in the middle 1930s and the growth of the mass industrial unions of the Congress of Industrial Organizations (CIO) often under the slogan of the Communist Left, 'Black and White Unite and Fight', that the notion of a multiracial working-class unity in which particular ethnic and racial identities did not wither away so much as interests converged became broadly available, plausible and institutionalized, competing with racially exclusionary visions of class. Whatever the historic failures of the US trade union movement might be, and however persistent exclusionary models of class identification and community among significant segments of organized labour, the vision of a common class interest across racial and ethnic boundaries, between native-born and immigrant, between men and women, among different crafts and job classifications remains not simply the property of radicals. Rather, it became and is still the official doctrine of most of the US labour movement, especially unions representing workers in the service sector, the public sector and manufacturing.

Not surprisingly, it was also in the Popular Front period that African–American-derived music, particularly swing and other forms of jazz, was used to consciously articulate a multiracial model of class consciousness and a popular, anti-fascist democracy among white, black and Chicana/o Americans. As Michael Denning notes, swing was basically the sound track of the Popular Front in many parts of the United States (1996, pp. 228–38). One might say that there was a dialectal relationship between swing and Popular Front visions of class. The Popular Front exerted considerable direct and indirect influence on some prominent swing performers, such as Benny Goodman and Artie Shaw, and their audiences. Long before the baseball player Jackie Robinson debuted at Ebbets Field in 1947, white band leaders broke with the apartheid practices of American mass culture and included such African–American musicians as Billie Holliday, Charlie Christian, Roy Eldridge and Lionel Hampton in their groups. While these breaks with Jim Crow caused the bands (particularly the black musicians in them) enormous difficulties, especially (but not exclusively) when touring in the South, while many white band leaders, such as Glenn Miller, were quite racist (and often anti-Semitic), and while such inclusions could be considered a sort of tokenism or exoticism, the presence of black and white musicians side-by-side in popular orchestras provided a powerful vision of a democratic multiracial, multi-ethnic working-class culture from which the Popular Front drew strength. From that moment at least until the present, music significantly and publicly associated with Africa–Americans, (jazz, rock and roll, disco, R 'n' B, rap and hip-hop) have been used by artists and audiences to articulate and advance models of class identity that are in contradistinction to more racialist notions of class consciousness.

Despite the work of George Lipsitz and others, it is easy to forget, for example, the early class associations of R & B and rock 'n' roll in the post-swing era as well as how it was inflected by race and age group. Again, as would the case in the 1960s, early rock 'n' roll and R & B frequently thematized class and class conflict. Chuck Berry, in particular, was a sort of poet laureate of working-class frustration (and solidarity) in such songs as 'Almost Grown', 'Memphis Tennessee', 'Too Much Monkey Business', 'Come On', 'Nadine' and 'Going Back to Memphis'. 'Too Much Monkey Business' can be seen as a sort of forerunner of Springsteen's 'Born in the USA' as the returning veteran finds himself pumping gas. Its litany of racially inflected, but not racially exclusive, working-class complaints also anticipate the list of urban ills in Grandmaster Flash and the Furious Five's 1982 'The Message'. But there are many other famous examples: Eddie Cochran's 'Summertime Blues'; Frankie Lyman and the Teenagers' 'I'm Not a Juvenile Delinquent'; Gene Chandler's 'Duke of Earl'; and, of course, the Silhouettes' 'Get a Job'. It has been a commonplace for decades that these songs figured an emerging youth culture and generational resentment. This may be true, but I argue that, in the 1950s, this youth culture was actually a vision of a significantly multiracial working class subculture, at least in the imagination, if not in fact – though early rock 'n' roll and R & B performances in many venues were often unusually, and for some disturbingly, integrated by the standards of that time (and perhaps our own). Again, the revisioning of this youth culture, grown middle-aged in the 1970s, retained what we might think might be considered the working-class accents of the original while significantly whitening the imagined community if not the performers. It was also a closely related revisioning of this pre-British Invasion working class youth culture combined with Dylan and 1960s soul and jazz that underlay the sound and many of the tropes (and the tremendous success of Bruce Springsteen) in the 1970s and 1980s – from the seemingly retro sound of Clarence Clemmons's saxophone to the use of Gary U.S. Bonds's 1961 'Quarter to Three' as an encore in Springsteen's stage show. Of course, in key respects, Springsteen's imagining differed considerably from that of much of the rock 'n' roll/doo wop revival in that he not only recalled, invocated and extolled black and white performers from the 1950s and early 1960s, but also pictured a young multiracial underclass in the badlands of the smaller cities of the north-east for whom the old laborist dream was failing or fading in the immediate post-Vietnam war era.

Closer to our own time, rap has gone through many stages and has had a variety of subgenres in its four decades. My particular interest here is the phenomenon of what has been characterized as a suburban fascination with hip-hop, particularly the thug end of the hip-hop spectrum. As I have mentioned previously, the participation of young white Americans in thug-inflected rap, has been frequently characterized as an extreme version of the sort of primitivist mimicry that has long attended white appropriations of African–American culture. In short, these white hip-hoppers hanging out at the mall are poseurs at best. Their consumption of rap allied to a sense that artists and the music industry is increasingly playing to the primitivist fantasies of middle-class white kids is then seen corrupting the music. These are plausible criticisms. However, it could be noted that the urban black and Latino audience of rap consumes dreams that differ significantly from their lives, also. Despite the real problem of youth violence, few of even the most devoted black fans of Biggie Smalls, Tupac Shakur or 50 Cent ever shot one another or anyone else with a Glock nine-millimetre handgun or an Uzi even if they might adhere to certain elements of a thug style. This does not mean, as will be noted later, the ideological and actual criminalization of black and Latino youth in the United States is not a fact – though one could argue that the so-called war on drugs and the particulars of its application in poorer black communities have more to do with the actual entry of young black men into the criminal justice system than Scarface, the rapper of the 'Dirty South' or *Scarface* the film(s). Its obsession with 'the real' notwithstanding, the thug dream resembles the long-standing figure of the old badman in African–American song and story. Again, most listeners to badman stories and songs did not emulate the original gangsta, Stagolee, who, among other things, shot a man with a family over a hat lost fairly in a card game. What thrilled them was imagining someone who recognized no limitations, legal, moral or physical, whatever the consequences when their lives were hemmed in by limitations and consequences.

To the thug dream one might add the somewhat related vision of black-consciousness rap artists from DJ Afrika Bambaataa through Grandmaster Flash and the Furious Five through Public Enemy to Mos Def, Dead Prez and The Roots. The beginning of this line of black-consciousness rap, which also imagines a sort of transcending of racial and class limitations, paved the way for NWA and, at the same time, eventually drew on the energy, anger and tropes of the gangstas, gathering a significant white, Latina/o and Asian–American audience. Of course, one might also say that the thug dream draws on the black love expressed in consciousness rap, focusing frequently, as Murray Forman points out, on the black neighbourhood as the site of black unity as well as of danger (2002, p. 185). Scarface's assertion in 'My Block' that he 'loves those ghetto boys and girls' of Houston's Third Ward is a prominent example of this side of the thug dream. One might also say that Scarface sounds a class as well as racial identity when he hyperbolically claims 'You either working or slinging cocaine on my block' (2002). The line, then, between thug/hardcore and consciousness/underground is not so clear – and the political side of rap remains an integral part of the hip-hop world of which almost all hip-hop fans are keenly aware, whatever the sales of 50 Cent compared to those of The Roots might be. It is also worth noting that one finds a considerable non-African–American audience for consciousness rap for whom a racialized model of underclass oppression and solidarity strikes a chord through a displacement of class on to race. So what attracted young non-African–American people to these inter-connected dreams of love, anger, thuggery and community? I suggest that the attraction is not because hip-hop simply provides a space where repressed 'middle-class' children can let go of their inhibitions through a minstrelized ventriloquism of a fantastic black man – though I certainly would not discount this attraction entirely. Rather, I raise the possibility that hip-hop allows the figuring of class- and class-consciousness through a model of class identification that is multiracial or cross-racial.

Whatever else you can say about it, the music of Marshall Mathers (aka Eminem), for example, is marked by an insistence on his identity as a member of the white underclass and rap as the natural vehicle for expressing that identity. Unlike, say, Vanilla Ice or R & B bandleader and impresario Johnny Otis, Mathers, for the most part, does not claim to be a sort of white Negro by virtue of his special individual connection to the black community. Rather Mathers posits a group model of a white underclass, rooted in the landscape of his hometown Warren, Michigan, whose interests intersect with its black counterpart without being completely subsumed.

It is worth noting that Warren in the allegedly autobiographical movie *8 Mile* (and in many critical accounts of Eminem) differs somewhat from the image presented in Eminem's music – not to mention life itself, as the saying goes. The character Mathers plays, BRabbit, is shown in the film as a sort of 'white trash', 'hillbilly' hip-hop hybrid, not, as characters note in the film, unlike the image of Elvis Presley in the 1950s.[4] No doubt this sort of hybridity is revealed most clearly when BRabbit and his friend Future (played by Mekhi Phifer) use the stereotypical 'cracker' anthem 'Sweet Home Alabama' as the foundation for rapping about BRabbit's life in the trailer park. The southern roots of BRabbit's identity are made even plainer by the accent of his mother, played by Kim Basinger. Both Southern 'white trash' and 'hillbilly' have long been connected to popular culture and minstrelized images of white people so degraded that they were virtually black in terms of cultural and behaviour. The type of the poor, drunken, shiftless, sexually promiscuous (and indiscriminate) 'white trash'/'hillbilly' remarkably resembles the portrait of African–Americans in popular (and 'high') culture – and in the line of liberal political thought deriving from the New Frontier/Great Society era in which Appalachia became practically synonymous with 'white' poverty. This black-southern 'white trash'/'hillbilly' connection is further strengthened in the movie's climax when BRabbit triumphs over his African–American nemesis, Papa Doc, in a hip-hop cutting contest by demonstrating that he is more 'black' than Papa Doc (who went to a private school in the suburbs) through a celebration of his 'white trash' trailer park roots. To a certain extent, the connection of BRabbit and his side of 8 Mile Road to a supposed 'hillbilly' subculture that has been transplanted north undercuts a multiracial class model since that subculture is strangely off-white whatever the melanin content of the protagonist's skin.

I have gone on at some length about how BRabbit's family is represented in *8 Mile*, because, remarkably, some commentators view this fiction as reflecting the actual reality of Warren and Mathers's childhood, and use this alleged reality as a tool for understanding Mathers' music and its appeal. Hilton Als, in an introduction to a recent collection of writing on Eminem, calls Warren 'a blue-collar suburb of Detroit populated by white laborers from the South who so longed for the "old country" and the old ways that they referred to their small community as "Warren-tucky". Confederate flags in the window, beer for breakfast, and watery hominy grits ladled onto chipped enamel plates by women split between being a waitress and Mom, if there is a distinction to be made' (2003, p. x.). This fantasy of Warren as Dogpatch north is empirically dubious. About two-thirds of Warren's largely blue-collar inhabitants claim Polish, German, Irish or Italian ancestry; significant numbers also are of French Canadian, Ukrainian and Arab descent. About 3 per cent of the city's residents are African–Americans; other 'minority' groups comprise about 7 per cent of the population. No doubt among the 10–15 per cent or so that declared English, Scottish, Scots Irish and 'American' backgrounds is a significant group whose ancestors came from the South.[5] However, the white population of Warren seems to be a pretty representative cross-section of white workers in south-western Michigan rather than an Appalachian ghetto. Linguistically Mathers' mother, Debbie Nelson, does not sound like the character played by Kim Bassinger in the film, but like the native-born Midwesterner from St Joseph, Missouri (a long-time meat-packing centre that has suffered from technological changes and contractions in the packing-house industry over the last few decades) that she in fact is. Debbie Nelson's story of spousal abandonment, poverty, welfare, multiple and often short-lived bad jobs, frequent moves and so on is in fact a common one, North and South, for young working-class families where the parents split up, leaving the mother with small children, relatively little formal education and few resources.

Rather than make the sort of 'hillbilly'/black connection present in the film, Mathers' music draws on the notion of his story as common class story. He does use the terms 'white trash' and 'redneck', which both have a certain Southern association in US culture, but empties those terms of their regional connotations to figure different aspects of white working-class identity in which 'rednecks' with relatively decent blue- and pink-collar jobs scrabble uneasily on the slippery slope above 'white trash' where all it takes is a broken marriage, a lay-off and/or a substance abuse problem to slide down. Of course, the racial implications of 'white trash' (and its dependence on racist notions of black character and proper social station for African–Americans) inform Mathers' music, allowing him to find a certain conjunction of style between himself and an imagined black underclass.

Yet one thing that Mathers makes clear throughout his music is that he is not black, either at skin or at heart. Although the speaker of his songs sometimes distinguishes himself from 'White America' to a certain degree, he both admits the benefits of white skin privilege (in 'White America' the speaker proclaims, 'Let's do the math / If I was black I woulda sold half') and recounts various sorts of conflicts he has had with African–Americans (in 'Brain Damage' the speaker is repeatedly beaten by a black school bully who shouts, 'You gonna die honky!') as well as close relationships (Eminem, 2000, 2002). What he does figure is not so much a convergence of identity as of interests. In this sense, the title of the film *8 Mile* does catch the vision of Mathers' recordings better than the scenes in the

trailer park, for the most part. As virtually everyone who has any interest in
Eminem or the film no doubt knows, the film's title refers to the street that serves
as the political boundary between Detroit and Macomb and Oakland counties to
the North, where Warren is located. Of course, this boundary is not simply
political. As Mathers commented, 'It's the borderline of what separates suburb
from city. It's the color line. I grew up on both sides of it and saw everything. I
had the friends who had racist redneck fathers and stepfathers. I had black
friends. It's just American culture' (quoted in Rich, 2003, p. 102). What Mathers
is talking about here is not a borderlands zone of liminality, but a sharing of class
interests and a cultural language with the more famous black underclass that is
embodied in his patron and musical associate Dr Dre, formerly of NWA. Again
– and here Mathers and his work differs from the visuals of the movie – this
convergence of interest and identity is not based on being the one white kid on
the block or in the factory and becoming black by osmosis. And, again, Mathers
rejects the movie's (and Hilton Als') positing of BRabbit (and in Als' estimation,
Eminem) as exhibiting a 'hillbilly' exceptionalism when he says, 'It's just
American culture'. Mathers's enormous commercial success is largely predicated
on this reading of 'American culture', invoking a common class experience that
does not negate racial (or, for that matter, ethnic) divides, but negotiates them.

One can find non-white hip-hop artists who draw on a similar notion of a
multiracial underclass – one can look at the videos of the rap group Dilated
Peoples, the name of which invokes a druggy, thuggy multiracial and multi-
ethnic subculture. Of course, the group itself, consisting of two 'mixed' rappers
and an Asian American DJ, embody a sort of 'Browning of America'
multiculturalism – a multiculturalism that, in the group's verbal and visual work
and in the public statements of its members, mixes a positive multiculturalist
celebration of diversity along the lines that one frequently encounters at
different levels of educational curricula in the United States with a sort of
*Bladerunner*esque vision of those fenced in the urban wastelands of post-
industrial Los Angeles:

> And being diverse and multicultural, what it's done for me personally is learning to
> tolerate differences, cultures and see it as an opportunity for myself to expand
> myself. The more cultures I find, the different types of foods, people and different
> perspectives I've experienced from people, are all things that have made me who I
> am. I can sit down with anyone, try their food, listen to them, and be open to
> whatever culture and appreciate it. (Rakaa, quoted in Yamaguchi, 2004)

This statement from one of Dilated Peoples' rappers, may sound a little like an
'It's a Small World After All' version of multiculturalism. However, videos like
This Way, in part a touching tribute to Run DMC's Jam Master Jay (and the
earlier music video framing of racial conflict and convergence in which
Aerosmith and Run DMC duel and collaborate on 'Walk This Way') in which
Rakaa follows Jay up an escalator to heaven, show an obviously multi-ethnic and

multiracial urban underclass confronting drugs, street violence, police violence, sex, racism, economic exploitation, and economic violence – an underclass in which young black people are at the centre, but do not form the totality. This multicultural notion of class that has black youth in a central role is a mixture of black consciousness and gangster tropes, at one point posing the contradiction from which the speaker (or multiple speakers) is trying to escape as choosing between 'getting paid or getting laid' (Dilated Peoples, 2004).

One does not have to be a Foucauldian to see that these hip-hop representations of the underclass draw heavily on social science, social policy and criminal justice, formulations of the post-Moynihan Report era, much in much the same way that youth-culture dreams of class identity, class conflict and class community were influenced by the interlocking academic, governmental and mass culture obsession with juvenile delinquency in the 1950s.[6] Like the earlier notions of juvenile delinquency, the post-Moynihan conceptions of the underclass were heavily racialized. In fact, one of the terrifying aspects of popular and scholarly visions of the underclass is not simply the social mayhem created by its members, but also a sort of racial contagion theory, familiar in the United States, in which white communities (and especially white youth) become infected by an underclass virus spread beyond its natural black and Latino habitat. While the notion of the underclass has something in common with the old Marxist concept of the lumpenproletariat, we recognize that it goes far beyond any normal Marxist sense of the lumpen, ideologically criminalizing (and to a frightening extent imprisoning) virtually an entire generation (or several generations) of black and Latino youth. At the same time, it makes available a powerful and widely dispersed imagining of racial and class oppression, racial and class community, and racial and class conflict. This imagining strongly appeals to young white people as a way of figuring class oppression and class community across racial lines even if, on the surface, they do not appear to fit into this category of the 'underclass' (for example, they have a job, they live in a household where both parents are present, their parents have jobs, and so on). And although such an imagining might rely on the model and rhetoric of the underclass in dubious ways, it should also be noted that, in many respects, this vision speaks to the condition of millions in the long-term unemployed, underemployed, temporarily employed and illegally employed floating world at the bottom of the late twentieth-century and early twenty-first-century US working class more convincingly than older Marxist concepts of 'labour aristocracy', 'lumpen' and so on.

Whatever one thinks of Marshall Mathers' music, which I find ideologically appalling in many respects, he and many white participants in hip-hop basically reject the contagion theory of the underclass. Mathers (and Dilated Peoples, for that matter) is, in essence, revising or expanding DMX's 'Who We Be' ('These motherfuckers don't know who we are'), saying that we have been here all along, that there is a sort of war going on (DMX, 2001). As has been the case for many years in US popular music, the artists and audiences that posit a multiracial, multi-ethnic working class draw on musical resources, themes and forms significantly rooted in the African–American community, in order to create these figurations of class and class warfare. Importantly, they publicly acknowledge these roots not simply as an act of respect, but also as a way of asserting the notion of a multiracial community of interest. It is a vision of a class solidarity that posits an African–American leadership. What it does not do is simply erase race and ethnicity in favour of a vision of class.

From a progressive standpoint, there are obvious problems with such visions of community influenced so heavily by racist and anti-working class ideological products of think tanks, government reports, assistant school principals, newspapers, television, Hollywood and so on. The homophobia, misogyny, random violence and so on, expressed in Mathers'/Eminem's work demonstrates some of these problems quite clearly. Even the work of more self-consciously progressive hip-hop artists finds itself constricted by the ideological limitations of thug tropes and rhetoric. However, I have gone through this rushed genealogy from swing to hip-hop to make several points that seemed worth remembering for scholars and activists. First is the obvious point that class identity and class community are figured and understood and significantly produced, through popular culture in a variety of ways. Second, rather than being a dirty little secret in the United States, or something talked about by certified (and generally marginal cultural) radical artists and intellectuals, popular culture, especially popular music, is now and has long been saturated with overt representations of class, class conflict and class solidarity that have had (and continue to have) a large audience for an equally long time. Third, while in some cases these representations draw on a racially exclusive model of working-class identity, sometimes, through a strange adoption and adaptation of racially identified cultural forms (as in the doo wop revival of the 1960s and 1970s), representations by black, white, Latino and Asian–American artists (and artists like Rakaa who view themselves as 'mixed' or 'multicultural') often use a model of a multiracial community of class interests that acknowledges an African–American cultural leadership. Fourth, people tend to figure class and class identification with the materials at hand.

We are increasingly far from the Popular Front and its multiracial ideology – an ideology that I argue underlies, in different ways, the structures of class feeling in 1950s youth culture and the 1970s doo wop revival in the United States. It is true that this ideology lives on in some institutions, most prominently in the labour movement. However, trade unions represent such a small proportion of workers in the United States, and the US labour movement has so little access to the institutions of popular culture, that most young people (and not so young people) have little direct exposure to this sort of labourism – except perhaps from their elders. Those multiracial models that are available are the criminal justice/sociology/educational discourse of the underclass, the more positive, but often relatively classless, educational discourse of multiculturalism, and nationalist discourses of black anger, love, pride and solidarity descended from Black Arts/Black Power. These discourses all have their strengths and weaknesses for figuring class identity and class community. However, what they mostly lack, with the partial exception of black nationalist-inspired visions, is the sort of democratic revolutionary optimism that attended the Popular Front. They are also extremely masculinist; men are the primary actors and women are often icons of class (and racial) identity and/or betrayal. Of course, as noted earlier, these sorts of masculinisms are not unique to rap, but typify the sounding of class conflict in popular music generally from at least the 1950s to the present, from Gene Chandler to Everclear.

However, this is not a nostalgic plea for a return to the Popular Front, nor a call for a move away from the alleged morass of identity politics back to a supposed halcyon era of class politics. As far as left-wing politics in the United States go, it has never been all about class – certainly not for the last 75 years or so – but always about how class intersects with racial (and ethnic) identity as it is understood in the United States. While these points are obvious, it may still be useful to keep them in mind as we strive for some sort of accurate scholarship about the relation between race, class and popular culture in the United States. As Tricia Rose pointed out some time ago – and it is still true, I think – we do not really have a clear picture of the racial/ethnic demographics of the rap audience (Rose, 1994, pp. 4–5). And I would add that we have an even less clear notion of the class background of the audience (both in terms of how members of the audience actually live and of how they see themselves), though clearly concerns and tropes that we would consider class-inflected are constantly sounded, as they have been in popular music for many years. These points might also be useful in reminding us that, if we want to change the world, there are popularly accepted models of class-consciousness circulating in the United States, not only models which imagine a multiracial community of class interests in ways that do not discount the complications of race, but also more racially exclusive models.

Notes

1. As Melnick notes, doo wop revivals began almost before the music died down enough to revive in the late 1950s. However, there was certainly a dramatic increase of rock 'n' roll revival/doo wop revival shows in relatively high-profile venues in the late 1960s and early 1970s, especially within the north-east. As Melnick also points out, '[r]egret infuses commemorations of Doo Wop' (1996, p. 219) – though I would put much more emphasis on the class content of this regret which, in my reading of the doo wop revival, elegizes the remnants of the Popular Front in sort of latter-day 'ghetto pastoral', to use Michael Denning's term (1996, pp. 230–58).
2. In an article on the United in Group Harmony Association (an association of what might be thought of as purist doo wop fans) in the 1990s, Martin Gottlieb claims that the majority of the UGHA members are blue-collar, suburbanite 'Reagan Democrats' who are nonetheless fiercely partisan to African–American doo wop artists (1993, p. E6).

3. For examples of this sort of doo wop revivalist integration reverie, see Gottlieb (1993, p. E6) and Groia (1983, pp. 10–12).
4. As Greil Marcus notes, Elvis Presley's early nickname as a performer, the 'Hillbilly Cat', was another way of calling him a 'white Negro' (1995, p. 152).
5. These numbers were compiled by city-data.com from, they claim, 'multiple government and commercial sources'. See http://www.city-data.com/city/Warren-Michigan.html.
6. Daniel Patrick Moynihan's 1965 study for the United States Department of Labor, *The Negro Family: The Case for National Action*, popularly known as the 'Moynihan Report', was a crucial document in the promotion of the idea of the pathology of the African–American family as a cornerstone of public policy in the United States, providing an underpinning for later formulations of the 'black underclass' (United States Department of Labor, 1965).

Chapter 7

Gender as anomaly: women in rap

Gail Hilson Woldu

In 1994 critic Danyel Smith wrote a provocative essay, entitled 'Ain't a Damn Thing Changed: Why Women Rappers Don't Sell', in which she challenged commonly held stereotypes about women who rap. Citing a variety of record executives, Smith attributed the following reasons to women's inability to attain commercial success in the world of rap: (1) women's versions of reality are perceived to be less believable than men's; (2) women have tried to be 'too hard – either trying to be just like men or trying to be raunchy beyond what people would accept'; and (3) listeners prefer not to hear 'aggressive, go-for-theirs sentiments from females' (Smith, 1994, p. 126). Rappers Salt-n-Pepa were acceptable, according to Monica Lynch of Tommy Boy Records, because 'they are pop-ish, not hardcore' (cited in Smith, 1994, p. 126). Two years later, in 1996, rapper Lil' Kim released *Hard Core*. With its teasingly pornographic title, *Hard Core* was a benchmark for women's presence in rap as it affirmed a brazenly discordant female voice in what Smith referred to as 'the almost exclusively male world of hip hop' (Smith, 1994, p. 126). *Hard Core* established Lil'Kim among rap's megastars; more importantly, it spat on the shoe of rap's male hegemony.

To be a rapper in the 1980s assumed three immutable truths: that the performer be black, urban and male. The success of Run-DMC, Fresh Prince and LL Cool J, for example, was due in large measure to their ability to project a street-savvy machismo that most audiences attached to – and expected of – young black men. By the early 1990s these criteria had shifted slightly to focus on a specific image: that of the hostile and angry black man, epitomized most exaggeratedly and cartoonishly in Ice Cube's scowl and the caustic disaffection of his lyrics. Whatever mutations and aberrations rap saw throughout the 1990s (most notably the phenomenon of Eminem), the fundamental criterion remained unchanged: its maleness. Trade magazines *Vibe* and *The Source* affirmed this every month on their covers and networks BET and MTV bolstered this tacit mandate on the air. The result, at least for most mainstream audiences, was the belief, reified through print and broadcast media, that rap was the exclusive domain of angry young black men who lived desperate, often criminal, lives in urban slums. Yet, within a culture and a business that at its inception deified black masculinity, women rappers – in particular Queen Latifah, Lil' Kim, Missy Elliot and Eve – have come to assume a distinct, if anomalous, presence.

Any discussion of women's role and place in rap must contain several layers. Not only must it consider rap's male hegemony, it must also explore women's participation in a variety of genres, including, especially, blues and the music of Motown. As such, a history of women in American popular music unfolds, here with an emphasis on the performance traditions of black women that focuses in particular on the performance and ideological similarities between the music of female rappers and their forebears Ma Rainey, Ida Cox, Bessie Smith and Diana Ross, as well as the marketing of women in rap and in other forms of popular music in the twentieth century. I begin my discussion with a brief overview of men's rap.

By most accounts, popular or commercial rap 'began' with the release in 1979 of 'Rapper's Delight' by the Sugar Hill Gang. This was pure house party music, with all the requisite ingredients for dancing the night away: catchy, apolitical and nonsensical lyrics accompanied by a repetitive, bass-driven rhythm. Women are not denigrated in this rap; instead, the performers vaunt their sexual abilities in the battling or toasting style that became a hallmark of early rap. 'Rapper's Delight' has since become a rap standard, appealing to partygoers of all races ('to the black, to the white, to the red and brown, the purple and yellow'), and the model, at least aesthetically, for the next wave of rappers – among them MC Hammer and LL Cool J – whose music sought more to entertain than to instigate. There followed in the late 1980s and early 1990s a particularly notorious period in popular rap, the so-called 'gangsta' era, in which the image of the black male as a violent, profane, woman-hating, sex-obsessed criminal was imprinted in popular culture. Arguably, this genre occasioned more bad press than any other black popular music; by consequence, not surprisingly, this species of rap is best known to mainstream listeners and is the type that most people identify as representative of all rap. With its ubiquitous references to gats, Uzis and hoes, gangsta rap was the domain of male performers, crystallized in the music of NWA, Ice Cube, Ice-T, Snoop Dogg and Tupac, and was not a genre many women rappers were eager to pursue. The sovereignty of men in rap, and the dominance of the gangsta style throughout the mid-1990s, is confirmed emphatically on the cover of *The Source* magazine's January 1996 issue, which features bubble snapshots of the 15 most important performers of 1995: all are male, all are unsmiling, and all, with the exception of Ol' Dirty Bastard, have affected some kind of thug or hoodlum pose. The gangsta era was succeeded in the late twentieth and early twenty-first centuries by what is most commonly referred to as the 'bling' phase. Mainstream media have referred to this cultural phenomenon as 'luxury fever', writing that 'some suggestion of luxury has invaded almost every aspect of our daily lives, whether it's an over-the-top diamond-encrusted crocodile Hermès handbag or an über-designed stainless-steel trash can' (Betts, 2004, p. 5). Countless numbers of these raps and videos have been written and produced; all are variations on the same theme – make money, spend money, flaunt money – the spirit of which is caricatured in the words of Cash Money: 'Everytime I come around the city, bling bling, pinkie ring worth about fifty, bling bling.'

Themes and traditions in women's rap

Lil' Kim's ascendancy as the 'queen bitch' of rap is intriguing. Although she reigned supremely on the bitch throne throughout the late 1990s and early 2000s, bedecked in a hip-hop queen's regalia of minks and boas dyed in a rainbow of pinks, blues and greens, her dominion was not easily attained; like most women who rap, Lil' Kim has decried hip-hop's misogynist attitudes and longed for 'a lot more respect for women' (*The Source*, January 1996, p. 49). Nevertheless, Kim, more than any other woman in the rap business, has defied its stereotypes and infiltrated areas that very few women have dared, including the use of lurid and pornographic texts. In fact, writes *Vibe* journalist Robert Marriott, 'Lil' Kim's mythology is about pussy, really: the power, pleasure, and politics of it, the murky mixture of emotions and commerce that sex has become in popular culture' (2000, p. 126). Her ability as a shape-shifter – as a black girl/white girl, a life-size Barbie doll with a wardrobe of platinum blond wigs, as ghetto angelic and as ghetto tragic – confounds the hip-hop world and stupefies the cultural mainstream. Annie Leibovitz, a photographer for *Vanity Fair*, writes that 'sociologically, [Kim] is really fascinating because she is not only dressing up to be a woman, but she's dressing up to be a white woman, with that blond wig' (quoted in Marriott, 2000, p. 132). In *Hard Core*, Kim is by turns a hardened gangster (not a moll), a vulgar, acquisitive hussy, and, always, a storyteller. She touts her lyrical abilities with the same bravado as male gangsta rappers, and in the track 'M.A.F.I.A. Land' she embraces the gangster lifestyle, rapping: 'It ain't a day in my life that rolls by, that I don't get high ... I used to roll hard with tons of bitches, now it's just me and my niggaz'. Kim the Vulgar reaches her highest level of sexually explicit nastiness in 'We Don't Need It'. Here, going toe-to-toe with 2 Live Crew and Snoop Doggy Dogg, Kim enumerates her demands for oral sex and insists that it be given properly and reciprocally. More important is the way in which she defines herself: as a 'diamond cluster hustler, queen bitch, supreme bitch, kill a nigga for my nigga bitch, by any means bitch, murder scene bitch, disease free bitch ... I'm rich; I'm a stay that bitch'.

The use of the word 'bitch' in rap is curious and duplicitous. In its broadest sense, 'bitch' is used to identify any woman between puberty and menopause and need not refer exclusively to one who is shrill and unpleasant. Not surprisingly, men and women rappers are often at variance in their depiction. In 'I Ain't Tha 1', for example, Ice Cube tells us that he 'spell[s] girl with a B'. The whining and manipulative 'bitch' in this rap uses sex to negotiate monetary favours from Ice Cube, and she implores her girlfriends to take men 'for all the money they got'. Ice Cube's response to the woman's incessant pestering? 'You want lobster? I'm thinking Burger King.' A completely different approach to the epithet is taken in MC Eiht's 'U's a Bitch'. Here the usage is not gratuitous, as in so many West Coast raps of the late 1980s and early 1990s. This rapper has been hurt by the song title's subject (a money-grabbing schemer) and he uses the term 'bitch' to vent his anger towards the woman who has used him badly. He even defines 'bitch' for us, explaining, 'I calls you a bitch: in other words, a dick teaser'. Biggie uses the term lovingly in 'Me and My Bitch', which is a bizarrely touching tribute to his main girl. Rapping 'a real bitch is what I want', Biggie enumerates the admirable qualities of this woman: someone who never snitches, who is dependable and trustworthy, and who understands that her man will beat her if she misbehaves.

By contrast, 'bitch', in women's rap, is usually not an epithet; like 'nigga' in so much male rap, 'bitch' becomes a term of endearment, a weapon of empowerment and a means of creating a sisterhood among kindred souls. As such, the word is transformed into a tangible expression of self-affirmation and worn like a regent's crown. The term, as found in women's rap, typically defines a homegirl, a young black woman between the ages of 14 and forty who comes from, and identifies with life in, the 'hood'. This definition can be narrowed even further to refer to a woman who uses men, who connives and who obtains lucre using whatever means are at her disposal. Importantly, there is widespread and tacit approval among women rappers that this behaviour is acceptable: that women, like men, can be lowdown players and hustlers. Rapper Da Brat opens 'All My Bitches' with the attention-getting question-cum-command to rally: 'Where is my bitches at? Where is all my bitches at? This motherfucker right here, this for all y'all motherfuckers'. In this rap about money, materialism and the necessity for women to be financially independent, the sisterly camaraderie is as palpable as is the utter contempt for men. Da Brat tells her audience of women – her 'bitches', to whom the rap is dedicated – that she is financially in charge. She takes care of the condo, the mortgage and the note on the Porsche, and she needs to depend on herself alone to survive: 'I'm talking to all of my bitches that live the hood life, good life; my bitches that don't need a nigga for shit. Bitches with a game plan, rock it, name brand, I dedicates this one to you.' The term assumes a different meaning in Trina's 'Da Baddest B***h'. Here, the 'bitch' is a scheming, street-wise hussy whose primary interests in men are carnal and pecuniary. The rap's language is thoroughly and unashamedly vulgar, and it is clear that Trina is trying to outdo Lil' Kim, the self-proclaimed 'queen b@#$h'. Trina and Da Brat join Eve in 'Gangsta B's', an uninspired piece that casts 'three of the illest dames' in rap as accessories to their gangsta men. Here, the 'bling' lifestyle is extolled (the women are 'studded in rhinestones and dripping in Chanel'), yet the lyrics do little to illuminate the women's professed roles; instead, we are told, repeatedly, that these women are 'gangsta chicks' with 'gangsta ice, gangsta clothes, gangsta money ... we the women that the gangsta's thirst'.

References to 'hood life' are a staple in most raps, as characteristic of the genre as are arpeggiated piano accompaniments in late nineteenth-century French song and blues texts that begin 'I woke up this morning'. This is especially true of male rap from the late 1980s through the middle 1990s. Every track from MC Eiht's *Compton's Most Wanted* is about life in the hood; each, like 'Hood Took Me Under', spins a tragic tale of violence, the gangster lifestyle that most urban black men must live in order to survive and the inevitable prison sentences that are as much a rite of passage as a first haircut or first kiss. Similarly, NWA's *Straight Outta Compton* chronicles a variety of hood woes, including, above all, police brutality, which is documented cleverly in the provocative 'F*** tha Police'. Virtually every rap written by Tupac and Biggie, both murdered while young men, centres on hood life, even if this is not expressly indicated in the title. Tupac's 'The Streets R Deathrow' is a story about guns, drugs, broken families and absentee fathers that reaches its peak with the words 'I hope I live to be a man; must be part of some big plan to keep a brother in the state pen', while Biggie's 'Juicy', arguably his best rap, about his hardships and triumphs, revolves around the refrain 'and if you don't know, now you know, nigga'. Interestingly, very little male rap written in this period contains messages that are uplifting, inspiring or positive. A notable exception is Tupac's 'Keep Ya Head Up', which stands out among all rap composition and whose lyrics about loving and respecting women will become a classic in the decades to come.

Women rappers' spin on life in the hood, by contrast, is less markedly angry, hostile and malefic. While some women pose as homegirl gangstas (most conspicuously, Lil' Kim), most present themselves as everyday homegirls whose raps are more exhortations and warnings to other women to take responsibility for their own welfare than they are confrontational threats. On occasion, the 'ghettocentric' messages are downright edifying, as we find throughout the music of Bahamadia and Lauryn Hill. The former's 'One-4-Teen', for example, is a mellow, jazz-influenced rap that exhorts listeners 'from the outskirts of the burbs to tenement blocks' to do little more than relax and get lost in the music's words and flow. Lauryn Hill's classy and classic 'Doo-Wop', on the other hand, is a strong message to black men and women about black pride, responsibility and self-respect. More often, however, these raps centre on the mundane issues of everyday life – working, partying and grooming – in addition to the ubiquitous themes of men and other women. Missy Elliott's raps are models of this style, with their humorous references to manicures, pedicures, visits to the beauty shop and nights at the club seeking out cute guys to take home.

The issue of independence – financial, certainly, but sexual and emotional as well – is a cornerstone in women's rap. This theme is as omnipresent in the music of early rappers Roxanne Shanté, Salt-n-Pepa and Queen Latifah as in that of Eve and Missy Elliott, and draws on a long tradition in black women's music that has its roots in the songs of the blues women of the 1920s and 1930s. Black women's ignoble social status in the early twentieth century was a double-edged sword; on the one hand, wonderfully liberating and empowering, enabling the women to exist outside the rigid strictures of the cult of true womanhood and, on the other, relegating and confining them to the lowest rung in the social hierarchy. Because blues women, in particular, 'were expected to deviate from the norms defining orthodox female behavior' (Davis, 1998, p. 38), they were able to address subjects considered taboo, like sexual love. The result was that black women's blues became 'a tangible expression' of that peculiar freedom; more importantly, their music was an affirmation of black women's individual and collective sexuality. Blues women 'preached about sexual love ... giving voice to the most powerful evidence there was for many black people that slavery no longer existed' (Davis, 1998, p. 9). Countless numbers of these blues were written and performed in the early twentieth century including, especially notably, Ida Cox's 'One Hour Mama' (whose sentiments appear, albeit far less cleverly, in Missy Elliott's 'One Minute Man'), Victoria Spivey's 'Toothache Blues'; and Bessie Smith's 'Need a Little Sugar in My Bowl'.

Independence as a theme, or even, as a trope, is depicted stunningly in Bessie Smith's 'Young Woman's Blues'. Following the obligatory 'woke up this morning' introduction, Smith tells a story of a woman who refuses to live within and be judged by conventionally acceptable social standards. Smith's young woman is a renegade whose manly preference for 'good moonshine' and her desire for a satisfying sexual life must have scandalized her contemporaries. Because Smith wrote this blues, we get a real sense of the autobiographical: that these words were written by someone who had lived them. In fact, as Angela Davis tells us:

> Bessie Smith knew how to ground her appeal in her own lived experiences as an African-American woman ...The attitudes of the female subjects in the songs she sang encouraged black women to be as strong and independent as they were loving and caring ... Her music issued an appeal as universal as the circumstances in which it was anchored were historically and culturally specific. (Davis, 1998, p. 143)

Every line of 'Young Woman's Blues' speaks to a woman's life outside normalcy and each demands that we reconsider our definition of 'good woman'. Moreover, we are shown that independence can be understood to mean, variously, self-sufficiency as well as not being subject to someone else's moral or social authority: I'm a young woman and ain't done running 'round / Some people call me a hobo, some call me a bum / Nobody knows my name, nobody knows what I've done / I'm as good as any woman in your town / I ain't no high yella, I'm a deep killer brown / I ain't gonna marry, ain't goin' settle down / I'm gon' drink good moonshine and run these browns down ... / And I'm a good woman and I can get plenty men. (Quoted in Davis, 1998, pp. 356–57)

Independence is depicted more literally in Smith's 'Lost Your Head Blues' and 'Hard Times Blues'; both, like 'Young Woman's Blues', centre on the 'good woman' and the consequences of mistreating her. In traditional blues, AAB-form, the former tells a straightforward story of a woman who is leaving her man because he treated her badly. Importantly in this as in other blues penned by Smith, the blues woman takes charge of her destiny, deciding when to stay and when to go: 'I'm gonna leave, baby, ain't gonna say goodbye, but I'll write and tell you the reason why. Days are lonesome, nights are long. I'm a good old gal, but I've just been treated wrong' (quoted in Davis, 1998 p. 309). The 'good woman' in the latter blues is a confident and feisty soul, intrepid enough to pack her clothes and leave her man behind. Here, the gender roles are reversed: the man is financially subordinate to, and emotionally dependent on, the song's protagonist who proclaims 'When your good woman is gone, you will see a hard time' and, later, 'I'm a good woman, I can get a man any place I go' (quoted in Davis, 1998, p. 286).

Among early raps, Roxanne Shanté's 'Independent Woman', written in 1989, addresses a host of young women's dilemmas that remain timeless. Featuring a very young-sounding Shanté who, in a voice that sounds much like an urban high-school cheerleader, this rap cautions women against depending on others to sustain, nurture and provide for them. This is pure storytelling cast in a preaching style redolent of blues women Ma Rainey and Bessie Smith. The accompaniment is spare, limited to a repetitive percussion background that allows the listener to focus on the anecdotal and rhymed text. Shanté summons our attention with the words 'ladies, listen up' and a refrain that reinforces the themes of the rap: 'so lend me your ears, dry up your tears and let's hear it for the year of the independent woman.' The yarn she spins is an archetypal late twentieth-century tale of women's dependence and benevolence born of neediness, and the virtues of being self-sufficient. Like an older sister, Shanté scolds, then comforts and reassures: How many runny-nosed kids can you have? How many nights / can you work on the ave? Your so-called man has a car and a Visa. / He's living large while you're living on pizza. Unemployed while / you're waiting for the perfect mate. Let's get one thing straight, / 'cause it's getting late. What you're waiting for is really never / coming ...You don't really need a man, all you need to know is you / can. Then you can stand on your own two feet and achieve anything / you want out of life. Do for yourself. ('Independent Woman', Roxanne Shanté, 1989).

Independence of a different stripe is expressed by Salt-n-Pepa, for whom music is often a vehicle for talking about sex and, particularly, asserting women's sexual independence. Critic Peter Watrous writes that 'their stance, both verbally and physically, implies women in control. Their sexuality is theirs, and if that means fulfilling the needs of a male gaze, so be it; it's still power and they'll use it' (1994, p. 12). Not surprisingly, as Mark Anthony Neal has written, most of Salt-n-Pepa's output falls into one of three categories: safe-sex recordings, public-service announcements, and support of feminist causes (Neal, 2001, p. 133). The messages in 'Independent', written in 1990, are crystal-clear: the woman in the rap is the breadwinning, responsible adult who has no qualms about telling her erstwhile partner 'I pay the rent; this is my apartment'. The chorus, especially, drives home the singer's resolve: 'I am independent. I make my own money, so don't tell me how to spend it. 'Cause you need me, and I don't need you.' The group's enormously popular rap 'None of Your Business' is about equality in sexual relationships. It challenges the separate conventions for women and men ('How many rules am I to break before you understand that your double standards don't mean shit to me?') and brashly announces a woman's equal right to promiscuity with the lines 'if I wanna take a guy home with me tonight', 'if she wanna be a freak and sell it on the weekend', and 'now you shouldn't even be getting into who I'm giving skins to' – each followed by the chorus 'it's none of your business'. The group's 'Let's Talk About Sex', although less aggressive in its tenor and message, is a rallying cry for women to find a level of comfort in frank discourse about sexual relationships. Unlike most contemporaneous male rap that has sex as a theme, this one is at once provocative and instructive.

If any one woman's name in rap is synonymous with independence, however, that name would be Queen Latifah. The performer whose name is Arabic for 'sensitive' was such a force throughout the 1980s that she epitomizes the female arrival in rap. Her formidable demeanour and her assertive lyrics trumpet the emergence of a distinctively and unapologetically non-male voice. Her important and best-known rap, 'Ladies First' is jazzy house music with lyrics that cajole, warn and admonish in an 'iron fist in a velvet glove' manner. The casual banter between Latifah and British rapper Monie Love deplores male stereotypes about 'female MCs' inability to create rhymes' (Keyes, 2002, p. 192). Importantly, Latifah claims a spot for herself (and other women) with 'Ladies First' as she affirms women's skills: 'Some think that we can't flow. Stereotypes they got to go. I'm gonna mess around and flip the scene into reverse with a little touch of ladies first'. Equally noteworthy but often overlooked is the rapper's 'Latifah's Had It Up to Here'. Here, in classic Latifah style that is 'lovely and lyrically loose, but ladylike', Latifah proclaims her role as a legitimate rapper, thumbs her nose at 'commercial entertainers' who are 'commercially a pain to my mind and my behind' and, as in 'Ladies First', shows pride in being a 'real' (that is, heterosexual) woman in the rap business, stating, 'I'm a woman, all woman. Keep your rumors to yourself'.

Marketing in rap: A hip-hop generation of bitches, hoes, niggas and gangstas

In an article that appeared in the December 1998 issue of *Vibe*, Foxy Brown announced that she was 'the new bitch'. She also paid obeisance to her idol Roxanne Shanté, because 'she's a pioneer for the type of shit I'm doing... She was a *bitch* back in the day – for having skills ... She was like, "I'm that bitch, I'm here, and these are my niggas, and this is how we roll"' (quoted in Smith, 1998, p. 113). That Brown qualified as the kind of bitch she considered herself –

'new' – is significant. It was clear that the image she wanted to project differed from the street-hardened hubris of her predecessor Shanté; what was not clear was how she intended to forge a unique identity among her counterparts who projected themselves in the same way. Although Brown, like Lil' Kim, has been marketed as a foul-mouthed, sex-obsessed hottie who uses her body to attract and then manipulate men, she, unlike Kim, does not appear to be as intentionally unidimensional. The whole bitch thing, she says, is but a part of her persona, on-stage and off. She uses her image to make meaningful social statements, and if her lyrics offend some, the real point of her music is 'to do things to keep people talking. To bring issues that the average female MC ain't raising. To talk about things average females talk about' (quoted in Smith, 1998, p. 114). She understands, too, the continuum between her role as a female rapper and that of her antecedents in blues and rhythm and blues: '[Females] have been fighting for respect; we've been fighting for equality since back in the Bessie Smith days. Millie Jackson, all that' (quoted in Smith, 1998, p. 114).

For women who rap, the relationship between equality, respect and popular image is complicated. The popular images of Brown and Lil' Kim as 'hoochie mama' clad in thongs and bustiers, mugging for the camera with legs wide apart or straddling some species of wild animal are difficult to reconcile with their claims to speak for all women. Yet, given the nature of hip-hop culture, and more generally the business of entertainment, it should not be a surprise to find hyperbolic representations of pedestrian lifestyles. In fact, the business of hip-hop is built on mythic and fantasized depictions of reality. Obviously, this is not exclusive to women. Throughout the 1990s we were beset with hip-hop's version of reality that wanted us to believe that every male rapper was a gun-toting gangster; this crystallized in the famous photo of Tupac sporting a handgun necklace. Performers (male and female) were regularly photographed in the company of their pet Rottweiler or pit bull; black leather, among women in particular, was *de rigueur*. In the early twenty-first century, the most pervasive popular image of male rappers has been of gold teeth, platinum jewellery, a harem of bumping, grinding, loose-hipped women and a fleet of custom-made Bentleys. And while some have defied these caricatures (witness, for example, the understated elegance of fusion artist Erykah Badu), these are the images that dominate – at least in the popular media.

There is, of course, a precedent for this type of sensationalist marketing. For over 80 years – from the blues queens of the 1920s and 1930s to Motown's 'dreamgirls' to the marvel of Lil' Kim – we find fantasy made into reality. Ma Rainey, as ordinary-looking a black woman as existed in the early twentieth century, was transformed from a nappy-haired, gold-toothed 'every woman' into a bespangled diva; Diane Ross became Diana Ross (and, later, 'Miss Ross'), known worldwide for her extravagant wardrobe of evening gowns and wigs; and Tina Turner, at the onset of middle age, became an ageless rocker, rhythm and blues's answer to Mick Jagger. Each became, for her generation, the unattainable but thoroughly desirable archetype to which so many ordinary black women aspired. Much has been written about blues women Rainey, Bessie Smith and the scores of courageous women who left their homes for their chance at celebrity. Daphne Duval Harrison gives a factual and detailed account of the lives of these women in *Black Pearls: Blues Queens of the 1920s*. Here she cites the music industry's kaleidoscopic vision of the ideal female performer who could be, by turns, light complexioned and petite or dark skinned and big boned (Harrison, 1988, p. 32). Ma Rainey dazzled Southern, largely black audiences in a 'lamé headband, necklace and earrings fashioned from gold eagle dollars, and a heavily beaded dress draped over her stocky torso' (1988, p. 37). Similarly, Edith Wilson, who was 'physically attractive, light complexioned, and charming' and who 'could easily pass in any Southern European country without being recognized as belonging to the aborigine race of Africa' (1998, pp. 166, 182) satisfied the tastes of her primarily Northern audiences with her sophisticated demeanour and swinging blues, cabaret style of singing.

The story of the women of Motown is more complex. In his fascinating look at the politics and social implications of Berry Gordy's Motown, Gerald Early discusses the record mogul's 'vision of reshaping and exploding the racial underpinnings of pop music' and his ability to move 'black music, largely on its own terms, within the popular-music mainstream, negotiating, with considerable aplomb, the enterprise of authenticating itself as a youth music, while acknowledging, even celebrating, the R and B sources of African-American music, reaffirming, in an astonishing cultural wave, the innovative power of R and B as a pop music' (1995, p. 85). Similarly, Mark Anthony Neal writes that 'Motown made no secret about its investment in the mainstream consumer public as a vehicle for black middle-class mobility' (1999, p. 89) and that 'Gordy saw black progress in terms of the integration of mainstream and elite American institutions by blacks with highly textured middle-class sensibilities' (1999, p. 88). Because Motown emerged and then rose to prominence in the racial, social and political upheaval of the 1960s and early 1970s, a time that Early describes as 'the height of the black power and black pride movement' (Early, 1995, p. 87), the images of its star performers attained an importance that surpassed their talents as singers and dancers. For many Americans, Motown's performers became symbols of a new black America; in particular, young, white Americans were attracted to Motown's meticulously-groomed singing groups and their polished, professional stage comportment. Interestingly, according to Early, 'many younger blacks thought Motown sounded too "white", too crossover, and not authentically "black" enough' (1995, p. 87). This reluctance to embrace the Motown aesthetic was due in part to young blacks' rejection of the image Gordy created for his black performing groups, which was intentionally reserved and, by consequence, perceived as 'white': in performance, male singers were dapper in tailored suits and spit-shined shoes; women were attired in full-length evening wear, complete with white gloves. In their interviews with the media, Motown's performers eschewed black slang and were instructed to enunciate crisply. A classic example of Gordy's resolve to attract white youth is the album cover of the Isley Brothers' *This Old Heart of Mine* (1966). Instead of featuring a photograph of the group's three dark-complexioned black men, the cover shows two white teenagers in love, sitting together on a beach and looking at one another affectionately. Everything about the cover is artfully contrived to court young, white consumer – from the surf of the ocean, to the young man's tan line revealed at the waistband of his trunks, to the pony tailed young woman's adoring smile at her beau, to the couples' multicoloured beach ball, which suggests youthfulness and innocence.

Mary Wilson recounts her years as a member of the Supremes in her tell-all memoir *Dreamgirl* (1986). If we are able to look past Wilson's gratuitous maligning of Diana Ross, diva, we get a sense of the Supremes' creation and Gordy's fashioning of their image. A good deal of Wilson's story centres on wardrobe and make-up. We learn, for example, that the group travelled with their 'own entourage of wardrobe people and hairdressers' whose job it was to hide their 'beauty secrets – the wigs, lashes, and falsies – which they smuggled in and out' (Wilson, 1986, pp. 216–17). Because the Supremes were 'Motown's greatest commodity' (1986, p. 200), their image in the public eye mattered more (to Gordy) than the money they earned; the 'show', as Wilson puts it, was their lives: 'We concentrated on what to wear, how to fix our hair, how to speak, what to say to journalists and other people we met, and so on ... Mrs. Maxine Powell was in charge of etiquette and grooming. She spoke and carried herself very properly' (1986, pp. 179–81). Not surprisingly, Gordy was obsessed with the group's clothes and the statement their clothing made about them. According to Wilson, 'Our two most popular outfits were red sleeveless spaghetti-strap dresses with tons of fringe, and a silver spandex costume, complete with tight pants, halter tops, and high heels. We looked hot' (1986, p. 174). Lead singer Diana Ross was the central link in Gordy's cross-over campaign. In addition to having a 'pop' voice that was not readily detected as being either black or white, Ross possessed one other important crossover benefit: her doppelgänger resemblance to British model Twiggy, who dominated runways and fashion magazine covers in the early 1960s. Both women were reed-thin, both had enormous eyes that made them look like unloved waifs in need of a hug, and both looked fabulous in the Carnaby Street fashions that were all the rage of the early decade.

Everything about the music the Supremes performed was calculated to appeal to mainstream America's sense of romance. With songs written largely by either Motown's famous trio of songwriters, Eddie Holland, Lamont Dozier and Brian Holland, or by the incomparable Bill 'Smokey' Robinson of the Miracles, the group projected a man's view of courting and love in which women are emotionally needy and thoroughly dependent on men for their own happiness and sangfroid. In 'Everything's Good About You', Diana Ross sings 'You're sweet, you're so fine, I'm so thankful that you're mine'; in 'I Hear a Symphony', Ross whispers, 'you've given me a true love, and every day I thank you, love, for a feeling that's so new, so inviting, so exciting'; in 'Baby Love', Ross pleads, 'Baby, baby, baby don't leave me, ooh, please don't leave me all by myself'; and in 'Back in My Arms Again', Ross is 'so satisfied' that her man has returned. 'My Baby Loves Me', recorded on the Gordy label (a subsidiary of Motown) by Martha and the Vandellas, expresses similar sentiments: 'I will never, ever give my baby no trouble. Whenever he calls me, I come running on the telephone'. While sappy and vapid lyrics abounded in songs by Motown's male groups as well – and, in fact, were characteristic of much popular music of the late 1950s and early 1960s – we do not find in them the desperate neediness that we find in the music of Motown's women.

Given the dominance of the Supremes throughout the 1960s, it is tempting to disregard the group's non-Motown contemporaries, including the Ronettes. For lead singer Ronnie Spector, whose talents as a singer were marginal, image was all. The title of her memoir in itself is revealing: *Be My Baby: How I Survived Mascara, Miniskirts, and Madness or My Life as a Fabulous Ronette.* Throughout this tabloid account of her career, the former Veronica Bennett (who married record producer Phil Spector) tells us how the 'half-breed' Ronettes, with their light brown skin, tight miniskirts, and long hair teased into ceiling-high beehive hairdos, captivated audiences and even tantalized John Lennon of The Beatles. Much of the first 100 pages of the book is about make-up and wardrobe; in fact, Spector entitles an entire chapter 'A Little More Mascara'. The image of the Ronettes was by turns exotic, bestial and teasingly little-girlish, a perfect foil for the staid look of the Shirelles and, certainly, of Gordy's elegant Supremes. Their only real hit, 'Be My Baby', recorded in 1963, is a classic girl-group song. Remembered best for the line 'Be my little bay-bee' and for Ronnie's sexually charged delivery of the syllables 'wa-oh-oh-oh', this song has been analysed variously by music critics and music historians. According to rock critic Maggie Haselswerdt, in this number 'Phil Spector and the Ronettes weave a gauzy curtain around the sexual impulse, diffusing and romanticizing it, blurring the focus with walls of vibrating sound, highlighting the drama of the encounter with a series of minute yet heart-stopping pauses' (quoted in Lorraine, 2001, p. 12). The issue of image and sexuality is taken up by feminist Renée Cox Lorraine, who writes that girl groups, like the Ronettes, 'were designed to appeal to girls and young women, and usually posited a sweet and sensitive boy as an object of desire' and that in 'Be My Baby', in particular, 'the female voice is not usually a passive one; the young woman urging the boy [here] is gently aggressive, somewhat maternal, more choosing than chosen' (Lorraine, 2001, p. 12). This song depended far more on the sexy stage presence of the Ronettes than on the text. Yet, as Lorraine points out, the song is not an expression of the sexually liberated black woman; rather, 'it is at least partly the conception of a young white male expressed through the voices of young women who were dominated both professionally and personally' (2001, p. 13).

The savvy marketing – and resultant image – of the blues women and Gordy's Supremes was clearly intentional. In both cases, a fantasy was the intended goal: the blues women as tiara-wearing, straight-shooting, 'ordinary' women, and the Supremes as pop music's *recherché* 'dreamgirls'. In both cases, the images allowed listeners to flee their own existences for the length of a song and indulge in a musical make-believe in which black women's voices, fashion sense, ideas and concerns were important. We find parallels in hip-hop. The whole 'bitch' thing, for example, is a carefully orchestrated marketing tool intended to carve out a space for women in a domain that, from its inception, was identified as black and male. If black men could be marketed successfully as 'niggas' and 'gangstas', then black women could find their equivalent success as 'bitches' and 'hoes'. Hence, if there was a profitable market for NWA, Ice-T, Snoop Dogg and Tupac, its counterpart could be created for the women whom we know as Lil' Kim, Foxy Brown, Trina, and Da Brat. The images created by these male rappers encouraged fantasy, particularly among white youth: far removed from the realities of life on inner-city streets, well-heeled young men from the toniest suburbs in the United States could blare Tupac from the expensive cars given them by their parents, call each other 'nigga', and pretend to be gang members from Compton. By contrast, young women (particularly young white women) have been far less amenable to fashioning themselves after Lil' Kim and Da Brat, preferring, when adopting a 'homegirl look', to dress in designer street gear. An answer lies partly in the greater visibility of male rappers in a domain that, in most circles, continues to be perceived as belonging to black men. A better answer might lie in the 'mystique of the black man' phenomenon, in which black men's swagger, machismo and sense of style – embodied by basketball legends Wilt Chamberlin and Clyde Frazier, contemporary icons Allen Iverson and Latrell Sprewell, R & B heartthrob Usher and, certainly, rappers LL Cool J, Tupac, Nelly and the very buff 50 Cent – have long been emulated by non-black men. Interestingly, both the 'bitch' and 'gangsta' genres were relatively short-lived, even within the vicissitudes of hip-hop culture: 'gangsta' rap reached its peak in the mid-1990s, while 'bitch' rap saw its heyday in the late 1990s.

It is easy to discuss Lil' Kim and her cohorts because their style and image are so amenable to facile categorization. It is much harder, on the other hand, to discuss female rappers who are less readily pigeonholed. Missy Elliott and Eve fall into this second category. Both women of robust proportion in the early years of their careers who slimmed down considerably by the late 1990s to boast figures in keeping with those of rap video's booty-shaking dancing girls, Elliott and Eve are the unwitting beneficiaries of grotesquely obese male rappers Biggie, Fat Joe, Heavy D and Big Pun, who paved the way for women rappers whose girth might have excluded them from celebrity. Elliott, typically attired in her trademark sneakers and oversized gold, hoop earrings, is best known for her lighthearted, purely entertaining raps. In the prelude to 'Back in the Day' she reminds us to 'just have fun; it's hip hop, man, this is hip hop'. She rarely preaches, proselytizes or moralizes; instead, her raps, like 'Work It', usually ask silly questions such as 'Don't I look like a Halle Berry poster?' or they tell her 'fly girl' female listeners to 'get your nails done, get a pedicure, get your hair did'. On occasion, however, Elliott, like so many other women in rap, tells her female audience to 'get that cash ...ain't no shame ladies, do your thing. Just make sure you're ahead of the game.'

When we attempt to assess women's rap, to quantify women's successes in rap or even to make a definitive statement about women's 'anomalousness' in rap we find ourselves in a quagmire. Far removed from the inchoate days of the late 1980s when women were just finding their voices, we discover that women's participation and presence at the beginning of the twenty-first century is more fully fleshed. We have witnessed a variety of styles – from Roxanne Shanté to Queen Latifah, Lil' Kim to Missy Elliott, and Bahamadia to Da Brat – yet no sole woman stands out as exemplifying all women rappers and, by consequence, succumbing to the 'woe' that Rachel Fudge says belongs to 'the woman who becomes singled out by the media, portrayed as a star or spokesperson or symbol' for her cultural constituency (2003, p. 35). We have also seen women move beyond the tit-for-tat bickering ('you call me a name, so I'll call you one') that characterized so much early women's rap. If, in 1994, Danyel Smith was comfortable – and correct – in asserting that 'women writers and MCs are too often satisfied by simply responding to men's music-flipping over the proverbial coin in a well-intentioned attempt to even the lopsided score' (Smith, 1994, p. 126), she would be unlikely to make a similar statement in 2004. True, we continue to find striking similarities in theme and trend in women's and men's rap; this is most likely attributable to the nature of faddism in popular culture and to the commercial viability of a particular image at a particular time.

If women remain an anomalous presence in rap, this is largely a question of numbers: fewer women than men have maintained careers in rap and fewer women than men have reached the upper echelons among decision-makers in the business of rap. By contrast, more women than men have appeared scantily clad in rap videos and more women than men have been demeaned sexually in rap texts and in rap's marketing. It is unlikely that these inequities will result in women's 'quitting hip hop', as Michaela Angela Davis warns (2004, p. 155). Instead, it is altogether likely that women in the twenty-first century will continue to negotiate rap's challenges and assert themselves more meaningfully in popular culture's most dominant form of expression.

PART THREE
THE PROBLEMS OF PLACE

Chapter 8

Protest music as 'ego-enhancement': reggae music, the Rastafarian movement and the re-examination of race and identity in Jamaica

Stephen A. King

[Rasta] held up that mirror in front of the faces of people of African ancestry and asked the question: 'What do you see, Snow White?' And life has not been the same again. (Rex Nettleford, personal interview, 23 July 1994)

Despite its prophetic vision, the Rastafarian movement's long-standing goal of returning its members to Africa remains a distant dream. Nevertheless, it is clear that the movement's persistent critique of Jamaica's 'ideology of racism' eventually allowed Africa to be reborn in Jamaica (Chevannes, 1990, p. 62). After Spanish colonialists decimated the Arawak Indian population (Jamaica's indigenous culture) through hard labour, Jamaica's second colonial ruler, Great Britain (1655–1962), began to import a fresh supply of slaves, West Africans, to the island to work in the sugar fields. Although the memory of Africa survived the Middle Passage, the British Crown employed a variety of dehumanizing strategies to destroy the slaves' African identity, including promoting Europe as a beacon of civilization and constructing whiteness as the normative racial type. Meanwhile the colonial powers rejected Africa as a savage, backward and benighted continent and marked 'blackness' as a 'curse by God' or, alternatively, as 'an attribute of the Devil and of hell itself ... ' (Chevannes, 1988, p. 139).

Although the vestiges of colonialism, including white supremacy and European hegemony, continue to have an impact on Jamaican society, the Rastafarian movement played a significant role in forcing the Jamaican populace, particularly the middle class, to re-examine their racial identity and cultural heritage. Rastafarian scholar, Dennis Forsythe, was correct when he asserted that the Rastafarians were the 'first mass movement among West Indians preoccupied with the task of looking into themselves and asking the fundamental question, 'Who Am I?' or 'What Am I?' (1980, p. 62). The Rastafarians found their answer by looking to Africa for its most potent symbols of dissent. The movement's visual symbols (African lion, dreadlocks), speech patterns (patois, Rasta talk), musical inspiration (drumming and chanting), living arrangements (communal), goals (repatriation to Africa) and religious beliefs (Selassie as deity) highlight and promote Africa as the movement's spiritual homeland. In a pamphlet entitled, 'Rasta: A Modern Antique', the Rastafarian Movement Association (RMA), one of the more 'political' Rastafarian groups, claimed that it was 'spearheading the African connection in keeping alive the reality of Heritage, Tradition, Custom and Culture, what makes us African' (1976, p. 6).

Despite efforts by the Jamaican authorities to neutralize the Rastafarian 'threat', the movement did, in large measure, succeed in promoting black pride and in rehabilitating Jamaica's African heritage. By the mid-1970s, more and more middle-class Jamaicans began to revise their negative impressions about the movement. Although most middle-class Jamaicans did not convert to Rastafari, many were now defining themselves 'closer to the Rasta than to the white reference point' (Chevannes, 1990, p. 78). In a study of attitudes of different racial and ethnic groups in Jamaica, Mary Richardson concluded that 'Africans' (black Jamaicans of African heritage) were ranked as the most accepted of all racial groups in Jamaica. In confirming this dramatic change in Jamaican attitudes about black as a racial category, Richardson concluded that the 'low self-evaluation of the negro in the society, and the low esteem he enjoyed from others is now a thing of the past' (1983, p. 158). In the end, as Chevannes has observed, 'By keeping alive the issue of identity and forcing it on national consciousness, the Rastafari movement has helped to expose and by so doing overturn certain assumptions of the ideology of racism, particularly among the middle classes' (1990, p. 60).

As a social movement, the Rastafarians employed a variety of methods to disseminate their message of outrage and liberation, including pamphlets, street preaching, church sermons and word of mouth within Rastafarian communities. Since 1968, with the emergence of reggae music, the movement increasingly relied on reggae music as its chief medium of communication. Although Rastafarian themes can be traced back to earlier genres of Jamaican music (for example, ska, rocksteady), reggae music more forcefully articulated the Rastafarian *ethos* than its predecessors, introducing terms such as 'Jah', 'Babylon' and 'Mount Zion' to the wider Jamaican society. Rastafarian scholar Horace Campbell noted that the influence of Rastafari 'on the development of the popular culture was evident by the fact that most serious reggae artists adhered to some of the principles of the Rastafarian Movement' (1987, p. 134). Historian James Winders echoed this sentiment, suggesting that, whilst not 'all reggae stars are Rastas', many are 'sympathetic to them' (1983, p. 69). Indeed, the 'language and orientation' of many reggae songs are 'nearly always Rastafarian' (Breiner, 1985–86, p. 38).

As the movement's main instrument of communication, reggae music was used as a vehicle to radically reconstruct the self-image of both those committed to the movement and Jamaican society at large. While numerous studies, both popular and academic, have analysed reggae's lyrical content and musical structure, few, if any, have examined how reggae songs served to redefine blackness as a racial category and promote Africa as a positive and legitimate cultural legacy (see, for example, Clarke, 1980; Cushmann, 1991; Hebdige, 1987; Warner, 1988; Waters, 1985). In writing this essay, I analysed over 100 reggae songs, recorded between 1968 and 1981, and I argue that reggae music ultimately served an important 'in-group' function for the Rastafarian movement, including intensifying group solidarity and transforming member's selfhood and identity.[1] I then go on to examine the relationship between social movements and protest music, provide a brief historical account of the Rastafarian movement, illuminate the self-directed nature of reggae music, and, finally, discuss the implications of this research on the study of protest music.

Social movements and protest music

Definitions of social movements vary widely and include the notion that movements are not in fact 'physical entities' or 'phenomena'. McGee contends that a social movement 'must be understood as an illusion and not a fact'. Social movements, according to McGee, exist only as 'meaning within the grounds/context of human communication' (1980, p. 242). Most scholars agree, however, that social movements are, indeed, 'unique collective phenomenon' (see Stewart et. al., 1989, p. 3). For example, in their comprehensive survey on social movement literature, Simons, Mechling and Schreier define a social movement as 'sustained efforts by noninstitutionalized collectivities to mobilize resources, resist counter pressures, and exert external influence in behalf of a cause' (1984, p. 794). Attracting the attention of scholars from an array of disciplines, the numerous and often contradictory definitions reflect particular academic boundaries (for example, the social-psychological school). In this essay, I argue that movements are collective phenomena 'intrinsically bound up with the management of symbolic resources' because its members 'organize symbols to persuasive ends', while at the same time 'seek change not through violence or coercion but through force of argument and appeal' (Morris and Browne, 2001, pp. 1–2).

Noting the rhetorical nature of protest music, Berger observed that music has been employed 'extensively in organizing social movements throughout the history of the United States' (2000, p. 65). For example, labour movements, such as the Industrial Workers of the World (IWW), used protest music at the turn of the twentieth century to solidify IWW membership. In 1908, three years after the movement's inception, the IWW developed the idea for the *Little Red Songbook*, a collection of protest songs previously printed on small red cards and distributed along with pamphlets at IWW meetings (Carter, 1980, p. 368). The songs polarized and radicalized the IWW from mainstream public opinion by portraying other labour unions, industrialists and capitalists as 'parasites' and 'fat grafters', while also encouraging the workers to organize, picket and hope for a brighter future (Carter, 1980, pp. 370, 373). In the 1960s American folk musicians, such as Pete Seeger, Joan Baez, Phil Ochs and Bob Dylan, wrote topical songs which became identified with the civil rights movement. A few years later, soul musicians such as Sly and the Family Stone, Aretha Franklin and James Brown served as 'messengers' who communicated 'the philosophy of the Black Power Movement to the masses' (Maultsby, 1983, p. 54).

As ever-changing phenomena, social movements typically attempt to target four primary groups: decision-makers, media sources, sympathizers and the movement itself (Owens and Palmer, 2003, p. 337). However unlikely it may be, a social movement's political objective – the capitulation of the existing order – is predicated on the movement's ability to positively persuade all four groups to accept the legitimacy of the movement's demands and goals (Mondak, 1988, p. 26). Not surprisingly, protest songs identify elites, the 'establishment' or the decision-making group that possesses political legitimacy and coercive power. Vividly describing the negative present as intolerable, protest songs use sarcasm, ridicule, parody or even direct invectives against its perceived 'devils' or main antagonists who are perceived by members of a movement to be primarily responsible for the undesirable conditions. At the same time, protest songs often contrast the inherited evilness of its enemy with the movement's virtues, with the hope of drawing 'sharp distinctions between the forces of right and wrong as they perceive them' (Mattern, 1988, p. 33). These efforts are particularly important when social movements employ the strategy of 'polarization' in an effort to further exacerbate the division between itself and the 'establishment', and encourage the uncommitted to join the ranks of the movement (Bowers et. al., 1993, p. 34). Furthermore, protest songs have, on occasion, targeted potential sympathizers, including individuals or groups who could enhance a movement's overall legitimacy. In perhaps the most comprehensive and systematic study of protest music, Stewart, Smith and Denton analysed 714 protest songs from the American Revolution to the 1980s and discovered that only 3 per cent of songs articulated appeals to outsiders (1989, pp. 226–27). Interestingly, according to the study, protest songs do not attempt to target, or even address, media sources.

However, the same researchers suggest that protest songs are most often directed towards a movement's own constituents. For example, protest songs increase the cohesion and 'groupness' of a social movement (Bowers et. al., 1993, pp. 24–25). In their study of American protest music in the 1960s Eyerman and Jamison agree, suggesting that protest music offers a 'sense of belongingness, a sharing in a collective vision', ultimately providing the 'basis of common understanding and common experience for a generation in revolt' (1995, p. 464). Summarizing the functions of protest music, Knupp concluded that the 'rhetorical patterns in protest songs suggest that they are largely in-group activities' (1981, p. 388).

Yet researchers have not rigorously examined how protest music serves to repair or, in some cases, transform the self-concept of protesters. According to communication scholar, Richard Gregg, protest rhetoric, for the most part, does not serve to persuade or appeal to outside groups, such as a political establishment; instead, the rhetoric of protest is 'self-directed' because protesters, suffering from damaged or inadequate egos, are in need of 'psychological refurbishing and affirmation' (1971, p. 74). Citing a number of social movements, from Black Power to Women's Liberation, Gregg claims that movement leaders and participants experience 'intense feelings of self-deprecation and ego-deprivation' (1971, p. 81). Through legal and extra-legal discriminatory policies, the 'establishment' has defined the Other as weak, abnormal, deficient, inferior and invisible. Protest rhetoric ultimately serves an 'ego-function' because it has the capacity to help members repair their damaged egos, assist in the construction of a positive self-image and even promote 'ego superiority' (1971, p. 84). For example, James Brown's 1969 song, 'Say It Loud (I'm Black and I'm Proud)', was a rallying cry for African-Americans to divest the negative imagery associated with 'blackness' (as defined by white society) and redefine the racial category as something distinctly positive and self-affirming.

Since Gregg's landmark article, a number of follow-up studies (Lake, 1983; Simons, Mechling and Schreier, 1984; Darsey, 1991; Tonn, 1996) have confirmed his findings. Most recently, however, communication researcher Charles Stewart questioned Gregg's claim that social movements are, by definition, self-directed. The problem, according to Stewart, is that scholars have primarily studied self-directed movements, including groups agitating for women's liberation, black self-determinism and gay rights. After examining other movements, including animal rights and pro-life groups, Stewart concluded that some movements are 'other-directed' because members agitate on the behalf of others. Moreover, 'other-directed' movements comprise of individuals who do not define themselves as members of a dispossessed class (1999, pp. 91–93). However, it can be argued that the Rastafarian movement is, in fact, self-directed because many of its members are from Jamaica's underclass and the movement has focused much of its attention on redefining racial and ethnic identities in Jamaica. The next section provides a brief overview of this self-directed movement.

The Rastafarian movement and reggae music

In the early 1930s the Rastafarian movement emerged from the ranks of the dispossessed black class, the most marginalized and despised sector of Jamaican society. Originating from the slum and shantytowns of West Kingston, some of the early members of the movement were also admirers of Marcus Garvey, a Jamaican black nationalist. Garvey migrated to the United States in 1916, formed the Universal Negro Improvement Association (UNIA) and encouraged his followers to resist white supremacy through a variety of measures, including supporting plans to return to Africa. After spending two years in an Atlanta prison for mail fraud, Garvey returned to Jamaica in 1927. Subsequently, he revived Jamaica's UNIA chapter, formed the nation's first contemporary political party and continued to preach his pan-African vision to the world (Chevannes, 1988, p. 140).

Garvey's influence on the development of the Rastafarian movement cannot be overstated. As the movement's 'prophet', Garvey's efforts to remind black people about Africa's glorious past and his repeated assertion that God was black would figure heavily into the movement's emerging religious and philosophical world-view. Most important, however, was Garvey's vision, as revealed in his play *The Coronation of the King and Queen of Africa*, in which a black king would eventually emerge from Africa. In 1930, Ras Tafari Makonnen ascended to the throne and was crowned the new emperor of Ethiopia. At the coronation, Makonnen took the name Haile Selassie I, along with other royal titles including 'King of Kings' and 'Lord of Lords' (Chevannes, 1994, p. 42). Convinced that Garvey's prophecy had come 'true', many of Garvey's followers became part of Jamaica's newest religious 'cult'. Through the Rastafarian lens, Selassie became transformed into 'Jah,' short for Jehovah, a 'God (Almighty) for his people and a liberator to all the oppressed on Earth' (Brown, 1966, p. 39).

From its inception, Rastafari has been characterized as a 'decentralised' movement. According to Rastafarian scholar, Yoshiko Nagashima, the Rastafarian movement 'as a whole cannot be organised as one monolithic political, religious, or cultural organisation' (1984, p. 26). Over the years, the movement has been composed of smaller and larger groups with names such as 'King of Kings Mission', 'Twelve Tribes of Israel', 'Bobo', 'Rastafarian Movement Association' and the 'Jah Rastafari Hola Coptic Church'. Some members belong to a specific group, while others belong to multiple Rastafarian groups because 'membership in a commune is marked by fluidity'. Still other Rastafarians do not belong to a specific group or organization even though they 'affirm the consciousness of Rastafari ...' (Edmonds, 2003, p. 68–70). Consequently, the movement has never unified around a central leader. According to Rastafarian expert, Leonard Barrett, Rastafarians are 'deathly afraid of leaders because they feel that a leader would destroy the movement'. Although each group may have a spokesperson, 'they do not speak for the members as leaders, but simply serve as an inspiration for their specific groups' (1988, p. 172). Rastafarian scholar, Rory Sanders, summed up the movement's heterogeneous structure: 'As to lifestyle, church or organizational involvement, and outward appearance, each Rasta differs from the next' (1982, p. 65). Yet, it would be incorrect to assert that the Rastafarian movement lacks a critical centre.

Douglas R.A. Mack, a Rastafarian, discussed how members of various groups find common ground, especially during periods of intense scrutiny and persecution by Jamaican authorities: 'During the turbulent period of 1961, when the Rastafarian brethren were being bombarded by the Jamaican institutional society, Brother Phil and I ... consulted and reasoned with the brethren to establish cohesion, continuity, and self reliance, in lieu of Babylon's continued ostracism ... The love, unity, and communal spirit that existed among us, made us weather the storm' (1999, p. 68).

Since the movement's inception, Jamaican authorities repeatedly attempted to quell the movement's efforts to spread dissent throughout the island-nation. Employing a wide variety of measures to control the movement, the Rastafarians were routinely harassed, arrested, imprisoned and even deported. Jamaica's national newspaper, *The Daily Gleaner*, ridiculed the Rastafarians as 'mental juvenile delinquents' (Parchment, 1960, p. 8). The Jamaican government and its surrogates also employed evasion tactics to block movement goals and there were also efforts to appease or mollify the Rastafarians. In response to the ever-increasing efforts to stem the tide of protest, members of the movement began to rely more and more on popular music as a means of disseminating its ideology to both its own internal constituents and various external audiences.

Although Rastafarian themes can be traced back to earlier forms of Jamaican popular music, reggae music disseminated the movement's ideology in ways not previously witnessed in either ska or rocksteady. By the mid-1970s, reggae music was experiencing unprecedented popularity in Jamaica and acclaim throughout the international community. The movie and soundtrack *The Harder They Come*, Toots and the Maytals's *Funky Kingston* and the Wailers's *Catch a Fire*, all served to introduce the Rastafarian ethos to an emerging international audience, which included white American college students and European youth. By the end of the decade the increasingly global popularity of performers such as Bob Marley and the Wailers helped solidify the 'marriage' between the movement and its protest music (King, 2002, p. 100). The Rastafarian movement, in effect, co-opted reggae music as its chief medium of communication. Since the Rastafarian movement is a self-directed movement, one would expect to find similar themes in reggae music. In this next section, I will discuss how reggae songs portray the image of dispossessed slaves, redefine 'blackness' in more positive terms and attack 'Babylon' as the source of personal misery and social ills.

Reggae music: 'Lively Up Yourself'

Image of the dispossessed slave

Almost without exception, Rastafarians blame 'Babylon' for their suffering and mistreatment in Jamaica, a country described by some members of the movement as a 'hopeless Hell' (Simpson, 1955, p. 134). In studying the Old and New Testaments, the Rastafarians associate Babylon not only with the ancient city of Babylon, but also with the excesses of the Roman Empire and its enslavement and oppression of early Christians and Jews (Owens, 1976, p. 69). Rastafarian scholar, Ennis B. Edmonds, observed that for the Rastafarians the 'experience of forced captivity in the West paralleled the Babylonian experience of the ancient Hebrews, and the constant subjugation recalled the Roman iron rule over its empire' (2003, p. 43). In turn, the term 'Babylon' has been applied to a variety of entities that the movement deems oppressive, including the Jamaican government, the police, the Christian church, the American and British empires and Western culture in general (Davis and Simon, 1982, p. 69).

For many Rastafarians, Babylon was responsible for developing and profiting from the institution of slavery. Many reggae songs act as alternative history texts, providing their audience with narratives of slavery, a subject historically downplayed in Jamaica's educational system, especially when the island-nation was under colonial rule. In the Melodians' song, 'Rivers of Babylon', the singer remembers when the 'wicked' transported African captives to the New World, a 'strange land'. On *Marcus Garvey*, Winston Rodney, Burning Spear's lead singer, vividly recounts the capture of slaves in 'The Invasion' and, in the hypnotic and haunting 'Slavery Days', he ask his listeners: 'Do you remember the days of slavery?'. In addition, pirates often profited from trading slaves for money and fortune. In 'You Can't Blame the Youth', Peter Tosh criticizes the colonial education system which portrays famous pirates such as John Hawkins and Henry Morgan as 'very great' men. Other notable adventurers, including Marco Polo and Christopher Columbus, are not spared. On 'Columbus', Winston Rodney contests Columbus' 'discovery' of the New World by asking why the Arawak Indians and the 'few black men ... down there before him' are not acknowledged as the true discoverers of Jamaica.

Even though slavery was abolished in 1834, many Rastafarians believe that 'slavery' – based in economic and social injustice – still continues in present-day Jamaica. In '400 Years', Peter Tosh laments 400 years of the 'same old philosophy'. Joseph Hill, the spirited lead singer for Culture, reminds his audience about the extermination of the Arawak Indians and the destruction of Jamaica's natural beauty in 'Pirate Days'. At the same time, Hill and harmony singers Albert Walker and Kenneth Dayes employ the call and response technique to develop an effective exchange on the issue of oppression: 'People let me ask you a question / How long do you believe slavery continue? / Tell them / 300 years, 300 years black man / Tell them again / 300 years, 300 years black man.' In yet another example, 'Redemption Song' opens with an unblinking description of how 'old pirates' purged slaves from the ship's 'bottomless pit' only to be sold to 'merchant ships'. In the second stanza, Bob Marley instructs his listeners to 'emancipate yourself from mental slavery' because 'none but ourselves can free our minds'. Other songs, including 'Israelites' (Desmond Dekker), 'Declaration of Rights' (Abyssinians), 'River Jordan' (Sugar Minott) and 'Too Long in Slavery' (Culture), envision a world where the oppressed, particularly the Rastafari, are 'slaving' in Babylon.

As a result, many reggae songs portray Rastafarians as modern-day slaves. Black Uhuru's 'Rockstone' vividly recounts the misery associated with throwing rocks into a 'dumper truck' and 'forcing jackhammers through the concrete wall'. At the conclusion of the song, Michael Rose (lead singer), Puma and Duckie Simpson (harmony) sing in unison 'We are the slaves / We are the slaves'. In the Abyssinians' 'African Race', the slave image is associated with separation, alienation, and loss: 'We are the slave descendents of the African race / African race, African race / ... I speak Amharic, my sister speaks Swahili / They put us together now / That's why we can't understand.'

As slaves, many Rastafarians and other poor Jamaicans attempt to survive in the world of 'Babylon' – a system which perpetuates social and economic 'slavery'; reggae songs paint a bleak and disturbing world in which inhabitants must face inadequate housing (Jacob Miller, 'Tenement Yard') and hunger (Toots and the Maytals, 'Time Tough') as well as street crime (Mighty Diamonds, 'Why Me Black Brother Why?'), police harassment (Wailers, 'Burnin' and Lootin''), imprisonment (Bunny Wailer, 'Fighting Against Conviction') and social upheaval (Junior Murvin, 'Police and Thieves'). Clearly, the Rastafarian movement is 'self-directed', and reggae songs serve to underscore the causes for the development of this negative 'slave' image. Persecuted by the Jamaican authorities, especially the police, and forced to live in abject poverty, many Rastafarians perceive themselves as innocent victims of Babylon's cruelty and greed. The image of the dispossessed slave suggests that, for some social movements, there 'appears to be a strong need to recognize and proclaim that one's ego is somehow ignored, or damaged or disenfranchised' (Gregg, 1971, p. 76). Unsurprisingly, reggae songs also play an indispensable role in redefining the 'negative self' in more positive, uplifting ways.

The African herbsman

Since Babylon is responsible for the enslavement of Rastafari and the poor, the term 'Rastafari' not only refers to a specific movement but stands as a potent symbol of protest – a reference point positioned in opposition to its enemy, Babylon. Reggae musicians reference the name of the movement in terms such as 'Rasta', 'Rastaman' or 'Rastafari'. Although reggae songs rarely refer to a specific Rastafarian group such as the Rastafarian Movement Association or the Twelve Tribes of Israel, the term 'Dreadlocks' appears on a number of reggae recordings. Emerging in the late 1940s, a group known as the Dreadlocks initially belonged to the Youth Black Faith, a 'radical' faction which criticized other Rastafarian groups for being too accommodating with the Jamaican state.

Moreover, the Youth Black Faith wanted to eliminate religious superstition from the movement's theology and challenged members to 'dreadlock' their hair; members 'locked' their hair by not cutting or combing it (Chevannes, 1994, pp. 145–58). Although the Dreadlocks shared the movement's belief in non-violence, these 'radicals' were a more menacing, more volatile subgroup, and their hairstyle played a role in symbolizing their 'aggressive posture ... toward the wider non-Rastafari world' (Chevannes, 1994, p. 208). With the eventual dissolution of the Youth Black Faith, the Dreadlocks later joined other groups, including the Jah Rastafari Hola Coptic Church, and became an increasingly popular 'figure' with members of the movement and curious sympathizers.

At the same time as the Dreadlocks were becoming a powerful and influential group among the Rasta brethren (1960s–1970s), reggae music was quickly gaining supremacy as the island's most popular form of popular music. Many reggae musicians identified with the Dreadlocks tradition and expressed their allegiance in song. Jacob Miller's 1976 hit, 'Tenement Yard', illustrates the problems of overcrowding in Kingston's poor communities and criticizes 'informants' for not allowing 'Dreadlocks' to 'smoke [their] [ganja] pipe in peace'. In 'Fort Augustus', Junior Delgado describes how the 'Dreadlocks' and other prisoners were held as captives in Jamaica's infamous prison. The Mighty Diamonds celebrate the Dreadlock's acetic lifestyle in "Natural Natty' ('natural man'), while reminding their listeners that Natty Dread works as a 'slave' for the 'big big boss'.

As suggested above, reggae musicians routinely selected the most radical, perhaps the most popular, Rastafari persona as the 'face' for the movement, and the Dread is associated with a variety of positive descriptors. Natty Dread is smart, strong, proud, fearless and, as suggested by a number of reggae songs, will not shrink from vanquishing their oppressors. Culture's 1979 release, *Cumbolo*, contains two songs of Rasta resistance, 'Natty Dread Naw Run' and 'Natty Never Get Weary'. In another example, the Gladiators's 'Mix Up' boasts of the Dread's defiance against the corrupting and dehumanizing influence of 'Babylon': 'Natty Dread, Natty rule / Natty cool (cool-cool Natty Dread) / Yes, the Dread / For they stand up in Babylon.' Rejecting the negative image of passivity and self-hate, these images depict black Jamaicans and others as 'Rastas', active agents of resistance against the tyranny of the 'Babylon System'. Yet, as many reggae songs suggest, the 'Dread' is also 'African'. Although many reggae musicians were born in Jamaica, reggae songs do not identify the 'self' as 'Jamaican', 'West Indian' or 'Caribbean'. By claiming African citizenship, Rastafarians ultimately reject Jamaica, a nation where the poor and dispossessed continue to 'weep' and 'wail' in perpetual bondage. By the mid- to late 1970s, more and more reggae musicians had increased their lyrical scope, focusing their efforts on 'reporting' about the African continent. For example, Bob Marley and the Wailers's *Survival* (1979) chronicles a number of social and political conflicts, including the civil war in the former British colony of Rhodesia. On that album, Marley sings of 'Rastas' joining forces with 'Africans' to 'unite Africa'; at other times, Rastafarians and Africans share a singular 'African' identity. Occasionally, songs will reference a particular African state, especially Ethiopia (Culture's 'Ethiopians Waan Guh Home'), and one reggae band even called themselves the 'Ethiopians'. In 'African' Peter Tosh summarizes the rationale for adopting 'African' as his new identity: 'Don't care where you come from / So long as you are a black man / You're an African.'

In addition to articulating the positive self, protest songs also routinely describe other members of the movement as 'brothers', 'comrades' and 'fellow soldiers', a strategy intended to reaffirm a sense of groupness and cohesion. Gregg notes that these terms are significant because they create the 'communal sharing of ego-well-being' (1971, p. 84). Reggae songs include unique terms which attempt to solidify a greater sense of solidarity than one would typically find in most protest music. For example, the phrase 'I & I' serves to transcend the impersonal distance between 'you' and 'me' into the unified 'I'. As Chevannes suggests, 'I' is the most important letter in 'Rasta talk', a subdialect which originated with the Youth Black Faith (1994, p. 167). Thus, Rastas have developed a number of 'I' words, including 'Irie', 'Ital' and 'Iman' (Pollard, 1990, pp. 85–87). In the case of 'I & I', the second 'I' is a substitute for 'you' as well as God (Jah) who dwells within each human being. In essence, 'I & I' suggests that 'disunity is an illusion fostered and imposed on the people by Babylon' (Steffens, 1998, p. 256). 'I & I' frequently appears in reggae songs, including Bob Marley and the Wailers's song 'Crazy Baldheads', a critical indictment of the 'conman' (Babylon) who forced 'I & I' to 'plant the corn' and 'build your penitentry [*sic*]'. At other times, the second 'I' refers to Jah (Selassie) who is also called 'Jah Rastafari', 'Rastaman', 'Jah Jah' and 'Father'. Meanwhile, reggae singers also refer to members of the movement as 'brothers', 'brethren' and 'sistren'. Although the Rastafarians have been criticized as a male-dominated, patriarchal movement, the term 'sistren' is a far more positive descriptor than one would find in other forms of popular music, especially rap (for example, 'ho' and 'bitch'). In any case, the use of 'I & I', 'brethren' and other positive descriptors are a necessary part of the 'discovery and enjoyment of group self-hood' which, according to Gregg, 'becomes easily transposed to a feeling of individual ego-satisfaction' (1971, p. 84).

In all, reggae songs function as powerful statements of self-affirmation and as a rejection of an ascribed negative self-image. Emphasizing the movement's struggle against the ideology of racism and its unwillingness to be perceived as passive and disorganized, reggae musicians have typically adopted the singular 'Dreadlocks' persona. Moreover, many reggae artists claim to be African citizens – an obvious rejection of both Jamaica and the wider Babylon world. Earlier, I discussed how reggae songs blame Babylon for the Rastas' damaged self-concept, the image of the dispossessed slave. In the next section I will discuss how reggae songs describe Babylon's 'wicked' persona, a technique specifically employed to underscore Rasta's superior ego.

Chant down Babylon

Almost without exception, protest rhetoric defines its adversaries, and reggae songs repeatedly identify, mock and ridicule 'Babylon' in order to enhance the image of 'Natty Dread'. 'By painting the enemy in dark hued imagery of vice, corruption, evil, and weakness', Gregg argues, 'one may more easily convince himself of his own superior virtue and thereby gain a symbolic victory of ego-enhancement' (1971, p. 82). In this sense, protest rhetoric serves as a counter-hegemonic response to political elites and institutions of authority (for example, mass media) that employ 'counterpersuasion' tactics in order to erode a movement's ideas and influence (Bowers et al., 1993, p. 49).

Reggae songs use animal metaphors, – particularly the vampire and wolf – to depict Babylon's parasitic greed (King and Jensen, 1995, p. 23). In 'Babylon System', Bob Marley describes the vampire as 'sucking the children day by day / Sucking the blood of the sufferers'. On 'Vampire', Black Uhuru's Michael Rose boasts that the 'wicked ... bloodsucker' has 'no control over I & I'. The vampire embodies the evil, parasitic nature of Babylon as well as the Rastafarian's notion that the 'wicked' will perish while the 'righteous' will enjoy everlasting life. According to Rastafarian scholar, Joseph Owens, many Rastafarians believe that if they 'remain faithful to the God of the living [Selassie]', they will not 'fear the spectre of mortality' (1976, p. 136). Many Rastafarians also believe in a type of reincarnation quite different from the Hindu doctrine which teaches that rebirth occurs after death. Instead, an individual may experience several incarnations during a 'lifetime'. That is, as a part of the 'regeneration of life' an individual will 'take on many diverse appearances and will at times simply disappear, but he will always be the same person' (Owens, 1976, p. 141). In contrast, Babylon is the vampire who did not transcend 'death' and will not enjoy everlasting life. The vampire is part of the 'living dead'. At the same time, the term 'wolf' often refers to individuals who exploit the external trappings of Rastafari (for example, dreadlocks, Rasta talk) in order to weaken or, perhaps, destroy the movement (hence, the term 'wolf in sheep's clothing'). On the title track of Dennis Brown's *Wolves and Leopards* album, the singer equates informants and other agents of Babylon as 'wolves' and 'leopards' 'trying to kill the sheep and the shepherds'.

Beyond the use of animal metaphors, reggae songs describe the corrupting influence of Babylon. Babylon quarantined the underclass in slums (Bunny Wailer, 'Fighting Against Conviction'), starved the poor (Junior Byles, 'Beat Down Babylon'), overexploited the working class (Culture, 'Pay Day'), intimidated and arrested the innocent (Max Romeo, 'Three Blind Mice') and institutionalized racial segregation (Peter Tosh, 'Apartheid'). For these reasons, reggae songs call for the destruction of Babylon, claiming that Babylon will be destroyed in 'fire' and 'brimstone' (Bob Marley and the Wailers, 'Revolution'). In sum, Babylon is depicted as 'weak', 'soft', 'vain', 'wicked' and 'brutal'. Babylon is ultimately a destructive force and its many embodiments – the slave driver, pirates, police officers, or preachers – are immoral, greedy, sadistic and evil. In turn, the Rastafarians are 'fearless', 'strong', 'proud' and 'righteous'. While Babylon perpetuates terror and oppression, the Rastafarians try to build 'one foundation' in order to establish a new global vision, one predicated on equity, justice and universal love. Reggae's scathing attacks against 'Babylon' ultimately promotes the Rastafarian's ego or self as distinctly superior to its evil counterpart.

Conclusion

For nearly 40 years reggae music has served as the Rastafarian movement's chief medium of dissent, challenging the ideology of racism which has historically permeated every sector of Jamaican life. Although numerous studies have examined the lyrical content of reggae, few, if any, have explored how the music functions rhetorically within the movement itself. Like to protest rhetoric from other self-directed movements, reggae songs describe the self as damaged or inferior ('slave'), praise the 'strength and virtues of the ego sought after' ('Natty Dreadlock') and condemn the 'ignorant or malicious qualities of an enemy' ('Babylon') (Gregg, 1971, p. 76). In this way, reggae music serves to develop and maintain a healthy and positive self-image of 'blackness' while, as the same time, intensifying cohesion and 'groupness' within the movement.

Although reggae music may suggest strategies for social and political change in Jamaica and advocate solutions to the problem of oppression, its main purpose seems to serve in-group goals. By the mid- to late 1970s, more middle-class Jamaicans, particularly the youth, began to join the movement, or to at least publicly express sympathy with Rastafari, as is evidenced by the adoption of the movement's more 'exotic' cultural symbols, such as dreadlocks. Although some of these new 'converts' have been criticized for their indifference to the movement's 'hard-core religious philosophy' (Burke, 1977, p. 15), the movement's new-found popularity suggests that Rastafari finally achieved cultural legitimacy in Jamaica. In addition, Rastafari gained the attention of academics, commercial entrepreneurs and Jamaica's political parties. By critiquing the inequities of Jamaican life, providing a new orientation to Africa and, most importantly, stressing a new and more positive image of 'blackness', the Rastafarians were able to make a significant impact on the island-nation's cultural landscape. In the song, 'Babylon System', Bob Marley sums up the movement's aggressive resistance against efforts to accept a negative, ascribed self-image: 'We refuse to be what you want us to be / We are what we are.'

Acknowledgement

I would like to thank P. Renee Foster for her suggestions, which improved the overall content of this essay.

Note

1. Although this essay focuses strictly on reggae's discursive discourse, I also recognize the importance of examining reggae's musical structure. For an analysis of the musical structure of reggae music, see King (2002, pp. 45–65).

Chapter 9

'We have survived': popular music as a representation of Australian Aboriginal cultural loss and reclamation

Peter Dunbar-Hall

It is not difficult to find descriptions of popular music by Australian Aboriginal musicians as music of protest and to imply that this is its most prominent social role. Often this is contextualized internationally, with Aboriginal rock songs likened to songs used for protest by other people suffering the effects of colonisation (Garofalo, 1992; Sakolsky and Ho, 1995). For example, Sweeney (1991, p. 179) explains Aboriginal rock music as having grown 'up in the late 1970s and in the 1980s, nurtured by the climate of rehabilitation of all aspects of the culture of the downtrodden and dispossessed original inhabitants of the huge country', while Breen (1994, p. 655) represents this music as an expression of black rights in Australia, noting songs that 'remind European settlers of their shameful history in respect to the Aborigines ... (involving) dispossession of land, denial of identity, dispersal and resettlement, the poisoning of water supplies, and as recently as the 1930s systematic massacres'.

Recordings from the early period of commercial releases of Aboriginal rock music in the 1970s and 1980s bear out this image, with albums such as *Rebel Voices from Black Australia* including songs which outline the demise of Aboriginal cultures and call for land rights, the redressing of the political mistreatment of Aborigines and improvement to their lifestyles and social well-being. The protest nature of Aboriginal popular music at that time was emphasized by the beginnings of a pan-Aboriginal civil rights movement focused on the public denouncement of the treatment of Aborigines who, it should be noted, were not counted in Australian censuses before 1967: in effect, they did not officially exist until the late 1960s.

In the early 1970s this new official recognition helped inspire the Aborigines to demand that their histories and present-day situation be acknowledged and redressed, and popular music was one means through which this demand was mediated to the wider Australian community (Robinson and York, 1977; Lippmann, 1981; Howard, 1982; Bennett, 1989; Moores, 1995; Neill, 2002).

Since then, songs which have become recognized as being representative of the Aborigines' position on their current status continue the links between the nascent Aboriginal black rights movement of the 1970s and the present day and can readily and correctly be interpreted as protest: these include Archie Roachs's 'Took the Children Away', with its autobiographical depiction of the removal of children from Aboriginal parents; Kev Carmody's 'Cannot buy my soul' which criticizes the effects of white invasion on Aboriginal identity; Tiddas's rendition of 'Malcolm Smith', telling of the death of an Aboriginal teenager in prison; and Ruby Hunter's 'Proud, Proud Woman' about loss of culture and personal pride. All of these songs remind audiences of Aboriginal histories and current conditions.

Reasons for how and why this impression of Aboriginal popular music has arisen and become entrenched in the Australian psyche and in analyses of Australian culture are not difficult to locate. One reason is the Australian population's low level of understanding about Aboriginal cultures. Aborigines account for approximately 2 per cent of a population of around 20 million and, despite federal government directives that all education in Australia, from primary (elementary) to university level should always include indigenous perspectives and despite the ease of access to Aboriginal artworks (from painting, to literature, music, theatre and film), understanding of Aboriginal cultures by non-Aboriginal people remains shadowy and Aborigines continue to be marginalized in the community. The fact that media coverage of Aboriginal issues favours the sensationalism of race riots, the high number of Aboriginal deaths in Australian prisons, and the endemic nature of alcohol abuse and petrol sniffing in Aboriginal communities does little to provide Australians with dependable and useful knowledge about Aboriginal people and their cultures. The popular misconception that Aboriginal rock songs are only protest songs has been furthered by the success and airplay of a limited number of songs at the expense of the wide range of popular music by Aboriginal musicians. The broader picture of this music to be gained by considering Aboriginal popular music as a national repertoire presents a different view of the roles and uses of music in Aboriginal communities and by Aboriginal musicians when they engage with the international contexts of popular music. It must be clarified, however, that whatever its topic, all music by Aboriginal musicians makes a statement of identity and thus acts, in whatever small way, to remind listeners of Aboriginal presences. How this is achieved provides a clue to reading Aboriginal popular music as more than superficially concerned with protest. Interpreting Aboriginal popular music as a representation of the survival of Aboriginal cultures and an expression of Aboriginal intentions to remain culturally strong is the primary means for demonstrating this position.

The concept of survival underpins much contemporary Aboriginal arts expression, and the word 'survival' is used in Aboriginal discourse with a semantic field beyond its use in standard English. That is:

... 'survival' in recent times refers not so much to physical survival, as to the spiritual and cultural survival of Aboriginal people (with the notable exception of 'deaths in custody' and of very poor community health). This survival is set against the enormous assimilationist pressures on the Aboriginal community particularly in the period from the 1930s until the 1970s ... the assimilation policies of the Australian government assumed that there would eventually be no distinctive Aboriginal community or culture. (Arthur, 1996, p. 240)

This expanded sense of the term in Aboriginal communities seems to have been adopted in the late 1980s, at a time when white Australia was obsessed with celebrating 200 years of English colonization. Alana Harris, for example, uses it in her description of an Aboriginal march on 26 January 1988 (officially Australia Day, commemorating the 1788 founding of Australia as a penal colony):

(Aborigines) came from all over the country, but they did not come to celebrate. They came to unite in peace, hope and justice and to show the world ... Aboriginal solidarity, Aboriginal needs for recognition, mourning for the past and present injustices and Aboriginal celebrations of the survival of our culture ... Despite all the changes that have happened in the last 200 years of our history, Aboriginal people and Aboriginal culture have survived. (Harris, 1995, pp. 138–39)

Another Aboriginal writer, Mark O'Connor (1988, p. 246), adds a further dimension to Aboriginal constructions of the 1988 bicentennial celebrations, one relevant to the reading of Aboriginal popular music presented here: '1988 may prove to be an important milestone for modern Aborigines and may yet justify Oodgeroo Noonuccal's belief that blacks should use the Bicentennial "to educate, not to celebrate".'

In addition to its indication that Aboriginal cultures continue to exist, Aboriginal use of the word 'survival' also argues against a common nineteenth- and twentieth-century view of the Aborigines as a dying race (for example, as espoused by famous quasi-anthropologist, Daisy Bates; see White, 1985). Use of the term by Aborigines reminds us that Aborigines remain, despite the proactive efforts by successive Australian governments to wipe them out or, by ignoring them, to assist in their demise. In the recent history of Aboriginal attempts to reclaim land from which they were dispossessed, the term 'survival' achieved increased strength in the 1990s after the 1992 *Mabo* decision, a landmark land rights victory that validated indigenous rights to land in Australia (Bartlett, 1993). The term is now also used as the Aboriginal name for Australia Day (see above); in this guise it gives its name to a day-long celebration of Aboriginal cultures, called Survival.

Rather than attempt to cover survival as it informs Aboriginal popular music by reference to a large number of songs and artists, this chapter focuses on the recordings of one Aboriginal rock group – Wirrinyga Band, from Milingimbi in the extreme north of the Australian continent – as a means of opening windows into the world of Aboriginal popular music and its role as commentator on the survival, maintenance and perpetuation of Aboriginal cultures. This group represents culturally-driven agendas by means of both music (in the manipulation of sounds which can be interpreted as typically 'Aboriginal'), and the issues that underpin the song lyrics. This approach highlights the fact that a number of issues recur as the topics of songs throughout Aboriginal popular music as a whole, and that musical practices through which Aboriginality and its survival are notified to the listening public demonstrate similarities on a national level. It also resonates with an interpretation of rock music albums by Aboriginal musicians as holistic statements of Aboriginality, reflections on the position and condition of contemporary Aboriginal existence in the Australian polity, and a means of representing the survival of Aboriginal cultures, and hopes for their continuation (Dunbar-Hall, 1996). In this way, although survival might not be explicitly broached as a song topic by Wirrinyga Band and, although the group's songs are not primarily explicit protest songs, they make implicit statements of Aboriginal presence and persistence. As another Aboriginal musician, Bart Willoughby (from the group No Fixed Address), sings in perhaps his most famous song: 'We have survived the white man's way, and you know you can't change that.'

Songs about the Dreamtime

The Aboriginal members of Wirrinyga Band refer to themselves as Yolngu, speakers of languages of the Yolngu language block that stretches across a wide region of the north-eastern section of Arnhem Land. In common with many Aboriginal people in Australia, while they might use the term 'Aboriginal' to refer to themselves when this term is required in government discourse, they more properly use the name of the Aboriginal nation of which they are members. References in their songs to Yolngu (people), therefore, are a way of stating a specific Aboriginality, of drawing attention to the coexistence of different Aboriginalities (a fact still unknown to most non-Aboriginal Australians), and a conscious strategy to encourage Australians to recognize Yolngu as a distinct people and culture.

This group has released two albums to date: *Dreamtime Shadow* (1990) and *Dreamtime Wisdom Modern Time Vision* (1996). It is significant in Aboriginal terms that both albums draw on the image of the Dreamtime (also referred to as the Dreaming) for their titles, as the Dreamtime lies at the basis of Aboriginal cosmology. Its appearance in rock songs attests to its centrality to Aboriginal expression of cultural continuity and reflects the continual appearance of the Dreamtime/Dreaming as album title and song topic throughout the repertoire of Aboriginal popular music. This can be seen in songs and recordings such as Baulu-Wah Bushrangers' 'Ngarrankany Dreaming', Coloured Stone's 'Dreamtime', Matthew Dolye's *Wild Honey Dreaming*, Kutcha Edward's 'I Have a

Dream', Little Piggies' *Dreaming In Broome*, Archie Roach's *Jamu Dreaming* and Tjapukai Dancers' 'Kurranda Dreaming'. Use of the word in album titles and rock songs indicates the manipulation of current forms of cultural expression to state belief systems dated by Aboriginal people to a period at least 40000 years before the current era. No more explicit statement of survival of Aboriginal identity by the means of contemporary media can be imagined.

The term 'the Dreaming' refers to the period of world creation, the assigning of land to Aboriginal people, the linking of languages to specific regions and the setting in place of protocols by which land is owned and cared for. Reference to it, therefore, goes beyond statements of events of the past. In an intertextual manner, it calls up beliefs and positions on land, and, through these, Aboriginal agendas for reacting to government treatment of Aborigines. Dreaming figures and their activity permeate both the physical landscape and the spiritual domain; they form a recurring topic of song, dance and painting over the many thousands of years of Aboriginal existence. Songs on both of Wirrinyga Band's albums refer specifically to the Dreamtime. Some, while retelling the activities of the Dreamtime, also call on understanding of the Dreamtime as a source of spiritual and cultural power. For example, 'The Land and My People' (also labelled on *Dreamtime Shadow* as 'Land Rights Song') addresses the spiritual dimensions of Yolngu knowledge stemming from the Dreamtime: There is a story about our land / It has got Dreaming tracks and sacred boundaries / The spirits of the Dreamtime move across the face of the land / Giving knowledge and understanding to all Yolngu men.' A call to be taken 'back to the Dreamtime', which resurfaces in numerous songs by Aboriginal musicians across Australia, is used by this group as a symbol of the pre-white past and in *Dreamtime Shadow* to equate the Dreamtime with the spiritual nature of (present) Yolngu existence through the metaphor of land: 'Take me back to the Dreamtime / Far away into Yolngu land.'

References to the Dreamtime are more explicit on Wirrinyga Band's second album. Here, it appears regularly as a song topic or as a place where the actions of song topics occur. For Wirrinyga Band, as for other Aboriginal rock groups, the benefits of the traditional past, symbolized as 'the Dreamtime', are called on to address the tensions of contemporary life. The songs on this album refer continually to images of the Dreamtime. It is an ever-present point of reference for Yolngu who, in the song 'Balanda's Totemic Waterhole' (*balanda*: white/non-Aboriginal person), are described as 'living so simply in the mysteries of the Dreamtime', and is linked to the concept of ownership of, and responsibility for, land that was ordained as Yolngu during the Dreamtime period: 'Yolngu people taking good care of our land.' In 'Indigenous Man Keep on Telling Those Stories', listeners are called on to 'hold on tight to our Dreaming' and that the 'Sound of the *yidaki* [didjeridu] and *bilma* [clapsticks] enriches our spiritual land . . . Forty thousand years of talking history / Within our culture and our Dreaming / One mob, one voice, one land'. This conflates a number of images and issues

Figure 9.1 *Dreamtime Shadow album cover*

that underpin contemporary Aboriginal conceptualizations of indigenous Australia and its continuation: reference to *yidaki* and *bilma* as aural symbols of Aboriginal cultures (see Neuenfeldt, 1997); 'forty thousand years' as the generally accepted figure for Aboriginal ownership of Australia prior to the white invasion in the late eighteenth century; 'talking history' as a reference to Aboriginal cultures as orally/aurally transmitted; and 'Dreaming' as holistic reference to the Aboriginal past as it continues in the present. This continual setting of the past against the tensions of the present forms part of this rock group's description of themselves, as on both albums they describe their music as influenced 'by the strength of [the band's] connection to their cultural background and deal[ing] with a number of issues encountered by living in the modern world as people strong in their Aboriginal identity' (Wirrinyga Band, album notes, *Dreamtime Wisdom Modern Time Vision*).

This past/present dichotomy informs the title track of Wirrinyga Band's second album, which relies explicitly on the Dreamtime as its central image in contradistinction to 'moderntime': 'People of the Dreamtime / And people of the moderntime / Take this message stick of the Dreamtime / And share it to the nation ...'.

Not only does Wirrinyga Band's use of the Dreamtime recur across Aboriginal popular music as a standard reference for the past, for Aboriginal identity and for a means of affirming cultural links to land, but the image of a 'message stick' (an Aboriginal means of spreading information), of the Dreamtime being taken to other (non-Aboriginal) Australians, also resonates with the way in which numerous Aboriginal musicians use rock songs as a means of calling for conciliation between black and white in Australia. This topic is particularly prevalent in the songs of Blekbala Mujik and Yothu Yindi. For example, in 'Nitmiluk', Blekbala Mujik states that 'this land's for you, this land's for me', while Yothu Ynidi, in their most famous song, 'Treaty', sing that although 'now two rivers run their course, separated for so long', they are 'dreaming of a brighter day when the waters will be one'.

Perhaps the major outcome of the Dreaming is Aboriginal relationships to land. Ownership of land and rights to it, as well as personal and group attachment to land, are the continuing basis of Aboriginal existence and identity. The history of Australian Aborigines since the time of invasion in 1788 has been primarily one of struggles over land. It is not surprising, therefore, that land always has been, and always will be, a major topic of Aboriginal arts expression; its appearance as the topic of rock songs permeates Aboriginal popular music in many ways. Some musicians sing land rights songs that openly call for return of lands. For example in 'Land Rights' the group Sunrize Band sings 'Give me back my freedom / Give me back my home'. Others sing celebratory songs occasioned by the handing back of land to its owners. This can be demonstrated by Blekbala Mujik's song 'Nitmiluk': 'A fight took place in court ... / The jury gave the answer / You're free for everyone.' Still others praise places significant to them,

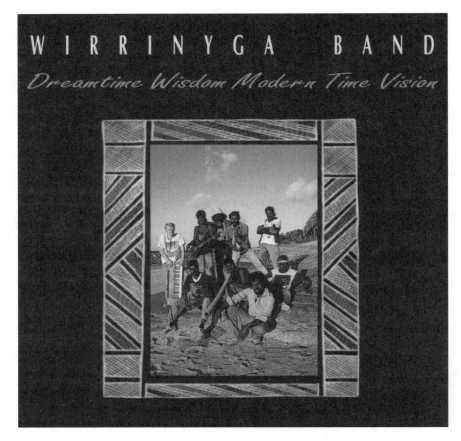

Figure 9.2   *Dreamtime Wisdom Modern Time Vision* **album cover**

as Kerrianne Cox sings in her 'Beagle Bay Dreaming': 'No matter how far I go / My feet will carry me home ... Beagle Bay dreaming.'

In addition to these specific treatments of land in songs, Aboriginal popular music is permeated by a sense of place, by the naming of places and the linking of people and events to places (Dunbar-Hall and Gibson, 2004). In these ways, Aboriginal connections to places, and thus either Aboriginal survival at them or statements of loss of ownership, are made. At the same time, a dominant topic of Aboriginal cultural expression of all times, Aboriginality, as represented through land-related belief systems, links contemporary music, in the form of rock songs, to the ongoing traditions of Aboriginal communities. The topic remains unchanged, while its musical representation continues to evolve.

The types of land song noted above from the repertoires of Blekbala Mujik, Kerrianne Cox and Sunrize Band are represented on the albums of Wirrinyga

Band, thus linking this group's output with Aboriginal music, both contemporary and of the pre-colonial past as a whole. Wirrinyga Band's songs are often set in 'the timeless land', sometimes specifically naming places important in their lives, as in 'My Sweet Takarrina', a song that tells the history of Yolngu interaction with Macassan sailors and traders (and incidentally establishes Yolngu ownership of Takarrina and continued Yolngu existence there today): 'They sailed across the great Java seas and navigated / The seas to an island called Takarrina ...' Other songs specifically mention the group's region, as in 'Arnhem Land Lullaby Blues': 'So let's sing this song of my favourite Arnhem Land blues.' The most important mention of land in songs by this group, however, is in songs that express attachment to land. This is heard in songs such as 'Dreamtime Shadow' with its call to 'take me back to my home country', and in 'The Land and My People': 'What does the land really mean to my people? / Land is our mother, it protects us all.'

Like references to the Dreamtime, references to land, country and places in Wirrinyga Band's songs and the survival of Aboriginal custodianship of them exemplify a regular topic of Aboriginal cultural expression, which is reinforced through other aspects of this group's recordings. To gain some understanding of these aspects of Wirrinyga Band's songs, it is necessary to consider the commercial contexts of this group's albums and to investigate links between these and Aboriginal agendas of cultural survival and perpetuation.

Wirrinyga Band and the Central Australian Aboriginal Media Association

Both albums by Wirrinyga Band were recorded and released by the Central Australian Aboriginal Media Association (CAAMA). CAAMA is one of a network of media production companies subsidized by the Australian federal government to provide radio, television, Internet and recording facilities to Australian indigenous communities. In terms of its broadcast footprint and the number of recordings it produces and markets, CAAMA, located in Alice Springs in the centre of the Australian continent, is the most significant of these media associations. CAAMA's recording catalogue ranges from albums by popular 1970s singer-songwriters such as Bob Randall and Herbie Laughton to those of current, musically harder-edged artists such as Frank Yamma and the bands Lazy Late Boys, Nangu and SPIN.fx. As with songs on Wirrinyga Band's *Dreamtime Shadow* and *Dreamtime Wisdom Modern Time Vision*, songs recorded by CAAMA artists adhere to a number of policies specific to the support of Aboriginal cultures. Two of these, observable in songs by Wirrinyga Band, concern Aboriginal health and lifestyle and Aboriginal languages.

To listeners not accustomed to Aboriginal popular music albums, the appearance of 'Antipetrol Sniffers' Song' and 'Balanda's Totemic Waterhole' on

Wirrinyga Band's second album could seem an unusual occurrence. Issues of health and lifestyle, such as petrol sniffing, alcohol abuse, sexually transmitted diseases (especially HIV and AIDS), and calls for the proper care of children, however, are common topics on the albums released by CAAMA. The message of 'Balanda's Totemic Waterhole', for example, tells listeners to be wary of alcohol: 'Yolngu women and Yolngu men / Don't you get fooled by the Balanda ways / Totemic waterhole now open and someone's calling / He's a stranger with a pub totem'.

In the case of three CAAMA albums, *AIDS: How Could I Know?*, *Unwankara Palyanku Kanyintjaku: A Strategy for Wellbeing* (consisting of songs about the health and care of children) and *Wama Wanti: Drink Little Bit*, these issues are considered important enough to warrant complete albums of songs. As with contemporary songs about land and the Dreaming, the appearance of health-related topics in Aboriginal rock song is a continuation of this practice in songs of pre-colonial times (see for example, Strehlow, 1971, who discusses songs against illness in order to bring about health by the Aranda and Luritja people of central Australia). Adaptation of contemporary music to the ongoing expression of song topics from the past demonstrates both another level of the survival of ideas and the means of recording and disseminating them among Aboriginal people. The practice of addressing these issues in rock songs is indicative of the poor levels of health in Aboriginal communities, of Aboriginal life expectancies which are drastically lower than those of other sectors of the Australian population, and the depressed living conditions of Aboriginal communities (Brady, 1992; Australians for Native Title and Reconciliation, 2004). CAAMA's position in responding to these issues through popular music is explained in the association's press releases. For example:

> CAAMA's charter [is] to provide full media service to Aboriginal people by arresting cultural disintegration through broadcasting educational material in language and song. Specifically, the CAAMA charter aims to alleviate problems ... in areas of health, law, social services and literacy experienced by Aboriginal people ... [and] to promote knowledge and understanding by the Australian community of Aboriginal culture and traditions. [This] is carried out through specific campaigns such as preventing alcohol abuse and recording and distributing the work of many Aboriginal artists through CAAMA's recording facilities. (Central Australian Aboriginal Media Association, n.d.)

> Music forms the bulk of (CAAMA's) program content, and as the organisation has grown so has its collection of locally recorded Aboriginal artists. Bands such as The Areyonga Desert Tigers, Wedgetail Eagles, Warumpi (Band) and Coloured Stone, and solo artists Punch Thompson and Frankie Yamma... have been able to utilise the airwaves to spread the word about substance abuse, land rights, and the discontent felt by Aboriginal people at constantly finding themselves on the margins of society. (Central Australian Aboriginal Media Association, 1989, p. 8)

Wirrinyga Band's 'Antipetrol Sniffers' Song' is sung in a Yolngu language, as are seven other songs on Wirrinyga Band's two albums. This indicates another aspect of CAAMA's work: the proactive use of popular music as an aid to Aboriginal language reclamation and preservation. It is in the recording of songs in Aboriginal languages that the work of CAAMA exemplifies one of the most noticeable examples of the use of popular music in Aboriginal cultural survival.

Linguists calculate that at the time of English invasion of Australia in 1788 there were approximately 250 mutually incomprehensible Aboriginal languages in use (Dixon, 1980; Schmidt, 1993; Walsh and Yallop, 1993). By the late twentieth century, only 90 of these were still alive. Of these, 20 were in a 'relatively healthy state' and 'the total number of surviving languages is expected to diminish to less than ten within the next thirty to forty years. Only ten percent of the Australian Aboriginal people still speak their indigenous languages' (Schmidt, 1993, 'Executive Summary'). This loss of Aboriginal languages is the result of numerous factors, some actively pursued by white colonizers, among them the prohibition of their use by government, church and educational authorities. A recognition that language loss means culture loss and that Aboriginal languages are in need of serious assistance if they are to survive has been the tenor of various Australian government reports. In these reports, the role of rock songs in Aboriginal languages as a strategy for supporting these languages is acknowledged. For example, a 1992 Australian federal government report, *Language and Culture – A Matter of Survival: Report of the Inquiry into Aboriginal and Torres Strait Islander Language Maintenance*, states that:

> Another objective of language maintenance is to reduce unnecessary pressure destructive of language. This involves maintaining pride in the language and maximising the use of language within the community ... The production of books, videos and contemporary songs in language are ... useful in maintaining pride in language. The recent success of Yothu Yindi and other Aboriginal bands ... while using traditional language in songs has raised the awareness of Aboriginal and Torres Strait Islander languages. It has also helped make traditional languages less 'old-fashioned' to ... teenagers. (House of Representatives Standing Committee, 1992, pp. 39–40)

Three years later, in 1995, another government report, *Alive and Deadly: Reviving and Maintaining Australian Indigenous Languages*, quotes Ashley Coleman, from Gudju Gudju band, explaining his group's use of Djabugay language in songs as being 'for the kids so they could pick up the language' (Department of Employment, Education and Training, 1995, p. 7). In another government report on this topic, *The Land Still Speaks: Review of Aboriginal and Torres Strait Islander Language Maintenance and Development Needs and Activities*, this time from 1996, specific examples of the benefits of rock songs in language are cited. For example, at Borroloola, in the Northern Territory, where Aboriginal languages have died out or are weak, 'a number of Aboriginal bands ... sing a lot of music in language. The children often know the songs' (National Board of Employment, Education and Training, 1996, p. 29).

The significance of Aboriginal rock songs in Aboriginal languages does not escape CAAMA's policy direction. Much of the repertoire recorded by CAAMA uses Aboriginal languages, and albums are compiled with songs in a number of languages as part of a strategy to preserve and teach Aboriginal languages. This is made clear by the notes accompanying the CAAMA album *In Aboriginal: Aboriginal Music in Aboriginal Languages*:

> *In Aboriginal* ... is the first in a series of compilation albums which feature Aboriginal language with eleven bands and two soloists singing in Warlpiri from the Tanami Desert, Pitjantjatjara from the southern desert lands, Gapapunyngu from the top end, Gumnadga from the Gulf country, and Arrente from the centre. Our languages are alive and vibrant, our peoples and our cultures are diverse and growing. The 'In Aboriginal' series can help all Australians to understand that we are not all the same but we are all Aboriginal. (*In Aboriginal*, 1994)

A follow-up album, *Strong Culture: Aboriginal Music in Aboriginal Languages*, picked up on the educational benefits of the first album, noting in its album notes that 'we have found that the first album (*In Aboriginal*) has been widely used in Aboriginal classrooms in remote Australia'.

The use of rock songs in Aboriginal languages, therefore, has multi-level intention. A primary objective is to record languages and provide concrete artefacts for teaching them. Making statements of and about cultural identity and emphasizing that different Aboriginal cultures have their own languages are also important considerations. Because they are popular and attractive to young listeners, rock songs are seen as an appealing way of encouraging Aboriginal children to learn and use Aboriginal languages (Dunbar-Hall, 2004); they also assist in disseminating important messages about topics that are socially proscribed in Aboriginal communities, such as the prevalence of sexually transmitted disease. Such songs not only notify that Aboriginal cultures survive, but also provide a strategy for that survival to continue.

Conclusion

In the reading of them presented here, songs by Wirrinyga Band are representative of numerous Aboriginal musicians' use of music. They celebrate, educate and remind. They address problems in Aboriginal communities, use local languages and rely on locally understood imagery mediated as symbolic of the Dreaming as a resource for understanding the past and for surviving the tensions of the present. At the same time, they are a form of post-colonial discourse. They show Aboriginal people refusing to accept non-Aboriginal constructions of the past, proactively putting forward their versions of history and becoming 'part of a process of "putting the record straight" on Indigenous issues' (Meadows, 2002, p. 265). In a national culture which misreads Aboriginality as frozen in a 'primitive' past, these songs raise the 'cultural visibility' (R. Smith, 2001) of Aboriginal people and demonstrate the ongoing and responsive nature of Aboriginal cultures, countering essentialist perceptions of Australian Aboriginal people as 'that of a "Stone Age" Aboriginal culture frozen in time' (Langton, 2003, p. 42).

That Aboriginal cultures continue to develop is an implicit message of these songs. Whether this is heard through the integration of the sounds of traditional Aboriginal music into forms of contemporary music through the use of didjeridu and clapsticks in rock music settings, or through using rock music to address topics which have been sung about throughout Aboriginal history, the roles, uses and values of music remain while the forms of expression respond to developments in the wider world of popular music. The result is an indication of survival of cultural principles and mores. Songs by Wirrinyga Band present this survival through reliance on beliefs underpinning Yolngu and Aboriginal cosmology and existence. As they sing in 'Indigenous Man Keep on Telling Those Stories': 'Through justice and peace we're battling / Say it's our survival and treaty in this land ... / Gotta hold on tight to our Dreaming / Better keep on telling those stories.'

Chapter 10

The bleak country? The Black Country and the rhetoric of escape

Ian Peddie

Introduction

No rivers, hills or county lines define the boundaries of that area of the West Midlands known as the Black Country. Stretching from the outskirts of Birmingham to Walsall and Wolverhampton still further north, through the western edges of Wordsley and Stourbridge, to Smethwick and West Bromwich on its eastern boundaries, the area is definable solely as an industrial entity, with economics rather than physical or administrative boundaries designating its identity. Taking its name from the thickest coal seam in Britain, the legendary 'ten yard seam', in 1862 Elihu Burritt, then American Consul to Birmingham, described the area as 'black by day and red by night' (1868, p. 1). This was a grim if accurate picture, perhaps inspired by a vision of the area as a Dickensian Coketown, dominated by ironworks, coal mines, and nail-making factories. But it is an image that has proven remarkably persistent. Travelling through Mexico in 1938, and chancing upon a desolate mining village, Graham Greene's barometer of choice could not have been more revealing: it was, he said 'worse than anything in the Black Country' (1993, p. 199). Yet if the topography of the Black Country is dominated by the Industrial Revolution, then so its contemporary image is bound to that same past. No more pertinent examples of the extent to which such images have penetrated the popular psyche exist than in popular music.

Discussions of music produced in the Black Country tend to evoke either a physical escape from a place envisaged by popular memory as blighted with disused factories, slag heaps and industrial spoil or, with equal tedium, a concomitant sense of shared community that can be 'read' from the fact of locale. Both of these complimentary positions continue to enjoy remarkable currency, so much so that they are often presented as axiomatic. In the introduction to *Judas Priest: Heavy Duty*, for instance, Steve Gett begins with the popular evocation of the West Midlands as 'a vast grey industrial wasteland' and continues by wondering 'why this particular district has spawned so many rock groups'. The coda to this familiar scenario is left to Rob Halford, lead singer of Judas Priest, who confirms 'there's an incredible desire to break out and make it other than in that particular environment' (quoted in Gett, 1984, p. 1). But perhaps the epitome of this theme occurs in Alan Clayson's *Back in the High Life*, a biography of Steve Winwood:

> Fouling the air and waterways, the thick black clouds and chemical waste percolating from the conurbation's blast furnaces and factories cake employees' poky dwellings with soot and grime as indelibly as Lady Macbeth's damned spot. 'It's called the Black Country,' escapee Steve Winwood informed an American journalist in 1970 ... It's really heavily industrial'. (1988, p. 3)

One *escapes* the Black Country. Like the previous example, Clayson's confirms the Black Country as a Dickensian stew from which music offers the possibility of deliverance. For all that, this perception nourished a vision that was, at least in part, in keeping with the life chances of so many in the Black Country; it was the same vision that, in *Bang Your Head: The Rise and Fall of Heavy Metal*, Black Sabbath drummer Bill Ward succinctly articulated: 'Growing up in Aston, there were only three options: work in a factory, join a band, or go to jail' (quoted in Konow, 2002, p. 5). These grievances were underwritten by a combination of genuine experience as well as popular conceptions of the Black Country.

If the critical ground under which the Black Country had been viewed was prepared by legions of writers eager to emphasize the area's desolation, it is but a short step to argue that such an area nurtured a culture that reflected the essence of its character. For the Black Country this meant the noise of hammers and drop-forges, the heat of furnaces and the soot of coal mines. These images, harsh, noisy and threatening, are invariably deployed as a means of rationalizing the propensity for heavy rock that has emerged from the Black Country. As Judas Priest put it in 'Monsters of Rock', 'It started many years ago, out of the black country . . . From the concrete jungle / The smoke, the dirt, the grime / Could not contain the hunger / It grew and grew in time, into a / Monster, Monster of rock'. Born in Tipton, this Prometheus is a synecdoche for the defining narrative of the Black Country. Yet, equally, such familiar and stereotypical descriptions of place and culture suggest a climate from which rebellion or escape become inevitable. Hence place and culture form their own legend; place 'informs' the culture just as the culture 'reflects' the place. The syncretic and twisted narratives that emerge from this circular logic have influenced popular music criticism and journalism to the extent that Black Country musicians themselves are often 'invited' to assume the positions created for them. In this light, Black Sabbath guitarist Toni Iommi's contention that the group 'all came from a pretty depressing area, [Birmingham] and I think it came out in the music when we started rehearsing' (quoted in Stark, 1998, p. 5) fulfils not only the expectation of Sabbath fans but also the position into which the group has been critically placed.

The metadiscourse through which Black Country popular music is read incorporates a number of genres themselves cohered by a narrative that circumscribes the music as derivative of the materially and socially impoverished area whence it came. Hence Black Sabbath emerges as 'prophets bred from the downside of English society, the unemployed – people regarded as morally suspect and of negligible social worth' (Christie, 2003, p. 1). Under this rubric, any number of musical genres are held together as long as they conform to the appropriate metanarrative through which Black Country popular music is interpreted and subsequently naturalized. That is, the value of 'serious' popular music as generically representative of the Black Country is determined by the nature, terms and direction of expression. In short, the music must 'reflect' the conditions and character of the place. Much of the impetus behind this belief is located in a desire to adhere to the conviction that music is more than an aesthetic pleasure – that it should be, as Robert Plant put it, concerned with 'social behaviour, social awareness' (Interview, 1990, *Led Zeppelin*).

In what follows, I want to examine how Led Zeppelin and Goldie complicate some of the rather simplistic assumptions applied to music from the Black Country. Although both construct a sense of social protest through strategies of escape, their music was not solely the product of a place or an era, but a battleground upon which cultural contests of significant political import were fought. In choosing to analyse their music, I remain conscious that the Black Country has produced a great deal of work that may well be topically appropriate for this discussion. Without overstretching the boundaries of what constitutes the Black Country, and in terms of the argument set forth here, any combination of Slade, Dexy's Midnight Runners, Judas Priest and especially Black Sabbath and UB40 would repay close analytical scrutiny. But Zeppelin and Goldie reveal a dimension of social protest that is perhaps more subtle than that offered by these artists. Not for them the outright antagonism of, say, UB40's 'One in Ten', Black Sabbath's 'Children of the Grave' or Judas Priest's 'Breaking the Law'. Instead, Plant's celebration of spontaneity and loss of control and Goldie's emphasis on a diasporic, hybrid community undermines established and often simplistic ideas of place through which the music of many of their fellow Black Country artists was read.

As arguably the most famous Black Country artists of the 1970s and 1990s respectively, Robert Plant and Goldie produced music that evinces certain *rapprochements* in consciousness, direction and critical reception, and theirs was an oeuvre that contributed to, and shaped, the culture from which they emerged. Equally, neither Plant nor Goldie subscribe to the critically established boundaries of rock decorum. Save one or two isolated examples, Zeppelin issued no singles; their music overturned the dominance of the three-minute pop song beloved of radio stations; at concerts their songs could run to half an hour and, as the mood took him, Plant would frequently sing improvised lyrics to long-established numbers. In various ways, all of these issues undermined the constructed identity critics applied to rock bands from the Black Country. Similar conclusions can be drawn about Goldie's music. More so than Plant's, Goldie's work defies categorization. It speaks of an alienated otherness that extends beyond prescribed notions of community, beyond mere place. In celebrating hybridity and the diasporic, Goldie invites identification with a discourse contingent upon heterogeneity. To a lesser extent, of course, Plant also gestured towards this position, challenging the orthodoxy which saw music as the slave of place. But Goldie took this still further, suggesting that the shared experience of inner-city life was marked by an alterity that involved not a uniform sense of local experience but a global sense of socially shared fears and aspirations. In their own ways, both practices were anti-hegemonic, just as both sought to escape formulaic impositions. Yet all this is not merely to suggest an exercise of comparison. Rather, at issue is an attempt to trace not only how and why questions of escape seems so influential in their respective work, but also to examine the social and political implications of its deployment.

Neither dazed nor confused: Robert Plant

On the few occasions when Robert Plant mentioned his background his remarks were often extremely revealing. In a 1990 interview with *Rolling Stone*, for instance, Plant suggested that his and John Bonham's roots ensured that a sense of alienation from the metropolitan centre of London was always present, even within a band as successful as Led Zeppelin. Despite the fact that the band's earliest jams were 'so intense', Plant lamented the fact that 'it was very hard to relax, sit down, have a beer and be the guys from the Black Country' (quoted in Considine and Preston, 1990, p. 58). The anxiety in that comment is palpable and reveals a sense of vulnerability that affected Robert Plant throughout his Led Zeppelin years. The distinction Plant makes, on the one hand, between himself and Bonham, 'the guys from the Black Country', and, on the other hand, Londoners Jimmy Page and John Paul Jones, successful guitarist and musical arranger respectively, is indicative of that familiar fear that afflicts provincial artists when faced with the alleged 'sophistication' implicit in London's cultural dominance. Yet there is more to this argument than issues of provincial deference. If the antagonistic, oppositional sense that Plant drew from the vissictudes of place became a catalyst for some of his most impressive work as Led Zeppelin's lyricist, so his identity within the band was contingent upon geographical, communal distinction. 'When we were kids', Plant recalled in 2002, 'Bonham and I were the toughest guys around. Nobody wanted to be around us, because we believed in ourselves so much and we were really unbearable. So when he passed [in 1980], I really didn't want to stay with the southern guys – the two guys from London' (quoted in Klosterman, 2002, p. 99). Plant's attribution of difference here underscores the extent to which his background played a crucial role in his own self-image – an image that remains as problematic to critics today as it did in Led Zeppelin's heyday. For all that,

Plant is rarely conceived of in terms of his Black Country background – inadvertent nods to stereotypes such as Zeppelin's 'sledgehammer' style apart. Instead generalizations, such as that offered by Tony Secunda, former manager of Procul Harem, function as descriptions, particularly in his characterization of Plant as 'like so many people from the Midlands – down to earth, basic, extrovert' (quoted in Yorke, 2003, p. 26). Even though, in terms of his relationship with Page and Jones, Plant too concluded that 'Bonzo and I were much more basic in every respect in how to deal with everything' (quoted in Klosterman, 2002, p. 58), such commonplace judgements do not square either with Plant's lyrics or his onstage persona. Instead, they fostered a paradox, for, on the one hand, if such assessments were in keeping with common perceptions of Black Country people, then Plant was happy to embrace them. On the other hand, assessments such as 'basic' and 'down to earth' arrived with their own sense of emotional and psychological restrictions – and these were the very issues from which Plant was trying to escape. But this is the key to assessing the very process by which Plant's ideas were formed. The dialectic, which pivots uneasily upon Plant as Black Country man and Plant showing little deference to the established limits of Black country rock decorum, occasioned some of the singer's greatest performances.

Nonetheless, one of the principal reasons why Plant is seldom associated with accepted versions of Black Country rock is that both his persona and the music with which he is connected do not subscribe to the essentialist narratives through which such music is filtered. Yes, Led Zeppelin were loud, powerful and often heavy, but their music was also humorous, self-reflective and extremely subtle. The latter point may seem odd given Zeppelin's image, especially so since much of what passes for criticism of Zeppelin is built upon a perceived reputation of the band as paragons of excess – a legend fuelled by alleged physical indulgences on a scale that have passed into rock folklore. Yet it was this very excess, symbolized powerfully by a stage performance that wilfully flouted accepted rock decorum, coupled with a sound both vast and broad, through which Plant enacted a world that appeared to take him away from the Black Country. Of particular relevance here is Susan Fast's contention that:

> The musical and theatrical hyperbole of Zeppelin is marked by *realism*. These excessive uses of the body, these emotional outpourings, were meant to be taken as unconstructed, as *real*, and this feature of white hard rock music has often been deemed laughable by the critical establishment. The 'theatricality' of the performances, their physicality (including the intense depth and volume of the sound), their enormous length, the sometimes meandering improvisations …were all pressed into the service of celebrating an ecstatic loss of control, and all transgress the boundaries of practices acceptable to 'high' rock culture. (Fast, 2001. p. 6)

This sense of a 'loss of control' is especially meaningful if we recall the stultifying ennui of the post-war Britain in which Robert Plant grew up. This was a world that, as Jeremy Seabrook puts it, 'confined women to domestic tasks of numbing monotony, and men to the only slightly wider circuit of factory, pub and football ground' and it was a world that 'denied sexual minorities and couldn't accommodate the unfamiliar' (2000, p. 33). Here more than anywhere was a bleak country from which escape was the only option. For the middle-class Robert Plant there was no choice to be made:

> You can go to a grammar school and never see the light of day again for the rest of your life. The moment you pass your 11-plus exams, it could all be finished for you. I'm afraid it upset my parents a bit when I got in with this musician crew, and the cleft between Mum and Dad and me got gradually wider ...Ten minutes in the music scene was the equal to a hundred years outside of it ... Fortunately my parents saw it too, but only *after* I'd proved it. Not before ... I'm a little sorry about that, actually. They just couldn't relate to it at all, not even on a musical level. I just wasn't toeing any normal line. (Quoted in Yorke, 2003, pp. 18–19)

Plant's parents were not the only people who found Zeppelin's music and image difficult to come to terms with. In *Melody Maker* Steve Lake's review of Zeppelin's 1975 show at Earls Court suggested that 'Moby Dick' epitomized 'the archetypal drum solo [so much] that it was hard to believe ... 20 minutes of stultifying indulgence crowned with laughable electronic stereo effects. John Bonham has no musical intelligence at all' (quoted in Godwin, 1997, p. 322). Equally typical is Nick Kent's 1979 *New Musical Express* review of *In Through The Out Door*, where the remarkable claim that Zeppelin's music is marked by 'empty virtuosity' concedes prominence only to the author's admission that 'they never really influenced any contemporary bands beyond the reactionary heavy metal combos' (quoted in Godwin, 1997, p. 425). No doubt it was comments such as these that led Plant to vigorously resist the moniker 'heavy metal'. Still, such attempts to denigrate Zeppelin based on the band's refusal to conform to established rock boundaries fails to take into account the fact that such calls to order were restricting in that they functioned as powerful symbols of the provincial world from which Plant had been determined to escape.

There are few Led Zeppelin songs that can be considered transparent expressions of social protest; lyrical storming of the barricades they left to others. Instead, although much of their music built upon a foundation of the blues, arguably the music of loss, their work almost always contains a sense of hope. This is one important element out of which a sense of escape and protest can be discerned. The quests of 'Kashmir', 'Stairway to Heaven' and 'Over the Hills and Far Away' are invariably read as incorporating this sense of searching for something beyond immediate knowledge, a place where experience and myth become intermingled. But if Zeppelin's use of mythology only compounded their bombastic image among critics, few of those same critics bothered to consider the implications of Plant's live performances as a subtle, yet crucial, attempt at resistance. Only one critic came inadvertently close to identifying the essence of Plant's live performances. Commenting on a 1975 concert, Charles Murray wondered, 'how can you be a controlled beserker?' (quoted in Godwin, 1997, p. 321).

Murray's comment is prescient only in that it approximates to the critical confusion over Plant's live performance. The release, in 2003, of *How The West Was Won*, a compilation of live performances recorded at the Los Angeles Forum and the Long Beach Arena in 1972, provides a point of departure from which to assess Robert Plant's provocative singing and stage presence. 'Dazed and Confused', regarded by many as Led Zeppelin's magnum opus, is an extraordinary *mélange* incorporating influences as varied as Plant's Arabic vocal echoing of Page's guitar, and his ability to build tension through repeated calls such as 'do it, do it, do it' and 'push, push, push', each of which contributes towards a number of crescendos. The song begins with a Zeppelin trademark: humour. Although Plant sings 'come on, come on, come on, come on, show me the way, I want to make love to you 25 hours a day', he quickly adds 'that's all I want'. If these hyperbolic lyrics seem to mock Zeppelin's own image of excess they also set the tone for a song that celebrates spontaneity, emotion and organic expression. But this is only one of a number of ways in which Zeppelin began, as Plant would have it, to 'push' further. The length of 'Dazed and Confused' provided the kind of sonic space within which Plant could work his emotive ejaculations, and, for Zeppelin, less scripted than others in terms of their live performances, this was one of a number of ways in which the band seemed more than willing to admit the unfamiliar into their concerts. Another was through Plant's Arabic-like wailing, which owed much to the influence of Egyptian singer Oum Kaltsoum. Plant employed all of these techniques and influences as a means of exemplifying the creative possibilities that breaking through prescribed limits of expression might offer.

To achieve this, Plant correctly assumed an identity of interests between his goals and his audience's desires. It is worth considering this point in light of a revealing comment that Plant made in Zeppelin's early days. 'In England at a concert before people jump up they look round and see if everyone else is doing it,' Plant offered. 'That's not the way to enjoy yourself. There are so many limitations for someone going to a concert – to appreciate a lot of the music being played in London now you can't be a bank clerk during the day and a hippy at night' (quoted in Godwin, 1997, p. 74). Such was Plant's faith in the loyalty of his growing audience that he could admonish them thus. The choice of a bank clerk as the epitome of social conservatism – culturally, spiritually and emotionally impoverished – not only is a reminder of Plant's brief training as an accountant but also emphasizes the opposing poles of banal routine and emotive creativity against which he measured himself. And so many of his comments had this quality. In the sense that 'There but for the grace of rock goes Robert Plant' carried its own rationale, so Plant's vocal rhythms and antithetical movements were deployed as a further means of illuminating his escape from the terrors of musical or quotidian routine. Paradoxically, this position bore traces of the dichotomous thinking that critics attributed to Black Country musicians for whom escape was said to be a logical corollary of the allegedly depressing worlds they inhabited. On the other hand, Plant was offering a more complex and subtle invective – one that required his audience to recognize his loss of control as both oppositional and a form of social protest. This involved a compact with his audience that, much to their chagrin, left critics out in the cold. 'The acclaim', Plant said of Zeppelin's success, 'always came from the streets, never from the written critique' (quoted in Considine and Preston, 1990, p. 58). While this is only partly true, Plant's alienation from most critics and his relationship to his audience was cemented through the implicit acknowledgement that spontaneity was itself a form of escape, that 'form or order implies limitation or restriction, whereas disorder suggests potentiality' (Fast, 2001, p. 78). This was an issue that provoked great intensity of feeling not only among Zeppelin fans but also in the person of Robert Plant. As early as 1969 he was of the opinion that:

> ... what happens now is that quite often the music is created during some improvisation on stage one night. Some of our numbers can go on for half an hour and during that jam something might emerge which will be the riff upon which we hang a new number. That's really part of the beauty of today's group scene that you can hear things being created at the time on stage and so little is *prefabricated*. (Quoted in Godwin, 1997, p. 84, emphasis added)

Both the strengths and weaknesses of this position were advertised time and time again through Zeppelin's live performances. And where critics saw fustian pomposity fans saw the kind of innovation and spontaneity absent in many of their own lives. The 'oohs' and 'aahhs' of songs such as 'Whole Lotta Love' affected their own protest, and the loud cheers when Plant incorporated the old John Lee Hooker line 'you gotta let that boy boogie' into 'Lotta Love' told their own story. 'I am a reflection of what I sing,' Plant once recalled. 'Sometimes I have to get serious because the things I have been through are serious ... our feelings of protest do reflect in the music ... there's [a] Whole Lotta Love in everything we do' (quoted in Godwin, 1997, p. 161). To the uninitiated this altruism of the spirit meant little; to others it was an eloquent testimony to Robert Plant's social conscience.

A sense of rage: Goldie

'Wide open ... it's wide open' (quoted in Collin, 1997). Thus Goldie, unofficial face of Jungle music. The ambiguities of these two phrases are as useful a way as any of approaching the vexing issue of popular music and place. And there exists no better example than Goldie for illustrating the way in which critical predilections towards ideas of place as sites of musical authenticity and community are now under considerable pressure. As the self-styled 'chameleon … shapeshifting all the time' (quoted in Collin, 1997), Goldie is the quintessential postmodern musician – his music emblematic of scenes rather than locales, his identity a composite of personas that run the gamut from graffiti artist and DJ to actor and musician.

For Angela McRobbie and Caspar Melville, Goldie's music is 'of no clear-cut origins, raw, unfinished, and flowing across urban soundscapes' (1998, p. 67). In one way or another, attempts to classify the music as Jungle, drum 'n' bass, breakbeat or any other loosely applicable description all seem inadequate. A more pointed qualification was offered by the artist himself: 'Some people might call what I do drum 'n' bass. But I'm not going to narrow it down to what the music industry thinks is commercially viable. I'm not really into narrow thinking' (Goldie, 2004). Such resistance to genre involves far more than Goldie thumbing his nose at music executives. In so many ways the equation of genre with 'narrow thinking' is a profound disavowal and escape from categorization on multiple levels. It is also at the very heart of Goldie's thinking.

Of equal and related importance to Goldie and his public image is a sense of contingent, shifting identity. Built on his own protean insistence that he is 'a chameleon' who can 'zoom in and zoom out, tune in, tune out' (quoted in Norris, 1998, p. 70), Goldie, like his music, functions as the ambivalent Other, the figure of alterity against which the normative discourse constructs its points of reference. Like so many Black Country musicians, Goldie constructs himself and is constructed as a 'prophet from the downside of English society', a disposition exacerbated by Jungle's roots in pirate radio, its alleged connection with drugs and its use of a beat that, to the uninitiated, can appear ominously tribal. To protectors of racial purity, from this perspective Jungle was as threatening as early rock 'n' roll. More troubling still, the prominence of drum 'n' bass suggested that the music was the atavistic preserve of blacks. The latter point Simon Reynolds has identified as concomitant with a white 'fear of degradation through miscegenation', and a subsequent 'loss of racial identity' (1998, p. 247). Yet to ascribe some kind of established racial identity to certain black musical forms and not to others is to fall back on what Paul Gilroy calls an 'ethnic authenticity that vernacular forms manifest and which critical discourses suggest only they can confer upon a range of other less obviously authentic cultural alternatives' (1997, p. 84). From Reynolds's aspect then, as a hybrid form that is neither black nor white, Jungle's authenticity is implicitly called into question. Hence what is really at stake in Reynold's claim is a corresponding anxiety which is reflected in Jungle's apparent *musical* miscegenation.

Yet the difficulties critics have in slotting Goldie's music into divisions discloses more than the limits of interpretive categories. Crucial here is the extent to which listening to music reflects a whole set of values revealed through recourse to genre. It is at this point that it is most difficult to draw a balance, for the danger remains that the absence of recognizable categories becomes a departure point for criticism predicated on the platitudes to which hybridity seems especially susceptible. In this light, consider the following review of Goldie's second album: *Saturnz Return* 'succeed[s] as a murky crystal ball, divining the music's future as a little bit of everything … the problem, ultimately, with the attention being paid to Goldie and other faces is that drum-and-bass, like most genres, is not an album field per se' (Strauss, 1998, p. 58). For this critic, Goldie's 'pillaging' of modern classical music and his appropriation of selections from hip-hop, jazz, punk, soul, and pop make him 'seem like the genre's Emerson, Lake and Palmer' (Strauss, 1988, p. 57).

At issue here is not so much the policing of genres but the discriminatory codes employed to authenticate inclusion or exclusion. That is, 'musical genre, as a seemingly coherent system of musical codes, is in many ways a collective memory-residue, and adjectival chain that encodes not only the way in which a particular musical work has been listened to but also the *way that work ought to be heard*' (Gunn, 1999a, p. 35, emphasis added). Hence music such as Jungle, which straddles a number of genres, poses particular problems for critics. About the only fixed categories critics can agree on in relation to Goldie's music is that it affects an urban aesthetic – one that is, by his own admission, ominous, threatening and dark. 'I'm just a dark brother,' Goldie admitted. 'I had a dark background and a dark upbringing and I come [*sic*] out a bit dark really' (quoted in Marcus, 1994). Here are the familiar tropes so often employed to describe Black Country music: the difficult upbringing, the 'dark background' and the invitation to conclude that these experiences define the parameters of the music. And, in so many ways, the kernel of this description, saturated with portentous vision, is as emblematic of the Black Country as it is of Goldie's music.

This relationship, even as one tries to escape it, emerges repeatedly, inevitably. As if to baffle expectation still further, it cuts across the vexing issues of race and class, at times privileging the former, on other occasions the latter, and at times employing both as markers of oppression. Born Clifford Price in Walsall in 1965 to a Scottish mother and a West Indian father, Goldie's mixed race, his inability to fit neatly into prescribed racial categories, underscores the fragmentary and diasporic character that now signifies race. 'In school', Goldie recalls, 'I was a fucking nigger.' 'They used to say, "Goldie, you're a fucking Paki or you're a nigger"' (quoted in Collin, 1994). Conflating terms of racist denigration in this manner suggests an alienated otherness consistent with the inner-city life about which Goldie's music is so concerned. But, as Goldie was at pains to point out, otherness was an issue where race and class had common cause: 'now that urban jungle isn't black or white', he asserted, 'it's everybody below a certain level that has socially been fucked by drugs or living in the inner city' (quoted in Collin, 1994).

The second clause in this statement is a sensibility held dear by any number of Black Country bands. But that clause encapsulates the centre of Goldie's social protestation. The conviction with which he asserted that he makes inner-city urban music suggests that he understood that the logic which connects class and place involves a sophisticated vision of locale as a constructed landscape of identities that are continually reproduced. In this respect, the 'now' which Goldie uses to distinguish Jungle from an undefined 'then' assumes crucial importance in that, as it evolves, Jungle refuses simple racial categorization while insisting on a connection with what Goldie calls inner-city 'pressure'. But if this notion of the inner city, particularly the Black Country inner city, with its historical correspondence to mining, heavy industry, enamelling, nail- and chain-making, engenders a visual reconstruction dependent on class, then it is, of course, the same ideology upon which much heavy metal is based. But Goldie's Jungle pushes this notion of vernacular musical expression away from geographical place and into the realms of social place. There is no better way of illustrating this than to take a line from 'Digital', Goldie's 1997 single, where, he concludes, his music 'represents like the internet'.

In one of the most revealing comments on the implications of his Black Country upbringing, Goldie admitted to feeling 'twice as proud because of where I've come from' even though 'I'm still the normal geezer I've always been' (quoted in Collin, 1997). In this admission shades of the Black Country man made good jostle with intimations towards escape. On the other hand, this partial insight into the foundations upon which Goldie's ideas were formed, coupled with his insistence that he makes inner-city urban music, invites the conclusion that just as his compositions comprise samples drawn from a variety of sources so they also sample the psychological and emotional terrain of inner cities. In this light, the music asserts a relationship that escapes the traditional explanations that posit a sense of correspondence between place and expression in favour of a 'postimperial model of an infinite number of local experiences of (and responses to) something globally shared' (Frith, 1991, p. 268). In one way, of course, this echoes the appeal of Plant's loss of control, which was something that also might be globally shared. But it is also the logic that informs Goldie's contention that the hybrid, diasporic appeal of his music means that 'you can listen to it anywhere in the fucking world and you'll hear it right' (quoted in Marcus, 1997).

Timeless, Goldie's 1995 album, is an attempt to articulate inner-city experience as a diasporic present, where the drum and bass challenge the primacy of vocals as the dominant means of expression. This is an act of liberation that functions on at least two important levels. First, the shift in emphasis away from vocals as the primary means of 'message' delivery implicitly challenges the hegemony of rock as the dominant defining genre of popular music. Also at stake here is the implied questioning of the dominance of heavy rock in the Black Country and, indeed, whether the traditional, ambiguous antitheticality central to heavy rock, defined by given historically established local traditions, which invariably meant white, working-class, is any longer even relevant. Hence Jungle advances a campaign of escape from a past that is inextricably bound to locale in favour of a narrative that is inscribed with heterogeneity, with *other* identities. This is why critical anxieties over the various forms of Jungle ought to be a cause not of concern but of celebration. A valuable qualification in this respect was offered by Greg Tate:

> What makes jungle distinct from every funky dance form that has come down the pike since the swing era is that the bass and drums are not locked down with one another. They are in fact liberated from one another. Jungle strives to free electronic drum programming from strict timekeeping in a manner remarkably akin to the work of free-jazz drummers Sunny Murray and Milford Graves, who emancipated the drum kit from that same role in the '60s ... What the absence of bass and vocals compels is a greater experimentation with drum sounds and timbres than we've ever heard in popular music...New musical forms are characterized by what they refuse to do as much as what they do. Jungle is about erasure as much as synthesis. (Tate, 1995, p. 73)

Form as liberation. Along with Will Straw's emphasis on 'the diversity of musical practices unfolding within particular urban centres, one of whose effects has been to undermine claims as to the uniformity of local musical cultures' (1991, p. 368), this issue remains fundamental to Goldie's music; in its implicit attempts to avoid specific connections to place, his work invokes a sense of community contingent upon the desire to escape traditional, fixed models of community. Rather, the emphasis is upon what, in *Timeless*, Goldie called 'living free'. Unpacking the apparent ambiguity of the term 'free' requires an understanding of the artist's entire project, for the term in fact links attempts to escape from genre with the grievances of the inner city and what Arjun Appadurai calls 'a constructed landscape of collective aspirations' (1996, p. 31).

Such landscapes, incorporating similar hopes and desires, shared relationships and experiences, form an anti-hegemonic practice that attempts to transform the foundational narratives through which we perceive culture. Only in this way can Goldie reinvigorate the local through reaching out to a transnational economy that, in turn, shapes and reconstitutes that local in a similar way that the local influences the global. To listen to Goldie's music through this lens is to acknowledge a sophisticated attempt to come to terms with the changing parameters of contemporary music. By the same token, the remarkable shifts between tension and despair in compositions such as 'Timeless' fosters a genuine sense that the music is an attempt to reproduce the kind of inner-city consciousness with which Goldie is so familiar. In this light, my sense is that much as we are invited to 'read' or 'interpret' songs, with Goldie's work the emphasis seems to be on *feeling*. 'Timeless', perhaps his most famous piece, is a good example in this respect. As this 21-minute *tour de force* begins, the lush, sonic spaces create an elegiac counterpoint to the forthcoming reality of 'inner-city life'. Five minutes of swirling, emotional musing give way as the breakbeats crash across the surface at the same time as the track's watchword, 'pressure', articulated as the plosive it really is, emerges, ghost-like, at the front of the spectrum. All this is orchestrated around a desolate howl that punctuates the soundscape. It is Goldie's version of a city of night.

A large part of the appeal of *Timeless*, then, lies in its panoramic attempt to encapsulate experiences common to inner-city life. 'In "Timeless"', Goldie offered, 'is everything I've learned, everyone I've met, everything I've experienced, and a lot of pressures that are going on socially ... the whole pressure you're living with in that whole inner-city situation' (quoted in Collin, 1994). A brief glance at the song titles on the album suggest that the project is arranged as a kind of progression of consciousness. In this way, 'Timeless', 'Saint Angel' and 'State of Mind' echo the reality of inner-city, working-class existence; 'This is a Bad', 'Sea of Tears' and 'Jah the Seventh Seal' affect the despair that, for many, is the reality of inner-city life, while the outright anger of 'A Sense of Rage' dissipates as 'Still Life', with its sporadic announcements on the difficulties of life, and 'it's hard', ushers in 'Adrift', which is an account of the lack of control the working classes have over their own lives. And the album ends as it began, as it surely must, with two versions of 'Inner City Life'.

Goldie is too intelligent an artist not to know that to some challenging received ideas about music, its forms, its limits and its categories is tantamount to insurrection. This is why in his music there exists little in the way of transparent social protest. Too conspicuous a demonstration of protest was simply not required. Instead, *Timeless* is, as Goldie puts it, 'a wolf in sheep's clothing' (quoted in Collin, 1994). And it is, of course, the subject-matter that turned the album into a predatory animal. But if *Timeless* captures an urban pulse so often denied representation, then its author emerges as a subaltern who can speak – and protest.

Conclusion

In their own ways, the music of Led Zeppelin and Goldie challenges the monolithic nature of rock so often taken as the benchmark by which critical judgement is made. In relation to Zeppelin this claim may seem rather strained, particularly since so much that passes for analysis of the band's work is effectively little more than a handful of recycled clichés that bear only the most tenuous of connections to the band's music. After all, we are now accustomed to conclusions such as those found in the influential *Rolling Stone History of Rock and Roll* where the reader learns that Zeppelin's music was 'cruel and powerful', that 'Stairway to Heaven' 'exerts a terrible, beautiful allure' and that the band codified 'the basic formula for heavy metal' (Ward, Stokes and Tucker, 1986, p. 484). If, on the one hand, such claims attribute a pioneering role to Zeppelin, on the other hand they also masquerade as monolithic axioms, each of which is presented as so patently transparent that it requires no qualification. But the impulse towards sweeping generalization elides the subtleties upon which Plant constructed his sense of protest. In the light of the argument mounted here, if, as Barbara Bradby concluded of mainstream rock, 'what has died is the ability of "rock" to impose a unity in the form of white, male subject/author upon the heterogeneity of "other" racial, sexual and gendered identities and musics on which rock music itself fed' (1993, p. 163), then Zeppelin must have played a crucial, yet hitherto unacknowledged, role in this process. Nevertheless, one wonders whether rock ever really wielded such power. If the loss of control by the white male subject is at the heart of discussions of the 'death of rock' then where does Robert Plant's celebration of a loss of control fit into this debate?

The line that connects Robert Plant and Goldie should not be conceived of in terms of a movement. But as both *were* from similar geographical worlds, their music coalesces at the junction of place. And their attempts to break out from the restrictions of place arise from their contestation of identity and power. Like Goldie's sophisticated radical postmodernism, which pivots on the celebration of a multiplicity of identities, Plant's emphasis on loss of control as a form of creativity is itself a manifestation of the postmodern ideal of fragmentation. For Plant, this position was played out against a more traditional modernist identity politics, one where the dichotomous ordering of society (black/white, man/woman etc.) encouraged the kind of polarized thinking that privileged exclusivity or, the kind of 'us and them' or 'insider/outsider' mentality that also nourished critical perceptions of Black Country music. These forces encouraged an essentialism that rejected challenges to the primacy of its own world-view. In this climate, the lengthy and multifarious variations of each song Zeppelin played live, Plant's stage presence and his repeated calls for spontaneity were interpreted and opposed through a dominant social identity politics that either could not, or would not, see beyond the limits of Manichean thinking. In this respect, Plant was ahead of his time; his celebration of fragmentation and loss of control bespeaks a postmodern politics of multiplicity of the kind taken up some 20 years later by Goldie. And the latter's music suggests a strategically deployed sense of difference among the marginalized – one that is neither black nor white, but is held together by common experience. In so many ways, then, these two artists have contributed greatly to the reordering of difference, challenging the established either/or logic upon which much identity politics is founded. In this sense, perhaps there is a passing of the torch, from modern to postmodern, from orthodoxy to ambiguity: the protest lies in the politics, the politics in the protest.

PART FOUR
THE PARADOX OF
ANTI-SOCIAL PROTEST

Chapter 11

Communities of resistance: heavy metal as a reinvention of social technology

Sean K. Kelly

In her 1969 text *On Violence*, Hannah Arendt describes the student rebellions of the 1960s as a 'global phenomenon' enacted by a generation that was 'everywhere characterized by sheer courage, an astounding will to action and by a no less astounding confidence in the possibility of change' (1969, pp. 15–16). Today, such descriptions read as trite truisms, but contemporary audiences who are tempted to read Arendt's words through popular constructions of the movement she describes should be warned that her reading of the impetus for the events surrounding and following 1968 does not reinforce the over-reductive conception that this young generation's optimism and inclination towards civic involvement admirably represented some humane form of social progress.

Instead, Arendt's protesters' discontent emerged from their awareness that a 'socially progressive' future for humans increasingly meant a technologically determined one. With the possibility of nuclear holocaust on the horizon, techno-scientific determination was hardly an acceptable model of progress for the human species. As such, the protesters had as much interest in decrying progress as they did technology. Moreover, because the socially progressive/ technologically determined model of the future represented the culturally dominant conceptualization of historical time, any protest against progress also represented discontent with the popular notion of temporality. If one were to protest technology or its sway one would also have to protest certain common-sense notions of the future, time and history.

Arendt follows her above-cited description of the generation by claiming that anyone looking for a cause for the movement cannot ignore the fact that the 1960s generation was the first that had to deal with the reality that 'technological "progress" [was] leading in so many instances straight into disaster' (1969, p. 16). What the protestors understood all too well was that their future would be determined primarily by the direction of modern technology; that technology (both mechanical and social) had infiltrated human institutions to such a degree that it, rather than humans, would determine the future's direction; and that the direction did not necessarily demand the continued existence of a human species.

So if the future was to be constructed as progressive, it was certainly no longer necessary for its 'progress' to be judged 'progressive' from the viewpoint of the human species.

From a philosophical perspective, Arendt's reading suggests that, by the late 1960s, a generation was forced to encounter a future *of*, or belonging to, technology – a future that had been reified to such a degree that the philosophical concept of the future as something temporalized by humankind (an idea that had driven phenomenological thinking since Kant) was significantly compromised. Moreover, because all previous popular constructs of the futures that were promised by technology had been associated with the myth of human progress and utopian outcomes, the idea of a humanized, teleological notion of temporality was also seriously challenged. While the philosophical reconceptualization of time is hardly an original philosophical process, what remained historically unique to the case under discussion is that the crisis that demanded that humankind reconsider its relationship to temporality was confined to neither a small philosophical circle nor to an insular municipality; instead, technology had forced this reconsideration into the framework of a global imaginary.

Simply stated, the future offerd by the technological dynamic of the 1960s put the modern conception of the future as humane and progressive at risk, or at least up for popular reconsideration. This does not merely mean that, because the student protesters understood technology's potential to shadow all historical, human futures under mushroom clouds, they somehow felt that reclaiming the future was their task. Though important, this position is only a minor part of the equation. More central is that the generation about whom Arendt writes found itself still imbued with a sense of futurity, an openness towards the radically new and personal, even though the dominance of technology had already dismantled most definitions of the future that were sanctioned by philosophers or the naive realism of the day. Once it had defined and reified one possible future that did not include humans, technology served to identify the concept of the future-applied as distinct from the human feeling of futurity and the manual process of future production.

While the protesters sensed that the 'future', – though it should in fact remain open to them – was to be determined by something that was not only not them, but also altogether inhuman and that this freed them to become conscious that the future and futurity were distinct philosophical entities, there was also a sense that this 'futurity' was, first, yet to be defined using linear/progressive notions of the future and, second, universally human. Consequently, a certain temporal awareness began to develop alongside this new mode of temporal consciousness, which eventually developed into a central paradox faced by the protest 'movement'. Insofar as this temporal awareness resulted from a face-to-face encounter with the possibility of technology's blind possession of the future of humanity *and* this awareness made it possible for individual humans to reposition their relations to future institutions, the protesters discovered that, although it is individual humans who not only dream and hope for the future but also (at least if one accepts the fact that temporality is at least partially determined by the structure of human cognition), *futurize* the future, technology's logic forced them to speak in the name of humanity and for a future human community. In short, the essence of the modern technological paradigm forced a generation of individuals to encounter their own deep-seated psychological need to, as existentialists say, temporalize time and to speak in favour of a world in which all humans have the ability to do such.

The differences between a demand to speak for humanity and the universalizing of 'the human' as a strategy for liberation are, however, not insignificant, and, although 'the human' proved to be an expedient strategy for producing effective counter-technologies variously named 'humanity', 'global community', 'world peace' and so on, it also restructured protest within a technological register that, once again, abstracted historical humans from their own care. These technologies of humanity, of course, presented the same dangers as the one against which the protesters rallied, and the violence of the paradox could, of course, be felt most radically at the local levels of the implementation of protest strategies, at the sites where individual humans found themselves held responsible for, and accountable to, 'universal' movements. In the USA, the most radical examples of this surfaced daily in the news. One need only look to the Manson family or to the Kent State incident to find individuals who felt the pressing requirement to produce the future as an open space for the actualization of singular human existences only to deny such a space to other human agents. In such instances, the technology of humanity became a tool to forcibly design a specific future of a set of individuals' choosing rather than a political strategy for combating the fact that the technological position of the era had absolutely threatened every individual's ability to project a life into a minimally open future.

The universal versus the particular was exposed as an historical antinomy that technology had literally forced human philosophers to confront outside of the confines of professional philosophy. Resolving this antinomy entailed the popular reconsideration of basic questions about both the future and human solidarity. Instead of people asking what 'their common future' or the 'future of humanity' would look like (questions which assume that we have an exhaustive understanding of the word 'future' while projecting certain assumptions about the community and humanity into that future), more authentic questions emerged. What might appear as humanity or universal human community if one radically reconsiders the very concept of the future? Where are there instances of human solidarity that explore or disclose concepts of temporality that resist assimilation into the sway of an historical framework determined by technology?

The rock 'n' roll scene that developed out of this era became one site where the actualization of alternative conceptions of both time and community in resistance to technology did realize itself. The Rolling Stones concert at

Altamont, at least in intention, provides just one example of the way in which rock's attempts at new relations to technology (Hell's Angels as security, a free concert, massive stage shows in non-municipally owned sites, and so on) were viewed as promising modes of community that respected the future-producing capacities of the people in attendance. But Altamont was, by all accounts, a failure that ultimately, and perhaps unfortunately, produced new technologies intended to control the public musical forum. Part of the problem with Altamont was one inherent to rock's general focus. Rock 'n' roll, as Lawrence Grossberg reminds us, names the unity of effects 'at the level of an (at least potentially) oppositional politics that produces a rupture between the rock and roll audience (in their everyday lives) and the larger hegemonic context within which it necessarily exists' (1990, p. 117).

Grossberg's account suggests that rock produces a fissure between the listener and the social hegemonies of his day. This 'rupture', then, provides a site in which the listener is freed to act in the name of a politics not determined by the said hegemony. The listener experiences a free space for thinking the future in a different way from that determined by the social technologies of the day. Altamont, however, underscored the problems that emerge when the emotive production of the rupture and the thoughtful appropriation of it remain in disconnect. The concert's organizers demanded new social relations. But they utilized overtly anti-social technologies (for example, Hell's Angels, rock-as-rebellion, beer, drugs, free admission and so on), rather than a thoughtful consideration in the space of the rupture itself, as the means to achieving such relations. In so doing, they allowed the political space to be occupied by activities, symbols and characters that stood in stark binary opposition to the social norms of the day. Thus, when political action was claimed by attendees, it was hardly surprising that it manifested itself in ways that mainstream society was already prepared to dismiss as immoral, violent and worthy of social contempt. The status quo's hegemony was not challenged, but reinforced.

Clearly, events like this Stones' concert were meant to allow participants to enjoy the effects of the rupture *without having to experience it or deal with the historical consequences of participation*. Altamont presents just one example of a gesture in the spirit of this philosophical crisis that I am discussing, but, because it opened the space for social being through a merely oppositional politics it inevitably doomed Altamont's participants to working within the same temporal dynamic within which the dominant social forces were already constructed. Furthermore, the participants' inability to successfully manoeuvre and/or claim responsibility for the violence, both personal and collective, surrounding the event only serves to emphasize the failure of the concert to significantly reposition community in the space it created. But at least one subgenre of rock succeeded in presenting an historical actualization of this strange philosophical community demanded from Arendt's paradigm: heavy metal. From its inception as hard-edged rock, as performed by groups like Rush and Black Sabbath, to its fruition in the bands that completed the logic of this production of a community *of* resistance (rather than a collective enjoined at the site of oppositional politics) *to* (both towards and against) technology, Judas Priest and Iron Maiden, the movement negotiated this philosophical dynamic in an exemplary manner.

In the musical world of the late 1960s through to the early 1980s, hard-edged rock (as a social institution rather than historical movement incorporated under the auspices of musical genre) emerged as a scene that repositioned the relationships between human temporality and technology. One cannot deny that bands such as The Who, Rush, Deep Purple, Led Zeppelin, Jethro Tull and Black Sabbath each expressed – through their very utilizations of the electric guitar, distortion, light shows and so on – an outright embrace of technology. Hard rock tours were touted as 'louder than Zeppelin' to emphasize the subgenre's love affair with the amplifier. Bruce K. Friesen and Jonathon S. Epstein observed that 'heavy metal musicians fully embraced the new technology and experimented with possible sounds, using different combinations of amplifiers, instruments, effects pedals and the like' (1994, p. 8). However, to claim that hard rock's uses of technology represented only an embrace of its advances means ignoring the deep-seated ambivalence that the music expressed in its relation to this very technology. Perhaps the attitude of hard rock is best understood by contrast. At the time of hard rock's birth, bands like The Grateful Dead were expressing the same cynical attitude towards decadent technological progress that the protest movements at large were voicing. These more progressive rock bands, like their hard rock counterparts, made use of most advances in technology to synthesize their respective musical texts into consumable cultural artefacts. But their deployments of technology, unlike those of heavy rock, would not appear in the mode of resistance. In the cases of The Grateful Dead especially, little, if any, physical dissonance was intended to be felt in the actual performance or in the way it was heard by the audience. Though loud, their music was meant to resonate nicely. In more mainstream circles of rock, like those orbiting the Stones and, later, Van Halen, there was a certain amount of sonic resistance in the music, but this was married to an oppositional politics that utilized fundamentally appealing social technologies (such as Van Halen allowing the audience to vicariously experience the sexual fantasy of sleeping with their teacher through their music) as its primary protest strategy, thereby providing for easy product consumption. (Rock, in general also, by always ultimately resorting to opening and occupying a space for political activity for the social underdog and the marginalized by empowering them with the gentleman's fantasies *de jour* – be they alcohol, sex, drugs, youth and the like – served to reinscribe the gentleman's *future* through such an act.) Progressive and psychedelic rock bands utilized technological advances as means for producing the possibility of a world in which human well-being and technology could co-exist; and rock's mainstream promoted empowerment through laying claim to objects prohibited by dominant social technologies, thereby sanctioning the futures presented by them. However, heavy rock took on a much more difficult task: it challenged technology at the site of the human encounter with technological production.

In heavy rock, distortion, feedback and reverberation functioned to drive the creation of unified, rhythmic texts. But they simultaneously disarticulated any illusions of a 'pure' or 'universal' note or song, listening experience or performance in those individuals who experienced them. Insofar as they caused the body to tremble at its limits, distortion, amplification and the like denoted material resistances in/of the song to the very technology needed to produce it. Once these became essential elements of heavy metal's textual production as a technical act, they worked to inscribe an historical, human resistance to technology within the musical scene itself. So if more progressive and psychedelic rock bands could use technology to get people to think about an alternative future use for it (say, to produce dance clubs rather than bombs, to get a groove on rather than enforce enlistment), hard rock's uses of technology functioned to produce a text that performed an historic-material rather than ideological-conceptual resistance to technological production. Bruce Dickinson, Iron Maiden's lead singer, characterizes this as follows: 'What makes a classic hard-rock record is not that somebody invents a new guitar scale; it's capturing a moment in time on a record ..., capturing a performance by somebody that is so real you feel like the person is with you when you listen to that record' (*Christian Science Monitor*, 1990, p. 13). Here Dickinson claims that the hard-rock record as technological artefact must produce the historical performance on technology to such a degree that the performer continues to resist full incorporation into a universal, reproducible entity.

Moreover, Dickinson's hard rock authentically appears only once the listener *feels* this contamination of the recorded by the live – once the listener feels as if the performer is 'in the room' with him 'when he listens to the record'. So the music's performance is less about an actual artist's recording a certain genre of music on some device and its being replayed later than it is about singular, embodied listening experiences – experiences that enable the listener to feel as if he occupies some communal space with one who is able to transcend technological determination (the live performance in the room with the listener) even though conditioned by a totally technological structure (the record).

While the use of mechanical technology to disarticulate the consumer from the listening experience differentiated heavy from progressive rock, thematic organization distinguished heavy metal from many of its mainstream rock contemporaries. Heavy metal's choice of Satanism and futurism, and its mythic and archaic themes, positioned the listener against socially sanctioned desires for the future – it promised apocalypse instead of sex, Satan rather than salvation. And although the genre undoubtedly attracted psychotic fans – Tony Iommi describes them as 'an unbelievable amount of nutcases' (Wall, 2002, p. 25) – who demanded that satanic blood orgies be the same publicly acknowledged as legitimate fantasies for the future like Van Halen's schoolboy dreams, the unquestionable majority of fans shared Iron Maiden's view from 'Number of the Beast' – that these themes of the occult were not vocalizations of prohibited, universal human desires to worship the Dark Lord, but mesmerizing, tortuous reflections of our 'warped' minds looking back at us (Iron Maiden, 1982). Heavy metal's thematic elements emphasized a here-and-now conceptualization of things by which the audience was equally fascinated and repulsed. This at once emphasized that this musical scene's experience must be one in which pleasure is experienced in resistance both to civil technology's sanctioned desires *and* to the general idea that desire is a unified faculty that exists other than as a mode of resistance. It is this latter point that dislocates temporality to such a degree that the listener can no longer imagine one self occupying historical space except as a self-in-resistance – a self touching itself at the point where the music warps it.

As these elements of sonic and conceptual resistance became essential musical values within the listening audiences and text producers, the axiological demand for the music to mark the historical nature of humans' relations with technology became unconsciously inscribed in the being of the scene itself. Rock in general had always, as Bruce Baugh reminds readers, most validly derived its aesthetic character from the 'way that it affects the listener's body' (1993, p. 23), thereby identifying the body's resistance to the music, but heavy rock demanded something more. It wanted to hear the body's resistance in the music; to witness this body leave its material mark on the technical production of the sound; and to produce the resistance as a universal activity. This resistance remains one of the most essential and underappreciated elements of heavy rock as one finds it immediately following the protest era described by Arendt and through its development into heavy metal.

It is important to explicitly emphasize that the historical resistance to technology must reappear in the music at all levels to avoid mistakenly understanding heavy-edged rock and heavy metal as utilizing technology as total sensory assault in order to open its audiences to a nihilism that could lead to violence, anarchy, fascism, violence and so forth. (This is an historically absurd claim if one considers that Black Sabbath constructs itself and is always constructed as a band that grew up in the rubble of Nazi devastation, that metal is contentiously constructed as helping to bring down the Berlin Wall, and that the genre's egalitarian relationship between producer and consumer and the metal's prevailing moral message is in fact inherited from the hippie movement.) The much discussed power chord of heavy metal certainly functions to carry the unity of song and sonic experience. Moreover, the volume at which it must be performed resonates, as Deena Weinstein reminds readers, in the chest of the concertgoer (1991, p. 145). Combine this with the fast-moving stage show, the lights, the speed of the rhythm and so on and it becomes easy to understand the body's resistance as giving way to a possession by the music, thereby allowing the devious artist to construct the community of possessed in his image. But heavy metal is not about immanence. The resistance must continue to perform itself in the body throughout the entire performance or else heavy metal, as a scene, has not happened – 'the show didn't rock'. Dionysian rapture thus remains one of the most unfortunate analogies employed to describe the experience of heavy metal. The enthusiasm (from *en-theos*) is not some possession from gods or music, but an impassioning of the body to exhibit its own historical resistance to such possession, and it is the band's/fan's joint ability to maintain this existence in historical time as their own production that remains heavy metal's primary accomplishment. One can write this about heavy metal primarily because its audience actually demands to hear the body resist technologies in the music. The fans want to hear the vocalist's screech as both a human voice *and* amplified sound; they expect to feel the fingers of the bass player in the mechanical vibrations of power chord. And while the pleasure associated with the body's resistance might lead one to reduce this experience to a mere expression of some universal Dionysian impulse, to do so in the case of heavy rock would be to ignore its primary contribution to sociopolitical philosophy and the historical movement's relationship to technology out of which the genre emerged. Allow me to develop this below.

In many ways, Rush illustrates exactly how well-articulated this resistance that is at once *of* and *to* technology permeates the post-protest years of hard rock. Early in the band's career, Rush established itself as a rock trio built upon the strength of two musical virtuosos – Geddy Lee on bass and Neil Peart on drums. Over the years, it also garnered a reputation for providing astute, sometimes heady, social commentary. Although songs such as 'Working Man', 'Closer to the Heart' and 'The Trees' demonstrate that, even early in its career, the band maintained affinities for expressing wider social concerns, not until the 1980s does Rush exemplify the fostering of social consciousness as its dominant lyrical project. Once this does happen, Peart's lyrics lean heavily towards exploring the problematic relationship that the human has with modern technology. On *Moving Pictures*, for example, 'Red Barchetta' (1981) explicitly addresses both the crisis of a future delivered over to technology and the ambivalence inherent in the conflict. At the level of narrative, the song presents a protagonist living in a futuristic world in which the 'Motor Law' makes the driving of automobiles a crime that is, presumably, punishable by death. Despite or because of this, the protagonist finds empowerment in driving the red Barchetta that his uncle has preserved for him. On the weekly drive recounted in the song, 'gleaming, alloy air cars' that hunt those who are reckless enough to violate the prohibition against driving engage the protagonist in a race – a race that, once won, allows the song's hero to 'dream with [his] uncle by the fireside'. At the level of lyrical plot, this song presents a human whose ability to claim a future for himself and his kin (represented in the song's final space for dreaming) depends on his successfully manoeuvring a 'deadly' encounter with a social technology that refuses his need to actualize himself. But unlike texts such as *1984*, in which love and human relationship provide the tools for engaging the oppressive technological powers,

'Red Barchetta' suggests that it is a technological encounter with technology that provides the ultimate resolution. The song's hero must demonstrate some synergy with technology in the face of technology in order to be released into dreaming.

This plot represents only the reification of a much more deeply expressed relationship between music and technology on the part of the song's singer. The lyrics call for the vocalist to relate the driving experience as follows: 'Wind in my hair / Shifting and drifting / Mechanical music / Adrenaline surge.' A physical experience with nature, freedom and a sense of physical empowerment liberate the narrative's protagonist to the sound of mechanical music but, more interestingly, the nexus of mechanization, liberation and music that the vocalist performs simultaneously tells the tale of a performing vocalist (indexed by the first-person pronoun) who feels a connection with his physicality through this mechanized encounter of music. Furthermore, in these lines the vocalist's experience as the driving, human force behind the technology of the song is identified as mechanical. In order to produce the feeling of the music, the vocalist is therefore called upon to perform the mechanized sound as a human voice, must strain the 'limits of machine and man' (something Lee's vocal quality can perform nicely). Proof of successful navigation of this limit only comes in the empirical experience that the body has with the song; shifting, drifting, adrenaline surges and so on must be felt. Although 'Red Barchetta' indexes this merely at the subjective level of the vocalist, the song is also emblematic of the relationships that must be achieved for the functional performance of heavy-edged rock to be deemed successful. I write 'relationship' knowing that the vocabulary of vocalist, listener, song, technology and so forth instantly emerges, although practically one finds each of these erased at the point of this limit of which I am writing. A limit is not a boundary. A limit, to paraphrase Aristotle, is simultaneously the first place that something is what it is and the first place where it is not what it is. The limit produces the being of the thing in its essential nature. So the musical scene emerges here as that strained limit of machine and man, with the 'and' conjoining, *at the register of this song's narrative*, the two against a broader decadent technology while also, *at the register of performance*, producing a new form of humanity that exists only from engagement with the site of technological production (social or otherwise).

By the time *Moving Pictures* was released this was clearly part of Rush's conscious political identity. Rush's previous album, *Permanent Waves*, had even presented this problematic via its most well-known track, 'Spirit of Radio'. But their representation of technical *polemos* as an overtly lyrical theme could only become a consciously valued narrative for organizing the band's more progressive identity for the 1980s onward if this mode of technical relationality had previously been established as a value for the band and their audiences. Looking back to the album *Rush*, released in 1974, one finds the seeds of such an establishment at the level of performance in the song 'Working Man'. Because this song is one from the musical phase of Rush's career that did greatly influence the direction of heavy metal, its portrayal of the resistance *of* technology will allow us to better understand the performative function/nature of this resistance within the genre as a whole.

'Working Man's' lyrics are straightforward. It is a song in which the title character comes to class-consciousness, vocalized in the line 'It seems to me I could live my life a lot better than I think I am'. From this recognition, a man who has already stated that he 'has no time for livin' cause [he's] workin' all the time', is able to 'guess' why 'they' call him a 'working man'. His status as working man thus opens at a strange temporal fissure: This man realizes that he has no time for livin' alongside the claim that he does live his life. He is then posited on the edge of irony: he is himself qua working man if and only if he gives all his time over to work (in which case he has no time for livin') *and* does so as a man who still 'lives' his life.[1] Because the narrative provides no resolution, the text's *reader* leaves with the hero held out into this ambiguity.

Meanwhile, the song's *audience* finds something quite fecund in this situation. Once one realizes that Rush is playing upon the multiple meanings of the phrase 'working man' the song's opening musical minutes can be reinterpreted. The slow, harsh bass playing of the song's first two minutes, which previously served to reinforce the lyrical strategy of presenting the song's hero as living at the service of social technologies, now simultaneously indexes the drudgery of the working man who has no time for livin' *along with* the working man who is producing vitality by playing the song. The performative voice of 'Working Man' is now constructed totally as the body working, the body demanding of itself that it live better while simultaneously not given a time to live outside of the context of the song's performance. For the vocalist, this paradox is clear: if the voice takes its own time to live by being quiet, all time is taken from it and it cannot sing better, but if it continues singing, it is totally at the service of the song. So the voice must forever work harder to perform a song better, only to find that its own success repeats the demand. This is emphasized by Rush's titling the song 'Working Man' – the voice becomes the very song that it performs. The cycle is endless and self-destructive unless the performer can simultaneously enter the song's performance and remain heterogeneous to it. When one expands this to the wider experience of this song – its simple lyrics begging memorization, its rhythmic chant calling for participation, the opening bass lines resonating in the physical being of the listener – 'Working Man' indexes this simultaneous heterogeneity, this crisis of temporality/consciousness of futurity opened at the limits of the musical experience of the song itself in all of the human bodies that engage in the performance. When this song is performed properly, the audience's bodies, as implements of the performance experience, at once *work* (to create the musical experience) *and* are *liberated* from any sense of un-freedom in this work. After all, it is precisely this work experience that teaches them that they can 'live better' than they think they are.

In the case of 'Working Man', Rush frames the resistance of hard rock within the ready-made confines of class protest rhetoric. But confining one's interpretation of the resistance of hard rock to this arena fails to account for the universal nature of the experience that this music is performing. Black Sabbath's 'Iron Man' (1974), for example, underscores heavy metal's insistence that a technologically determined future should be equally disconcerting to the working class and the techno-scientific elite. Sabbath's 'Iron Man' is as much a thought experiment in human/technological relations as any that philosophers have ever offered. The Iron Man possesses first-hand knowledge of the damage produced by humans giving themselves over to technology, *even to a technology that promises a future for mankind*. His being turned to steel, an event that evokes his most-human emotion of revenge, occurred only because he became the instrument for a social technology deceptively operating under the guise of 'universal humanity', a technology that exhibits its inhumanity precisely by the fact that no one will help, or even acknowledge, the returned, deformed Iron Man. Like 'Working Man' the song indexes its performance: 'Now the time is here / For Iron Man to spread fear'. By identifying the time and place of the performance as the locus of the event of Iron Man's reminding humans of their humanity, Sabbath, first, identifies *the song* as that which has been rejected for its inhumanity and has returned from the grave of mechanization to produce a new set of human possibilities and, second, locates the temporal here-and-now as contaminated both by the mythical future promised by technologies and the technology of the song itself.[2] As in 'Working Man', the chilling bass riffs and amplification that the song demands serve to contaminate the listening audience with the type of physical resistance that present any successful performance of 'Iron Man' as having taken place upon the flesh. Far from confusion, this song successfully produces an historical call for community alongside a warning against a technology of community *and it does so in an historical space that cannot be reduced to a linear temporal dynamic – the body of resistance.*[3]

Rush and Black Sabbath both index the musical performance as serving the important function of locating a space for human production from within a present claimed by technology. By constructing the material experience as the body of resistance, moreover, the ontic status of the entities that emerge from the performance (producer and consumer, voice and instrument, body and song, performance and community) only find articulation insofar as the limit experience, the body of resistance, is held out into time. The unique facet of this holding out is that this human resistance to technology, because it appears as feeling, can emerge only at the singular sites of touch for each (qualitative) listening body. By multiplying the points of bodily resistance in any one quantitative body, the metal arena functions to produce the body in a plurality of resistances. The listeners' bodies, then, occupy socially ambiguous positions. Acting as both instruments of performance and narrators of history, they perform the time and space of Iron Man's resurrection. In these functions the bodies, which are no less technological than the Iron Man himself since they work in his service, resist the 'people' who, according to the lyrics, persecute him. Moreover, insofar as the bodies are *humanized* through the intense pleasure of the experience, they demonstrate solidarity with the humans upon whom the Iron Man seeks revenge and thereby resist techno-conceptual appropriation – a resistance to the Iron Man, becoming 'Iron Man'. So, like the 'people he once saved' who turn upon and resist the song's protagonist, the listeners' bodies resist full techno-appropriation by the song. They are both 'saved' by and in 'fear' of 'Iron Man' – both technologies of, and resistances to, 'Iron Man'. Insofar as the experience itself is multiple, the body of resistance cannot enter this space as if it were an oppositional party for resistance politics – even though the experience unifies itself around the pleasures of resistances within one historical clearing. The performance of heavy metal is, therefore, the *performance of one singular historical being who derives a claim to existence only insofar as the feeling of being-with-others-in-resistance is maintained*. The anonymity of the technological fact of the resistance only serves to emphasize the experience with alterity that emerges at this site. That heavy metal provides the vehicle for such communication is evidenced most clearly in the caricature of two heavy metal fans physically straining to hit notes on their air guitars. Each one produces the joy of enacting the multiple sites of resistance for the other so that the other will, in turn, reproduce the demand. Here there is no oppositional resistance, only the production of resistance as a demand for a universal, humanly produced need to touch the world differently (futurity). The partners in the air guitar scenario demand and produce the pleasure of this differential structure.

Bands such as Iron Maiden and Judas Priest, who emphasized the performance of the heavy metal scene, became masterfully adept at conjuring the body-of-resistance command.[4] Iron Maiden, by meticulously attending to the multiple sensory sites at which bodies encountered the band's work, was especially successful at reproducing the structure of the body as multiple sites of resistance, as a community in resistance. This is not to say that they merely assaulted the senses. They simply prevented the audience from becoming comfortable in any one mode of resistance. If an audience were banging their head, playing air guitar and singing along they still remained aware that they should be watching the show, thinking about the lyrics and admiring the stagecraft. Maiden does not even allow the audience to remain in the present: the mummies from the *Live After Death* tour emphasized neither empty fantasy nor theatrical production, but served to stress the temporal shift within a performance dynamic that was consistently calling the audience to be here-and-now. How one reads this experience is vital to the position of this essay. Robert Walser, like most critics, focuses his analysis on the feelings of empowerment and freedom promoted by the performance of decentralization rather than on the fact the audience at an Iron Maiden concert finds itself having to work for such an experience through a mode of resistance to the experience itself, not to merely society or some other already predefined world structure (1993, pp. 152–57). The

Maiden concert's decentring of the audience member's identity does allow for the imagining of, in Walser's words, 'other possibilities' for social construction, but only in a transcendental manner. This means that reifying either the experience that makes this imagining possible or the possibilities themselves ignores the fact that the essential performance of heavy metal opens the body as a *working of present technologies in disarticulation, as the body working its hegemony*, rather than as merely existing in the mode of breaking from past social technologies, imagining future ones or transcending them altogether. Calling this a 'religious phenomenon', as Walser does, even if one keeps 'religious' under erasure, fails to recognize that Maiden themselves understood the danger/lure of this limit experience (1993, p. 154). If one was looking for religion in Maiden's rock, they offered only Satan and damnation, desolation and apocalypse in every possible religious afterlife, thereby occupying the 'religious' space with technologies that promised to demand one's resistance for all eternity.

By maintaining the plurality of such resistances within a larger framework of *the show*, Maiden opens a heterogeneous temporal framework that is faithful to a type of radically plural democratic activity. And while other bands also succeeded in doing such, this is not to say that metal ever knew exactly what to do with the space that it opened or with the radical politics of being together in resistance differently that it promoted. Many bands simply began to reify the space of production, becoming so enamoured by it that ballads to the rock experience became commonplace within the genre and the musical scene itself became entirely self-referential. This side of metal began to spawn tunes like Twisted Sister's 'I Believe in Rock and Roll' (1985), in which the experience of rock is reified as an entity that they equate with religion and patriotism and then historicized within a linear temporal dynamic that is legitimized by biblical rhetoric. In many ways, unfortunately or not, the period of heavy metal that produced thrash and death metal alongside moshpits of horror and exhilaration became the logical consequence of the objectification of this experience – the fans of metal were now called upon to feel themselves resisting themselves. Leaving aside metal's later years, one thing that metal's production as a scene of community of resistance to technology may have accomplished was to prove that a site for the preparation of historical engagement to a generation of hegemonized bodies was possible, desirable and enjoyable if offered a space for the heterogeneous expression of the multiple sites of resistance that the body, in effect, is. Offering the historical space for this social consciousness to perform itself, beyond all doubt, is a significant accomplishment for an era that was worried that even causes such as 'racial equality' or 'women's rights' worked as hegemonies that utilized historical agents in ways that disrespected their singular, future-producing potentials. Moreover, metal, by asking headbangers to 'stand and be counted' in their historical modes of resistance, produced a model for a future democratic community that thinks resistance and universality as mutually compatible expectation.

Notes

1. See Jacques Derrida's discussion of a similar temporal fissure in his *Given Time: I. Counterfeit Money* (1992).
2. The historicizing of this future is remarkably complex in 'Iron Man'. The future is identified as mythical through the song's plot but has been temporalized as past through the mode of storytelling. Moreover, the effects of this mythical future must happen here and now in the performance of 'Iron Man' and the Iron Man that performs it must do so because he is the victim of a future that has not taken real historical humans into account. One can easily understand why the transformation that makes the plot possible could only be the [']Iron Man's['] having 'travelled time'.
3. In the case of Black Sabbath, the parts of the band's history that have been preserved emphasize that the historical encounter of the limits of man and machine that the genre most values extends beyond the thematic content of its anthems. The band continues to describe Sabbath's original sound as a product of their physical encounters with technology. And this is not only due to the fact that Iommi basically had to create his own light-gauge strings and metallic fingertips because he had lost his fingers while working a machine. In their interview with John Stix, Iommi and Geezer Butler talk about their progression into hard rock as developing out of boredom with the 12-bar blues bass line that drove experimentation with three chords. So, for Sabbath at least, it was the resistance that they felt to the blues bass line that drove them to progress within the technology of those same bass lines as a way of producing their own identity (Stix, 1994).
4. That heavy metal had become spectacular rather than merely musical is an uncontroversial claim. Judas Priest, in 'Monsters of Rock' (1988), recounts the genesis of metal from Zeppelin and Sabbath to the post-NWOBHM years. They write the following about the completion of the logic: 'And millions roared, and millions cheered / This spectacle on stage.'

Chapter 12

The handmade tale: cassette-tapes, authorship, and the privatization of the Pacific Northwest independent music scene

Kathleen McConnell

Though the Earth, and all inferior Creatures, be common to all Men, yet every Man has a Property in his own Person: this no Body has any Right to but himself. The Labour of his Body, and the Work of his Hands, we may say, are properly his. Whatsoever then he removes out of the State that Nature hath provided, and left it in, he hath mixed his Labour with, and joined to it something that is his own, and thereby makes it his Property. (Locke, 1960, p. 305)

The emergence of a cassette culture

In the early 1980s the International Federation of Phonogram and Videogram Producers launched a campaign for a blank tape levy with the slogan 'Home-Taping is Theft'. At the same time the Recording Industry Association of America (RIAA) printed the slogan 'Home Taping is Killing Music' on all their materials in an effort to respond to the perceived threat of new and increasingly popular home recording technologies (Frith, 1987, p. 60). These campaigns targeted two different activities: the dubbing of commercial music, which eroded industry profits, and the practice of home recording in which individuals recorded audio texts using consumer cassette decks. With the advent of the home cassette deck with recording capabilities, any consumer could potentially be an audio pirate or a recording artist, and a network of home recording enthusiasts did in fact exist, united under the banner of 'independent music'. With the advent of the affordable and convenient consumer cassette deck, the cassette-tape became emblematic of the potentiality of independent music and a cassette culture emerged that championed the use of home-based recording technologies thus challenging the RIAA's allegation. The culture of independent music supported the proactive, do-it-yourself musician, rejected the perceived homogenization of mainstream music, and challenged the property rights that music corporations enjoyed over cultural resources. Enthusiasts hailed independent music, especially cassette-tape recordings, as a 'new model of cultural interchange' that challenged the 'ideology of copyright' and provided an 'activity available free to all' (McGraith, 1990, pp. 83–87).

In the American Pacific Northwest, an independent music scene first took shape in the late 1970s with the rise of interconnected activities such as home recording, small press music journalism and live music shows hosted in private homes or small venues. Olympia, Washington was a particularly notable site of independent music practices (Humphrey, 1995). It was there that the Evergreen State College radio station, KAOS, implemented a policy requiring that 80 per cent of all music played on the station be produced by record labels other than the six big music corporations. In 1979 the person responsible for that policy, John Foster, founded the Lost Music Network and launched a small press publication about independent music called *Op*, which resulted in the catchy acronym LMNOP. Two of *Op*'s contributors, Calvin Johnson and Bruce Pavitt, recorded local bands and distributed cassette-tape compilations under the respective names of their new record labels: K Records and Subpop.[1] Around the same time, a music venue called the Tropicana opened on Olympia's main street and hosted bands such as Calvin Johnson's Beat Happening, Rich Jensen's The Wild Wild Spoons, and The Young Pioneers. This small network rejected the homogenizing tendencies of mass-produced culture, and the corporatization of everyday life in favour of the crafted artefact and singular experience.

The first major overhaul of US copyright law since 1909 coincided with these activities. Among other significant revisions, the US Copyright Act of 1976 granted authors copyright protection for their work from the time a text was 'fixed' in tangible form, thereby no longer requiring individuals to register works with the US Copyright Office. In the spirit of John Locke, this revision established the act of creation as the basis for ownership over a text. The authorship granted by US copyright law resulted from a 400-year-old legal discourse that first emerged in tandem with printing technologies and the book trade in England in the seventeenth and eighteenth centuries (M. Rose, 1994), and it is this discourse that later allowed independent musicians in the Pacific Northwest to sign their name to audio texts and thereby claim authorship of their work. After the 1976 revisions to the legal code the law would formally recognize their signature as such a claim. These cultural and legal shifts further naturalized the now common-sense notion that an individual could declare a particular grouping of words, images or sounds as their private property, which served to further privatize cultural resources.

Home recording and cassette culture, which entailed not only the recording and listening to, but also the trading and documenting of, cassette-tapes, dovetailed with the concomitant rise of other independent music practices.

Cassette-tape enthusiasts shared a general dislike for mainstream music, an indifference to sound quality, a passion for singular experiences, a preference for limited editions over mass-produced copies and an interest in do-it-yourself music projects. In addition, they lauded originality and sincerity over the presumed filters and glitz of mass-mediated music. In their home recording endeavours, they protested copyright law while simultaneously employing rigid notions of originality in order to establish authorship and ownership of the texts they created. Inspired by the emergent technologies of home recording, cassette-tape enthusiasts defined original as 'homemade' and 'handmade' texts and demarcated a space of independent music distinct from the mainstream music industry. The initial passion for all audio recordings along with the celebration of home recording practices as a 'democratic art form' eventually gave way to standardization within independent music and uniformity across localized scenes (McGee, 1992, p. VIII). Cassette-tape enthusiasts and other independent recording artists forged cultural logics required to appreciate their creations, which resulted in the formation of a conceptual space accessible only through appropriate knowhow. In this way, home recording technology was used to exercise the historical function of authorship and limit 'the cancerous and dangerous proliferation of significations within a world where one is thrifty not only with one's resources and riches, but also with one's discourses and significations' (Foucault, 1984, p. 118). Home-based recording artists associated authorship with individual ingenuity and employed notions of authorship to fashion privatized texts and constrain, via exclusion and choice, a proliferation of interpretation. Despite their general hostility towards copyright laws, cassette-tape enthusiasts fixed audio texts with a private preferred meaning over which individuals claimed ownership.

The reviews of cassette-tape projects in three music-related, small press publications provide evidence of the shift from an initial celebration of a democratic art form to an eventual Pacific Northwest music scene. *Op*, *Sound Choice* and *Snipehunt* all featured articles, interviews and reviews about independent music, including home recording projects. Circulated in succession, they collectively span a period of 17 years between 1979 and 1996. *Op* was the pioneering publication that ran from 1979 to 1984. Like *Op*, *Snipehunt* was Pacific Northwest-based with an editorship in Portland, Oregon. The quarterly first started as a fanzine in 1988 and ran until 1996. *Sound Choice*, which ran from 1985 to 1992, was California-based but featured Pacific Northwest writers and musicians. The reviews featured in these publications established the criteria for originality within the independent music scene and helped readers adopt the appropriate sensibilities for the appreciation of independent music. The reviews of cassette-based projects offer a narrative that illuminates why home recording technology was adopted, what the cassette-tape in particular allowed that could not be done with other audio technology, and the aural and visual qualities associated with these projects. The earlier reviews, in particular, captured the spirited excitement for the potential of the relatively new phenomenon of home recording technologies.

Home recording technology eventually succeeded only after several decades of failed marketing strategies in which manufacturers and retailers attempted to forge an association between the home phonograph and the camera by selling sound recording as an artistic hobby akin to amateur photography (Morton, 2000, p. 138). Despite these efforts, the most popular use of recording technology proved to be the reproduction of eight-tracks and cassettes, and by the 1960s 90-minute blank tapes were available which allowed the recording of an entire LP. By the late 1970s the standardized and increasingly affordable home cassette deck, car stereo or Sony Walkman made audio technology ready to hand for consumers. Consumer audio technology allowed for small-scale production as well as listening, and also provided a way of personalizing or individualizing musical tastes; for this reason, the cassette-tape simultaneously represented methods of mass production as well as customization. While Pacific Northwest musicians, such as Beat Happening who released their first recordings on cassette-tape, were in some ways exceptional in their enthusiasm for cassettes, they were making use of technology that was, by 1980, a commonplace feature of the everyday landscape (Azerrad, 2001, p. 465). Pacific Northwest recording artist Cory Brewer, for instance, used his parents' stereo equipment to start a cassette-based label featuring Botan Rise Candy, The Shitsters, Sunday Driver, Bland, and Chrysler Stuart and the Stewardesses: 'Almost all of the stuff that I put out…was just recorded on the hand-held, low-fi tape recorder…[copies were made] on my parents' tape deck; I would just sit for hours on end and I would just put it on high speed dubbing and watch television while I was doing it' (Brewer, 2002, personal interview).

As with any technology, the cassette deck required a particular knowhow, and its everyday uses in turn acquired an ethos. Cassette-tape enthusiasts cultivated this knowhow and drew a distinction between the common audio technology user and the cassette-tape connoisseur. In order to establish such a distinction, cassette-tape enthusiasts negotiated and modified legal discourses concerned with music pirating. In addition to extending legal protection to sound recordings, the Copyright Act of 1976 had codified fair use doctrines. The 1976 Act, however, did not extend fair use to the burgeoning, non-commercial practice of home-based audio dubbing. The legal discourse regarding the dubbing of music intersected with cassette culture in two places: first, anywhere an individual copied or 'pirated' an audio text, in which case the individual was either knowingly or unknowingly technically in violation of the law; second, anywhere cassette-tape enthusiasts employed the notion of authorship, in which they knowingly or unknowingly borrowed legal constructs in order to establish criteria for what constituted an original text. A letter to the editor of *Sound Choice* gives a sense of the degree to which cassette-tape hobbyists were aware of copyright law, and how they perceived it to affect their own recording practices as well as the distribution of music:

> And while I must confess to buying an occasional bootleg album, I have no respect whatsoever for the parasites who manufacture and distribute unauthorized products. The record companies' stance is clear, although at times some of the legalities get blurry. (Is [it] legal, for example, to tape a live show off the radio then make a copy for a friend?) My experience with tape traders leaves me with the impression that most are highly ethical and are simply fanatical fans and collectors of music, even given some of the possible contradictions involved. (A bootleg album, for example, must of necessity originate from somebody's tape ...) (Mills, 1985, p. 8)

The extent to which the letter writer engaged the technicalities of the law was not exceptional. The criminalization of dubbing practices prompted a need for a clear definition of originality in order that individuals could distinguish, if to no one but themselves, the difference between audio projects that involved copying, and those that were singular creations. Dan Fioretti offers an example of this distinction in his how-to essay for potential cassette-tape enthusiasts titled 'What Do You Do With Them Tapes'? He suggests that there is more to home recording than just dubbing:

> The very next thing you could do with cassettes is use them to make nice little original noize [*sic*] ... [let] us say right now that not all blank tape purchased in this country is for the use of recording copyrighted material-that not everyone buys a blank C-60 or C-90 just so they can tape a Bon Jovi LP or tape their fave toonz [*sic*] off the radio ... I remember when me and all my cousins and my two sisters and brother would get together and do weird audio tapes. We even did a parody of The Brady Bunch once! (Fioretti, 1992, p. 19)

Where the letter writer above drew a distinction between the retailer who pirated copies for profit and the enthusiast who dubbed a radio show for a friend, Fioretti drew another between the reproduction of an existing audio text and the creation of a new text. This second distinction was essential to cassette culture, which expanded the definition of originality to include captured sounds as well as those that were intentionally constructed. For instance, another cassette-tape enthusiast suggested using cassettes 'to record things that have never been recorded before. Just what does a bowling alley sound like? What did your kid sound like when she was born? What happens outside your window while you are at work?' (Jenson and Robin, 1992, p. 41). In this case, the distinction is between recording an original audio text such as a newly composed song, and capturing an original act of expression that is original in the sense of its moment of inception, such as a child's first words. A fascination with this last distinction is perhaps what most set apart the early reviews featured in *Op* from later reviews featured in *Sound Choice* and *Snipehunt*.

The Lost Music Network, *Op* magazine, and the ABCs of independent music

The Lost Music Network (LMN) published 26 issues of *Op*, one for each letter of the alphabet before discontinuing. According to *Op* editor John Foster, the motivation for the project was an altruistic desire to network musicians with potential listeners. As he explained in an early editorial:

> I want to help independent artists and labels be heard by people who would like them. I want people with an interest in certain types of music to be able to get in touch with each other. I'm not very interested in being a critic, but I want to see and hear what other people are doing and thinking (Foster, 1980, p. 1).

For Foster, music corporations enjoyed too much control over people's listening practices despite a proliferation of independent music recording, and his mission was to make obscure music accessible: 'We think you should have a greater opportunity to find out about music out of the mainstream' (Foster, 1982, p. 1). In this sense, the Lost Music Network was an explicitly political project that challenged corporate control over music. When *Op* was launched, there was nothing quite like it, and Foster's project was ambitious: to document all projects by musicians practising outside the corporate music industry. Since there was no precedent, any catalogue system of the independent music scene was a starting point, and LMN started with the first letter of the alphabet. Issue 'A' featured reviews of, interviews with and information about musical projects that started with the letter A, such as Laurie Anderson, the Alabama sound, and a cappella. Beginning with issue 'F', *Op* reviewed cassette-tapes separately from vinyl in a column called 'Castanets', by Graham Ingels. The purpose of 'Castanets' was to 'introduce the reader to the wide and wonderful world of cassettes – the ultimate in decentralized production, manufacturing and distribution' (Ingels, 1981a, p. 3). Ingels' reviews offer a glimpse into an emerging cultural phenomenon for which there was yet no standardized language: '[This cassette-tape] is poorly recorded, live, conjuring up a vision of a place where performances only takes place behind closed doors' (Ingles, 1984a, p. 17). His main objective was to document the new phenomenon of cassette-based home recording, and he drew from the values of cassette culture to establish criteria by which to judge projects 'recorded in living rooms and basements' (Ingels, 1984a, p. 16). He always noted, for instance, captured or ambient noise: '[This tape] has some fascinating things done with ambient sounds recorded in and from Perkins's apartment' (Ingels, 1981b, p. 8). He also praised spontaneity and other evidence of home recordings: 'this 3-song cassette EP includes … a piece recorded underwater, and a recorded prank phone call that was very disturbing to listen to' (Ingels, 1983, p. 19). Along with the aural appeal of ambience and spontaneity, Ingels valued the exclusivity, 'home-made styles', and obscurity of these projects (Ingels, 1984b, p. 11). Frequently he noted handmade covers suggesting the artist had made an extremely limited number of copies and perhaps no two copies exactly alike: 'Nice clear folky home-made songs in handsewn pouch with a little book of song titles, words, and pictures' (Ingels, 1984c, p. 18).

Ingels' descriptions of homemade and handmade projects contrasted sharply with the recordings he described as 'polished', 'professional' or 'squeaky-clean'. Within the logics he employed to celebrate 'homemade styles' and to disparage 'polished' recording techniques, Ingels' forged an association between the physical cassette-tape and the individual who recorded sounds on to it. The sounds on a tape were the unique expression of an individual regardless of the origins of the sounds captured in the recording. Consequently, his reviews reinforced the now common-sense notion pioneered by John Locke that a person's 'astigmatic recasting' of cultural resources was the private property of that person (Litman, 1990, p. 1012). In this way Ingels extended the established notions of authorship to the practices at play in cassette culture.[2] While Ingels and other cassette-tape enthusiasts recognized the dubbing of music to be a legal issue, it is not clear that they recognized notions of authorship as such. Cassette-tape connoisseurs' celebration of the homemade and handmade sensibilities emblematic of the do-it-yourself musician not only challenged corporate control over musical production and distribution, but also seemingly challenged the copyright laws that rationalized that control. Cassette culture did not, however, subvert or resist the logics of intellectual property rights so much as fortify the historical function of authorship. The cultural logics employed by Ingels to establish the value of home recording artists drew from legal discourses now naturalized into civil society. These discourses were the reason why cassette-tape enthusiasts could appreciate all recorded sounds, including ambiance, voices in the background and the inadvertent squeak of an instrument as 'authored' by a person. Legal discourses informed musicians' abilities to claim audio texts as private property, a claim that was implicit each time an individual or band recorded sounds and then signed their name to the recording. The protocol of crediting individuals undermined efforts on the part of the Lost Music Network and cassette-tape enthusiasts to democratize music practices, although establishing musicians' credentials was less of a priority for *Op* than was the distribution of information. This changed as Pacific Northwest bands grew in popularity and a Pacific Northwest independent music scene began to take shape.

Sound Choice and the rise of the author in independent music

As Foster had planned from the outset, *Op* did indeed discontinue after 26 issues, despite objection from its subscribers. With the same pragmatic tone of his earlier editorials, Foster opened issue 'Z' by redirecting readers' attention to new projects that aspired to pick up where *Op* left off. Two publications in particular, both California-based, positioned themselves as the *Op* legacy: *OPtions* and *Sound Choice*, published by the Sonic Options Network and Audio Evolution Network respectively. *Sound Choice*, based in Ojai, California, and first published in the spring of 1985, identified itself as the less 'glossy' of the two and more in the spirit of *Op*. Like *Op*, *Sound Choice* lauded home recording and cassette culture. With their first issue subscribers received two cassette-tapes that represented 'artists who have taken control of their audio explorations from start to finish preserving the unique, interesting, provocative or idiosyncratic nature of their art as expressed through the cassette medium' (*Sound Choice*, Spring 1987, p. 6). Despite these similarities, *Sound Choice* marked a significant departure from the motivations of the Lost Music Network. This shift reflected broader changes within independent music practices. As independent recordings became increasingly accessible, the preservation of authorship became an overriding priority for the magazine as it did for the musicians who submitted their recordings. Whereas Ingels reviews typified a general fascination for recorded sound, *Sound Choice* reviewers focused their attention on who authored the texts. Despite their commitment to cassette-tape enthusiasts, *Sound Choice* was also not quite as democratic as *Op* in its reviews policy, as the publication primarily focused on the offerings of independent labels. Although *Sound Choice* encouraged home recording and reviewed individual submissions, its review section reflects the growing centrality of a label-oriented music scene. With formated columns and illustrations that corresponded to the texts, even the layout of *Sound Choice* adhered to more conventional magazine practices than had *Op*. Up until the 1989 Fall issue, the magazine alphabetized reviews by artist or project name, but beginning in the autumn of 1989, the publication changed the format of the review section and listed all projects by musical genre. The shift away from *Op*'s pioneering catalogue system suggests increased standardization of independent music practices.

When preservation of a music scene took priority over making music, independent recording artists and reviewers increasingly employed notions of originality and authorship to protect their audio texts. While *Sound Choice* reviewers adopted the homemade and handmade criteria for originality and authorship established in *Op*, their reviews modified these notions. Reviews in *Sound Choice* frowned upon unoriginal material such as covers, and although it was customary to acknowledge influences on a musician, reviewers distinguished between influences and what they considered to be mere imitation. The standards for originality in home recording had changed, and *Sound Choice* reviewers expressed a sarcastic frustration with what appeared to be a tape of collaged sounds: 'Let's cut up some tapes of fundamentalist preachers recorded off the radio and TV! This is not a particularly new idea in 1986. And the less well it is actually done, [the] older and staler it sounds' (*Sound Choice*, Winter 1987, p. 45). For *Sound Choice* reviewers the novelty of home recording had diminished as had experiments with captured ambiance. A cassette-tape entitled

Idiot-Savant: Live 86'd that might have fascinated Ingels was dismissed by *Sound Choice* reviewers as insignificant: 'More idiot than savant and more eighty-sixed than live. This is mostly a tape of a bunch of people fooling around, presumably in their garage. There was apparently no attempt to do anything here but turn on a tape machine and record whatever happened. Nothing did' (*Sound Choice*, Winter 1987, p. 53). By the evolving standards of independent music, to simply turn on the tape recorder and capture some sounds no longer qualified someone as an artist, nor did using commonplace home recording technologies. The fact that anybody with a cassette deck could record an album was no longer sufficiently compelling reason to document home recorded projects. Despite this shift, *Sound Choice* reviewers continued to note homemade and handmade qualities, although the term 'homemade' began to refer to attributes other than where the recording was made. In some instances, reviewers used the term unfavourably to indicate that the recording sounded cheap, as in the review of the band Balcony of Ignorance: 'Sooner or later there had to be a dark side to the record-it-at-home, do-it-yourself ethic this magazine promulgates... Sooner or later people with absolutely no talent at all were going to start making tapes of zero quality. And here it is ... Probably recorded on a cheap walkmate style recorder' (*Sound Choice*, Spring 1986, p. 37). Another review chastizes the artists for using recording technology that, by the mid-1980s, was outdated: 'Much of this tape is very poorly recorded which seems inexcusable with all the adequate, inexpensive recording equipment in this day and age' (*Sound Choice*, Spring 1986, p. 63). While *Sound Choice* reviewers disparaged cheap home recording technology, the term 'homemade' maintained a positive connotation as a reference to a particular kind of musical sensibility bearing little relationship to where or how the recording was actually made. Musicians could now affect 'homemade', and reviewers used the term to mean sincerity, as in: 'There is an under produced, homey, personal touch to all this' (*Sound Choice*, Winter 1987, p. 53). The term 'homemade' and related terms such as 'DIY' or 'low-fi' that at one time referred to particular production methods now referred to an aesthetic and style of music that came to define the Pacific Northwest independent music scene.

Towards the end of its run and with the eventual change in the review section format, *Sound Choice* all but ceased reviews of home recorded cassette-tapes. Pacific Northwest cassette culture had lost two network hubs in *Op* and *Sound Choice*.[3] In addition to the loss of small press resources for cassette-tape projects, Sub Pop and K Records began to release their recordings on vinyl and compact disc, as did the small forest of independent labels that had sprung up in the Pacific Northwest in the 1980s. Despite these changes, the notions of originality, 'low-fi' aesthetics and rejection of mainstream cultural enterprise that had emerged in tandem with the rise of cassette culture continued to influence a general sensibility around which a Pacific Northwest scene was organized.

Snipehunt and the privatization of the Pacific Northwest music scene

In the early 1990s what were still obscure and disparate practices in the Pacific Northwest that were loosely identified under the banner of independent or alternative music received widespread media attention, coalescing those who wished independent music to remain as distinct as possible from mainstream popular genres. As the notoriety of the Pacific Northwest independent music spread, those who identified with it fashioned conceptual boundaries around associated texts and practices and insisted that appreciation of independent music required the mastery of particular culture logics. As Will Straw suggests, the significance of these logics is 'neither in the transgressive or oppositional quality of musical practices' but in the processes 'through which particular social differences ... are articulated within the building of audiences around particular coalitions of musical form' (Straw, 1991, p. 384). The Pacific Northwest independent music scene is, then, significant not because it challenged the homogenization of popular music or democratized musical practices, but because it produced a new musical aesthetic, appreciation of which was more than matter of merely opening one's ears and simply listening. A person's ability to determine the significance of any given cultural artefact, and thus appreciate it, requires consciously or unconsciously learning the knowledge, language or 'internal logic' available to name it (Bourdieu, 1984, p. 2). The ability to register a given text as representative of a particular author is dependent on the reader's or listener's mastery of relevant modes of perception: 'to see (voir) is a function of the knowledge (savoir)' (Bourdieu, 1984, p. 2). At the same time, the pleasure of appreciation is also an act of forgetting the acquisition of cultural skills so that the experience of listening to low-fi punk, for instance, is perceived as sublime. In short, the text seemingly transcends cultural impositions. Bourdieu suggests that all forms of culture, including popular culture, require a particular knowhow to navigate them 'properly', but mastery of the skills effaces the learning process and conceals the acquisition of cultural logics. More than either *Op* or *Sound Choice*, the quarterly newspaper *Snipehunt* was most explicit in defining what constituted the proper cultural logics for appreciation of the Pacific Northwest independent music scene.

Printed in duo-toned colour on newspaper and freely distributed to coffee shops, record stores, theatres and nightclubs, *Snipehunt* featured as many comic strips as it did reviews and was a miscellany on scene-related endeavours such as Stella Mars' postcard art. Although reviewers did track musical phenomena outside the Pacific Northwest, *Snipehunt* was most dedicated to regional music and each issue featured 'scene reports' from a handful of Pacific Northwest towns. In her regular column titled 'My Eye', editor Kathy Maloy stated her goals for *Snipehunt*, which extended beyond merely providing music news and information:

It's not enough anymore to tell people what kind of music they should listen to. I want to tell people how they should live their lives. Information that is useful like where to buy your food, how to fix your bicycle and how to make the first move and still smash the patriarchy. Real life matters not rock journalism. (Maloy, 1996a, p. 4)

For Maloy, punk rock was not just a musical genre, but a way of life explicitly positioned in opposition to all things corporate, from corporate jobs and corporate clothes to corporate music and corporate media, a sentiment she shared with her predecessors at *Op* and *Sound Choice*. However, rejection of mainstream culture took a different turn in the pages of *Snipehunt*. Whereas John Foster rejected the homogenizing tendencies of mainstream culture by encouraging a proliferation of music-making, Maloy wished to preserve the private preferred meanings she assigned to independent musical enterprise and, in that way, protect Pacific Northwest independent music from becoming itself homogenized. Increasingly, Maloy felt that the popularization of independent music threatened her way of life, and she expressed fears about the encroaching masses that had suddenly arrived on the scene. 'What I am most afraid of is that people who don't even live here are coming to make money at the expense of a cute little scene that has thrived so nicely in its semi-obscurity' (Maloy, 1995, p. 6). Maloy linked her anxieties to the fear that people might not respect the proprieties of her scene: 'Portland is changing. People are moving to my community. Will they know how to behave when they get here? Will they live up to my code of behaviour?' (Maloy, 1996b, p. 7).

In the face of such threats, the fascination with home recording technologies characteristic of earlier independent musical endeavours all but disappeared while notions of authorship did not. There emerged a band-focused style of journalism that sought to establish credit and credentials as well as demonstrate mastery over the cultural logics used to exercise judgement.[4] Only ongoing musical projects with a signature style such as Hazel, Bugsküll, New Bad Things, Irving Klaw Trio and Unwound made the *Snipehunt* charts as the emphasis shifted from playing music to establishing a name.[5] Whereas *Op* and *Sound Choice* defined the term 'independent music' broadly to include a variety of musical genres such as jazz, new age and, in effect, all non-major label recordings, *Snipehunt* focused on the subgenres of punk and rock 'n' roll. In addition, *Snipehunt* did not discriminate between 'independent' and 'major' labels in their feature articles or reviews and had no policy against reviewing 'demo' tapes (*Op* and *Sound Choice* refused). Reviewers noted the format of recording projects (for example, seven-inch vinyl, full-length vinyl or cassette-tape), but there was no longer a dialogue about the advantages of cassette-tape projects versus vinyl-based recordings. Instead, the cassette-tape came to represent an early stage in an artistic endeavour rather than a respectable medium in its own right. Small labels, such as Union Pole, released compilation tapes until they acquired enough capital to release projects on vinyl. *Snipehunt* reviewers still used terms such as 'DIY' and 'low-fi', but 'homemade' rarely appeared. The primary difference between *Snipehunt* reviews and those in *Op* and *Sound Choice* was their intention.

The purpose of *Snipehunt* was not to make independent music accessible, but rather to police the property lines of the bands that constituted the scene. *Snipehunt* was so band-oriented that the handful of reviews of cassette-tapes assumed the recordings to be merely one aspect of a larger effort to establish name recognition: 'I wonder what the band's live show is like. There's not a lot of originality on this tape' (Anonymous, 1992–93, p. 36). Unlike Ingels' reviews that considered the cassette-tape itself to be significant, the *Snipehunt* reviewer saw the tape medium as wholly unrelated to the band's project. At the same time, *Snipehunt* reviewers employed the cultural logics forged in part by Ingels. They heard recordings, regardless of the actual source of the sounds, as the organic self-expression of the musician and, by these cultural logics, it made sense to speak of an artist's 'own voice' coming through on the recording: 'I hope that this is just the start for the Dharma Bums, that they are now coming into their own with the confidence to do and say what they want in their own voice' (Anonymous, 1992, p. 41).[6] In the hope that the Dharma Bums spoke 'their own voice' lay the implicit notion that such a voice was possible.

As the Pacific Northwest scene crystallized, the appeal and usefulness of the cassette-tape faded as artists no longer needed to record at home in order to express originality and sincerity. Consequently, reviewers treated the rare mono reel project, such as Sid Merrt's home recorded project, like a relic – impressive if only because anyone still used it: 'This cassette was recorded over the course of four Saturday night "salons" at Sid Merrt's southwest Portland apartment …All of these songs were recorded on a mono reel to reel using only one microphone, yet the sound is quite impressive…This is more than a music cassette; it's a document' (Anonymous, 1994, p. 29). For the reviewer of 'Sid's Apartment', the cassette-tape no longer represented accessibility to sounds and sound recordings, but it did retain the stamp of originality, a kind of proof that the recordings really came from the artists themselves. In the end, the legacy of the cassette-tape was not that it liberated sound as much as further facilitated its privatization.

The *Op* legacy

In the short time since the advent of the battery-powered Sony Walkman in 1979, a range of new consumer technologies have emerged that allow people to create and listen to music in a variety of convenient ways, and each new technology prompts another round of corporate campaigns against music 'pirating'. *Tape Op* represents a new generation of sound engineers who wish to realize the potential of these technologies. The Portland, Oregon-based magazine pays homage to its ancestors in its name and a column titled 'Under the Radar' by Matt Mair Lowery, who reviews 'homemade CD-Rs and cassettes'. In the Spring 2003 issue of *Tape Op*, Lowery reviewed three CDs; the first was 'a collection of originals and traditional tunes' recorded in a backyard shed; the second was an 'honest recording of sounds', and the third consisted of 'really personal songs ...cut right to a mono tape player' (Lowery, 2003, p. 20). Lowery's reviews suggest that the fascination with home recorded sound and the accompanying charm of homemade personal expression has anything but faded. Looking back at the history of the cassette-tape, it seems as if home recording technologies became popular precisely because they allowed anyone to 'author' music and therefore allowed people to claim slices of cultural material for their own under the guise of the self-inspired artist who worked with raw sounds to create unique singular productions. Such a perspective fails to see that recording artists had other options available, but chose to reinforce historical notions of authorship. Similarly, to read the eventual commercialization of the Pacific Northwest independent music scene as another example of corporate 'co-optation' is to fail to see how the mass culture the scene rejected created the very technological and conceptual conditions that made the scene possible. Such analysis can only conclude, as Scott Marshall does, that each new round of technological innovation results in the loss of a better form of communication. '[Cassette-tapes] were labors of love for ourselves, and for our friends in the cassette-net ...we were all privy to a deeper and more personal, private, and inspiring aspect of communication' (Marshall, 1995, pp. 212–14). The irony in Marshall's encomium to the 'International Cassette Underground' is that corporations campaigned against home recording technologies because they diminished the viability of their recording rights and therefore eroded profits, while cassette-tape enthusiasts trumpeted those technologies as the answer to the corporatization of music because they allowed for the privatization of music. As Marshall himself puts it, the 'thrill was in receiving a personally hand-crafted audio greeting card ... Exchanging cassettes was like exchanging elaborate cultural calling-cards of information virus rather than consuming empty marketing commodity' (Marshall, 1995, p. 112).

If the purpose of independent music practices is really to curb the homogenization and corporatization of everyday life, then an appeal to 'author' more texts is ineffective. The paradoxical nature of authorship suggests invention while it serves to constrain discursive anomalies; consequently, more authors do not result in a proliferation of musical ingenuity. If the home recording artists of today wish to recover the radical potential of recording technologies, they would do well to reconsider their investment in laying claim to a particular sound. Somewhere between recording rights, personal expression and anonymity lies a democratic musical sphere. It is for this reason that the Lost Music Network remains remarkable. For LMNOP, the only thing a proper name determined was in which edition of *Op* you were featured.

Notes

1.   In 1984 Patrick Maley, then a student at The Evergreen State College, spent a recent inheritance on a Task-AM38 mixing board and other professional recording equipment. Other than the recording studio at Evergreen used by Bruce Pavitt, this was the only professional recording equipment in Olympia and, consequently, Maley's launch of Yo-Yo Records marks a shift in the town's independent music scene. According to Maley, up until that point, 'people weren't that interested in having really slick recording sounds necessarily; people would record a lot of stuff right into cassettes' (2002, personal interview, 29 June).
2.   As one *Op* reader put it, 'That was the brilliant thing about LMNOP in that it granted authorship, it granted the status that goes with authorship, to everyone who was capable of turning on a cassette recorder, and was brave enough then to bray into it whatever weird little sounds they could concoct' (Fred Nemo, personal interview, 11 June 2002).
3.   Other publications continued to support cassette-based recordings such as Massachusetts-based *Cassettera*; *Gajoob*, a Salt Lake City publication with connections to a radio show, and *Kentucky Fried Royalty*, 'a non-profit world-wide independent cassette tape distribution network', located in California (*Sound Choice*, Winter 1990, p. 11).
4.   These logics did not hinge on musical virtuosity. A mode of perception developed that allowed for distinctions between good awfulness and bad awfulness. The members of Beat Happening, for example, had little working knowledge of their instruments, but at some point listeners learned to appreciate this lack of skill as a kind of skill in and of itself (Azerrad, 2001).
5.   *Snipehunt* featured a 'Top 69' list of bands in every issue.
6.   This particular review is of the cassette-tape version of 'Welcome', which was also available in vinyl. The cassette-tape medium in this case holds no particular significance.

Chapter 13

Gothic music and the decadent individual

Kimberley Jackson

You know, if more people understood what society is trying to hide, a lot less people would be inclined to try and recreate it – Ian Curtis (quoted in Thompson, 2002, p. 42).

Because of its associations with punk and the music of rebellion, on the one hand, and its subcultural cohesion on the other, discussions of late twentieth-century gothic music most often centre on the themes of assimilation and identity. In his edited collection entitled *Gothic: Transmutations of Horror in Late Twentieth Century Art*, Christoph Grunenberg writes of contemporary Gothicism that 'at the end of mainstream appropriation inevitably stood commercial exploitation and semantic exhaustion, reducing stylistic idioms to innocuous mass-market caricatures devoid of their original subversive power and meaning' (Grunenberg, 1997, p. 173). Joshua Gunn, in his article 'Marilyn Manson is not Goth: Memorial Struggle and the Rhetoric of Subcultural Identity' (1999b), would include such statements as Grunenberg's in what he calls 'the assimilation thesis'. Gunn argues, using the 'Goth' subculture as his model, that there is a fecund relationship between, on the one hand, what is assimilable, or what has been assimilated, of a subculture (including misconceptions and misrepresentations) into the 'mainstream' and, on the other hand, what remains only within the 'memory' of the subculture itself – relationship that is often antagonistic. Gunn wishes to employ this site of antagonism to show how 'both popular representations of the subculture and the thoughts of goths themselves are needed for an analysis of their dynamic interaction in the creation of individual and community identities' (Gunn, 1999b, p. 409). While Gunn's analysis offers us access to what is still vital and 'dynamic' in the negotiations of identity taking place between the subculture and the mainstream, it is my intention to highlight the characteristics of gothic music prior to its creating a 'subculture' and to describe a point of radical disjunction at the site of emergence of this particular form of Gothicism. In theories of gothic music, and within the gothic subculture itself, the violence of this site of emergence has been forgotten. This forgetting was perhaps necessary if there was to be any 'memory', subcultural or otherwise, to inform a determinate 'scene', since what is revealed when one looks closely at the beginnings of this musical form is a movement which explodes the only 'atoms' (the individualized identities and communities) that could have contained it.

If Gothicism serves as an effective model for discussions of semantic exhaustion and exploitation, it is because in all of its media – architecture, film, literature, music – and its many historical emergences, the gothic, due to its excessive nature, is always poised on the edge of ridiculousness, always in danger of going too far, of losing its efficacy by the very means it employed to gain it. But in its seminal stage (a stage which has been re-created time and again), in the works that come to define Gothicism for a genre or an age, the gothic becomes the mirror in which a society, a culture, a genre, reflects its own Mr Hyde – that underside of itself, its self-destructive nature, turned into an aesthetic figure.

The vampire is a defining figure in this regard. The vampire, the gothic figure *par excellence*, does not simply produce cultural-subcultural misunderstandings at the level of the (superficial) image – on the one hand, an evil, heretic, blood-sucker with no capacity for human emotion and, on the other hand, a tortured yet glamorous and sophisticated figure – but, rather, presents (prior to the cultural-subcultural distinction) the decadence (excess and decay) of the cultural imagination itself and the society from which it originates. The vampire is the exemplary individual, the individual absolutely detached from any association with others in community, the individual who exists by draining life from his surroundings.

It is such an individual vampirism that, for Friedrich Nietzsche, characterizes modernity and is presented in decadent art. It is not surprising that certain aspects of Nietzsche's thought, particularly those aspects highlighted in *The Case of Wagner*, should correspond with the inception of a musical scene which could easily be described as 'decadent'. Nietzsche's definition of decadence is as follows:

> What is the sign of every *literary decadence*? That life no longer dwells in the whole. The word becomes sovereign and leaps out of the sentence, the sentence reaches out and obscures the meaning of the page, the page gains life at the expense of the whole – the whole is no longer a whole. But this is the simile of every style of *decadence*: every time, the anarchy of atoms, disgregation of the will, 'freedom of the individual,' to use moral terms–expanded into a political theory, '*equal* rights for all.' Life, *equal* vitality, the vibration and exuberance of life pushed back into the smallest forms; the rest, *poor* in life. (Nietzsche, 1967, p. 170)[1]

While the 'decay' of Nietzsche's decadence involves the disintegration of 'life' and its confinement in the individual (the 'atom'), making 'the rest, *poor* in life', what one might call a 'postmodern' decadence involves the overinvestment in this figure of individuality and the inability of that figure to sustain itself any longer. The relationship between decadence and Gothicism lies in this 'disgregation' that Nietzsche describes – an essential connection between excess and decay, exhaustion and deterioration. Decadence need not manifest itself in gothic darkness, but Gothicism does provide a convenient vehicle for its presentation, particularly when the decay is so deeply ingrained that there is no way of presenting any one aspect of it (in other words, when it seems as if all modes of expression have been absorbed by its emptying force); in this case, it is only the very movement of exhaustion and decay itself that can be presented. As Patrick McGrath writes in 'Transgression and Decay', 'the Gothic has always been fascinated at the prospect of *undoing the human*' (1997, p. 155). Thus while decadence does not always necessarily entail Gothicism, gothic excess is most often a signal of social decay.

Nietzsche is critical of decadent art, as it merely *signals* the decay of society, fascinating it with magnificent and mythical scenes of its own banal and mundane deterioration, but he is nonetheless 'grateful' for it, as this staging and the consequent fascination are necessary for the philosopher to view decadence as a whole and effectively be able to isolate the 'sickness' it signals. The 'healthy' reaction to such art on the part of the many is, for Nietzsche, resistance. The problem is, of course, that society at large, particularly when faced with a 'tyrannical' talent like Wagner's, becomes so enamoured of the decadent art that they see the art itself as their 'redeemer', while redemption (if, in fact, this is what Nietzsche wants for us) is only possible if one is able to renounce the sickness signalled by the art. But if one falls in love with the sign of decay, then one surely does not want to give up the sickness itself. Hence Wagner continued to be popular long after Nietzsche was gone, and gothic music has gained a place of its own long after Ian Curtis committed suicide.

Although it may seem strange to place Ian Curtis of Joy Division alongside Wagner, Nietzsche's discussion of decadence, decadent art and the resistance it provokes positions an aesthetic experience not simply as a reflection of a sociopolitical condition but more specifically as a presentation of a movement of resistance whose energy is garnered from, and is thus implicit in, the sociopolitical condition itself, and which is only *thus* able to provoke it. This same decadent relation presents itself in the performances of Ian Curtis and some of his contemporaries. To demonstrate this parallel, I will be characterizing a particular grouping of bands, including Bauhaus, Joy Division and The Sisters of Mercy (three of the seminal bands of what would later be referred to under the names of gothic rock, gothic music, dark music and so on) as 'decadent art'. Working from Nietzsche's particularly modern definition of decadence, I will show how these bands begin to move towards a 'new' decadence corresponding to their own age.

For Nietzsche decadent art presents to a society its decay in aesthetic form, and thus the most 'pure' primary response to decadent art is resistance. This form of resistance was apparent in the relationship between bands like Bauhaus and Joy Division and their audiences. The difference between the 'original' Goth bands and many of the ones that would follow is that whereas the latter would come to characterize the 'gothic scene' as a 'community' devoted to a more passive acceptance of the 'dark side' of life, the former, in presenting a darkness that resisted assimilation into, or creation of, any sort of subculture, waged war both on the solidarity of their fan base and ultimately on their own existence. Fuelled by the fear of nuclear holocaust and the conservative politics it spawned, bands such as Bauhaus, Joy Division and The Sisters of Mercy both created and suffered from their own 'atomic' energy. Rather than representing a particular political stance or form of protest, these bands offered the *spectacle* of the social-in-decay, an image capable of sparking a bare (one might even say 'primitive') resistance.

While the British bands of the late 1970s and early 1980s, which were later to be called the 'fathers' of gothic rock – Bauhaus, Joy Division, The Sisters of Mercy, The Cure, Siouxsie and the Banshees – wrote and performed music that did indeed depict the darker aspects of various sociocultural movements and tendencies, they did not deserve the critical reputation earned by their gothic heirs. Bands and music labelled 'gothic' have faced harsh criticism in recent years. The common themes of dark music (death, destruction, decay, madness and so on) are rarely attacked in and of themselves; it is the *presentation* of these themes which is apparently objectionable. Some critics, like James Hannaham in his article 'Bela Lugosi's Dead and I Don't Feel So Good Either: Goth and the Glorification of Suffering in Rock Music', write that there is an essential apathetic distance to the horrors contemporary gothic music depicts, that it attempts to aestheticize tragedy, to make it a beautiful object, so that it does not have to be experienced at the private or personal level. Others attribute its success (and its excesses) to the boredom and dissatisfaction of its audience. Its excesses are often seen as insincere. The most ludicrous of assumptions is that Joy Division was the most sincere dark band because its lead singer, Ian Curtis, committed suicide, as if this were the only way to be authentically Goth. Hannaham writes that 'perhaps not all of the Goths who flocked to Joy Division's posthumous releases, who dressed as creatures of the night to prove their love of death, really wanted to die ... They wanted an Ian Curtis to die for them, so they wouldn't have to discover for themselves that death had no sting' (1997, p. 92).

Those critics who speak in defence of the contemporary gothic scene are writing about gothic music as it stood in the mid- to late-1990s, when it had already become 'popular'. (Notable exceptions are Mick Mercer and Dave Thompson, who write from Goth's inception). Whether the purpose is to attempt to define the 'goth scene' as a distinct subculture or to defend it against misconceptions, the message seems to be the same: the goth scene involves a calm, peaceful and thoughtful contemplation and embracing of the 'darker' aspects of life (death, night, nostalgia, melancholia). For instance, in his article 'Gothic and Dark Music: Forms and Backgrounds', Ansgar Jerrentrup, describing the scene at concerts of such contemporary bands as Rosetta Stone and The House of Usher, writes that:

The stage shows of dark musicians are generally not full of energy or turbulent. They contain few actions . . . The instrumentalists frequently give the impression that they are playing apathetically, only for themselves . . . The atmosphere of (the more intimate) dark concerts is comparatively calm, and active attempts to please the audience do not occur on stage. A 'civilized' manner is usual and arguments are avoided. (Jerrentrup, 2000, p. 36)

In her article on gothic as 'cult/ure,' Julia Winden Fey writes: 'Serving as a conduit to life's darker side, Gothic music thereby seeks to uplift its listeners rather than depress them ... Gothic music's affirmation of death and darkness serves to reinforce Goths' own beliefs about the value of all aspects of life, providing both reassurance and comfort to its listeners' (2000, p. 36).

Those theorists who study the 'goth scene' in the USA and Germany as it appears in the mid- and late-1990s are faced with the mere vestiges of a once-vital movement. What became a 'scene' of sombre, non-violent, brooding apparitions in black did not begin that way. Nor, of course, were the 'original' bands responsible for the crimes that would later be committed by those who claimed to be in various sorts of 'goth cults'. But the live shows of bands like Bauhaus and Joy Division, whether intentionally or not, did tend to create violent outbursts. While Andrew Eldritch of The Sisters of Mercy 'maintained an aloofness [from the audience] that bordered on absenteeism' (Thompson, 2002, p. 132), other front men were just that; they confronted and sometimes affronted, the audience. In any case, it was clearly not adoration that these bands were after. If they were to be popular, it had to be because their *resistance* was attractive. If the 'Fields' of Fields of the Nephilim were supposed to be magnetic fields, it was because people were drawn in not by glitter and glamour, but by a race of marauding giants who would just as soon kill a man as look at him. The first response to a movement which exists to represent to a culture its weakness and decay is naturally a certain horror and resistance. As such a primal impulse, free from the rationale that would allow for the incorporation of even the most scathing critique of culture and society, this initial response is always the most pure. Nietzsche saw such a reaction to Wagner amongst his fellow Germans and sought to highlight its purity: 'But formerly it was strong, it was terrible, it was like a dark hatred – through almost three quarters of Wagner's life. The resistance he encountered among us Germans cannot be esteemed too highly or honored too much. He was resisted like a sickness – not with reasons – one does not refute a sickness – but with inhibition, mistrust, vexation, and disgust ...' (1967, p. 181).

So while theorists like Fey and Jerrentrup write of the peacefulness of the gothic music scene, now that it has emerged as one subculture among others (and now that its practitioners wish to shield it from any kinship with the types of 'cult' violence that have resulted in murder and mayhem amongst the teens of America), the bands that these same non-violent Goths identify as seminal to the movement had no use for peaceful demonstration. In *Dark Entries: Bauhaus and Beyond*, Ian Shirley writes of Peter Murphy, lead singer of Bauhaus, 'He would do absolutely anything to get across to an audience. He was a live wire; angry, vicious, and totally commanding. He would actually attack the front few rows of people – in fact in the early days he picked up two convictions for GBH (Grievous Bodily Harm) for assaulting members of the audience' (Shirley, 1994, p. 33). In an article in *Melody Maker* Gill Smith writes: 'I've known Peter to insult an audience beyond belief and literally attack them. One horrific night at the Rock Garden he single-handedly took on the entire front of the crowd' (Smith, 1980, p. 13). Ian Curtis of Joy Division was no less violent. In Deborah Curtis's book *Touching From a Distance*, she quotes one of the other members of Joy Division describing the group's front man:

> It was the contrast of being nice and polite, and then totally manic when he was on stage. One night, during a performance at Rafters, he ripped the whole stage apart, pulling off these twelve-inch-square wooden tiles with nails in them and throwing them at the audience. Then he dropped a pint pot on the stage, it smashed and he rolled around in the broken glass, cutting a ten-inch gash in his thigh. (Curtis, 1996, p. 52)

The violence between these bands and their 'fans' is an indication that the goal was not to bond together for a common cause or against a particular evil. Far from being a protest *against* the state of the society out of which it grows, decadent art, as Nietzsche explains, is a reflection of its time. If, at the end of the nineteenth century, decadent art reflected an atomizing movement towards the individual and equality, then at the end of the twentieth we might expect that this artform would tremble with the possibility of the explosion of these atoms. And so it does; in its image, its dancing, and its mad arrangement, decadent gothic music, in the late 1970s and early 1980s, delivers the atom bomb in aesthetic form.

What distinguished gothic music from its closest relatives was precisely its adherence to a *figure* of decadence. Rather than confront their sociocultural reality with the scene of its dismantlement, as punk had, rather than present the world with the impossibility of freely choosing this 'order' (and thus the preference for 'anarchy' and chaos), the gothic spin-off adhered to a theatrical-metaphoric figure *of* that very order and held to it so tightly that it began to tremble in its own excess. The vampire, the undead individual who is immortal and infinite became gothic rock's sign for the underside of the 'star', the very epitome of individuality. While the individual-as-star gained its immortality through 'fame', the individual-turned-vampire, the undead decadent individual, garners his through condemnation, to forever live by draining life from others. This is a presentation of the suspicion, even the pronouncement, that the star is emblematic, even part and parcel, of economic, political and social mechanisms of 'bloodsucking' and thus that the individual exists at the expense of its surroundings.

The relationship between the role of the 'star', or hero, and the atomization of the social is taken up by Irene Traviss Thomson in her article 'The

Transformation of the Social Bond: Images of Individualism in the 1920s versus the 1970s', in which she writes that '[c]ritics in the 1970s portray a society that lacks ideals, heroes, and common purposes ... Instead of heroes, we have celebrities ... Whereas the hero idealized the community, celebrities idealize only isolated individuals' (1989, p. 856). And, further, Wilfred McClay demonstrates the tropic relation between individualism and atomic theory. In an article about the evolution of the concept of individualism in the West, McClay writes, 'Just as in atomic physics, where the unsplittable entity (the a-tomos) turned out to have an unnumbered multitude of particles and subparticles in its makeup, so too, the self has proved to be a complicated and vulnerable entity, as vulnerable as the idea of truth itself' (2001, p. 6). Gothic bands would take advantage of this vulnerability.

Describing the cover of Joy Division's *Unknown Pleasures* album, Robert Palmer writes that the 'rectangular graph of peaks and valleys ... was reproduced from a text on radio-astronomy, a graph representing 'the scream of an exploding star' (1988, p. 85). Rather than presenting the 'star,' the 'rock star', in its shining glory, Joy Division seemed to make a spectacle of the star's explosion. And just as the star, the celebrity, was the sign of individualism, so the exploding star would represent its 'disintegration' (as in the title of the 1989 Cure album). The aesthetics of atomic explosion was also a preoccupation for Andy Eldritch, lead singer of The Sisters of Mercy. As Simon Price writes in an article in *Melody Maker*, 'The Sisters of Mercy arose in an era when the threat of thermonuclear holocaust seemed very, very real. The music reverberates with that dread' (1993, p. 36). This is true, for instance, in The Sisters' single 'Mother Russia' which, according to Dave Thompson, was an 'anti-American diatribe flavoured by the Chernobyl nuclear disaster' (2002, p. 186), or in lines like 'I like Ike and his itty-bitty A-bomb' ('Doctor Jeep', 1990). Andrew Eldritch reflects that '[i]t is the scenario that the music was set in ... But my attitude towards that is very ambivalent anyway. I always found it quite exciting... I always said it was going to *look* good' (quoted in Price, 1993, p. 36).

The relationship between the dread associated with the possibility of nuclear war, the explosion of the atom, and the energy created by that dread manifested itself, particularly in bands like The Sisters of Mercy, Joy Division and Bauhaus, in an aestheticization of atomic fission. Gothic music, then, in its inception, is the sound emitted when a ball of energy can no longer sustain the tension of its existence. As Dave Thompson notes in his book *The Dark Reign of Gothic Rock* (2002), '[w]ith the Banshees and Joy Division at its heart ... a tiny dark ball had coalesced in the soul of all that was going on elsewhere ...' (2002, p. 46). Inside this 'dark ball' raged an immense amount of energy. In a 1999 interview, Peter Murphy of Bauhaus explains, 'I tend to store up a lot of energy and let it out in one main burst, and it's that energy that constitutes the power you hear on the records' (quoted in Thomson, 1999, p. 15). In another interview, Murphy continues:

We were just clicking with energy … The energy that came off that band was quite amazing. It was very high-butane, very confrontational. You could touch the atmosphere in the air whenever Bauhaus were around. It was kind of heavy at times, but we made it so. There was an over-emphasis on the importance of what we were doing and the doors we were breaking down. But, really, there was no door there at all. We were just breaking. We were breaking down doors but the doors were absent. We were just breaking, breaking, breaking. (Quoted in Thompson, 2002, p. 117)

It was not long, for Peter Murphy and Bauhaus, before the previous statement became passive. It was soon the 'we' that was 'breaking, breaking, breaking', cracking under the strain of its own force. 'We were victims of the very energy that we were generating, and we weren't really protected with wisdom, we didn't know how to control this. We'd split the atom, but we had no idea what to do with it' (Thompson, 2002, p. 137). Like The Sisters of Mercy, Joy Division, Siouxsie and the Banshees, The Cure and many others at the time, Bauhaus would itself split up. As Peter Murphy explains above, the band's very concept precluded the possibility of its lasting very long. While Siouxsie and The Cure would continually pick up the pieces, the initial explosion of the musical form of which they were a part provided only this impetus for breaking. As a presentation of 'breaking, breaking, breaking', breaking with 'no doors', with nothing *to* break, there was no goal, no end in sight, except for exhaustion and disintegration.

For bands like Bauhaus, Joy Division and The Sisters of Mercy, 'darkness' did not merely entail the doldrums of depression, but rather the seizure of possession – something that would not let them sleep, that took over their bodies and pushed them beyond their capabilities. While many are critical of the 'theatrics' and 'excesses' of certain Goth bands, there was something in the music and the times that required it. And it was required not only in the performances, but also in the writing and recording (Andy Eldritch apparently had a breakdown after each completed album). Despite the bands' desire to become 'IMMENSE' – Andy Eldritch of The Sisters of Mercy states in one 1982 interview, 'There's no reason we shouldn't be able to carry on playing more or less like we do at the moment and be IMMENSE. Darkness and decay and The Sisters of Mercy hold illimitable dominion over all' (quoted in Sweeting, 1982, p. 11) – there was always something that would not allow this to occur. Just when these bands would be ready to crest the pinnacle of success, something would happen; the band would break up, or someone would kill himself, or someone would have a physical or mental collapse.

Although breakdowns, drug abuse and tragedy are common amongst bands in many music genres, these occurrences in goth bands were not necessarily due to the rigours of fame and a heavy tour schedule. Gothic musicians used their bodies as instruments; they used their bodies to inform their audiences that there was something not entirely 'human' about the workings of society, the world, the music industry, politics and so on. Performers such as Peter Murphy and Ian

Curtis danced away from themselves, danced themselves to pieces, and used their bodies to demonstrate an explosion at the level of the individual, the supposedly indivisible. If Ian Curtis of Joy Division was notable in this respect, it was because he in fact suffered from epilepsy; nevertheless, the energy of the band itself was so great as to lead him to an attack. Tony Wilson tells us that 'something was happening within a set, doing what he did, that actually took him to that point, that actually overcame the drugs and made him have an attack' (quoted in Curtis, 1996, p. 114). However, Curtis's wife Deborah, suggests that his dancing in this way was *not* an epileptic attack, but an extremely convincing imitation: 'Certainly Ian's dancing had become a distressing parody of his off-stage seizures. His arms would flail around, winding an invisible bobbin, and the wooden jerking of his legs was an accurate impression of the involuntary movements he would make' (Curtis, 1996, p. 74). Mick Middles writes that: 'During the set's many "peaks" Ian Curtis often loses control. He'll suddenly jerk sideways and, head in hands, he'll transform into a twitching, epileptic-type mass of flesh and bone' (quoted in Curtis, 1996, p. 83). In a 1988 article in *Melody Maker*, Paul Mathur writes that:

> By now Curtis had become the focal point, and to witness his deranged stage behaviour was to see a soul turned inside out, a body caught up in an almost brutal entropy. Imagine the bit in 'Tom & Jerry' when Tom swallows a bomb. Now imagine it all taking place in 'The Exorcist.' It was there. And nowhere. To try and touch it would be to suck yourself into their darkness ... The external and the internal had crumpled into a quiet hurricane. The music, the sound, the faces, were no longer important. This was a dirty, drenching apocalypse. And the screams came out silent. (Mathur, 1988, p. 16)

This apocalyptic imagery – an individual swallowing a bomb and being 'caught up in an almost brutal entropy' – can be found everywhere in commentary on these bands. It abounds in the bands' descriptions of themselves, in descriptions by those who went to see them perform and in the words of those who interviewed them. Describing Peter Murphy's dancing at a Bauhaus show, Gill Smith writes, 'I was dimly aware of the stick-like figure on stage dancing like a speeding ostrich, limbs flailing in the air uncontrollably, while fragments of guitar alternately howled like a trapped wolf or splintered like plate glass' (1980, p. 13).

There is nothing in these descriptions to suggest that this music was intended to 'comfort' and 'reassure' its audience. It might be said that Ian Curtis had what Nietzsche calls 'the virtue of decadents: pity' (1967, p. 172), as Penny Valentine does in her article on Joy Division: 'Curtis's voice mixed back lends to the music poignant sorrow – not just for himself, but for us all' (1980, p. 24). Yet he did not offer us condolences, but rather the spectacle of an individual who had 'lost control', the individual at the limits of its indivisibility, acting out atomic fission. Arguably, Bauhaus did not last because it took its 'vampiric' self too seriously; it could not sustain such an excessive image. What cannot be said is that there was no violence at the conception of gothic music. Gill Smith writes of a Bauhaus show, 'I felt totally assaulted, my senses brutally raped by the splotches of shifting tones and dynamics which roared one moment, and whispered the next. The tide of force was utterly overwhelming. It tore me in two and trod on the pieces' (1980, p. 13). Even those critics who were not impressed with Bauhaus as musicians, like Steve Sutherland of *Melody Maker*, admit that their shows were 'exciting live pantomimes' (1981, p. 9). Yet Sutherland is perplexed at the band's inability to 'push their considerably promising projects through to any extreme, logical or satisfactory conclusion'. His position is that all bands after David Bowie's pinnacle fall prey to 'the symptom of the age; the cruel, inescapable legacy left ... by one man – Bowie' (1981, p. 9). For Sutherland, bands such as Bauhaus are 'pathetically imitative' of Bowie's 'trademarks – preoccupation with stage persona, absurd ego-gratification in the name of entertainment and, worst of all, the whole-hearted subscribing to the seductive lure of the star system so strong that even punk succumbed in anarchic self-parody' (1981, p. 9). I would not argue with any of these criticisms; where I would take exception would be in the implication that, successful or not, the first gothic bands were not *affective* in a way in which no band had been before. If they were 'imitative' of the epitome of stardom, David Bowie, it was to expose his underbelly and to such an extent, I would add, that Bowie himself appeared alongside with Bauhaus in the 1980s film *The Hunger*, in which Bauhaus performs 'Bela Lugosi's Dead' at the beginning and *Bowie plays a vampire*. The theme of 'Ziggy Stardust' and Bowie's 'descent' into Gothdom (in his 1995 album *Outside*) suggest that Bowie himself recognized the declining state of the star.

The suspicion that 'rock 'n' roll' was moving towards its 'death throes' (Sutherland, 1981, p. 9), that perhaps there was nothing new to say, did not mean that no one was saying anything. Voicing the fact of exhaustion and forcing it into frenzied motion was, at the very least, *something* to see and hear. In 'Joy Division Meant It', Tom Carson writes that '[t]he way he [Ian Curtis] keeps resorting to every cliché of language and pose which might apply to his situation, in fact, only makes his desperation more convincing; he seems to be doing it almost against his will, driven by a naked need to convey the truth of that situation ...' (1981, p. 63). Steve Grant writes, '... Joy Division transformed a moribund music into a vital if difficult experience' (1982, p. 33). When Ian Curtis died, when Bauhaus broke up, when Andy Eldritch was silent for some time, even their absence was palpable. Like the fans who would gather at Peter Murphy concerts and 'Love and Rockets' shows (both spin-offs of Bauhaus), looking a bit out of place and confused amidst the mainstream, so too was New Order (the band that formed from Joy Division) conscious of the empty space left by Ian Curtis:

> Guitarist Bernard Albrecht hugs the left-hand wall, bassist Peter Hook crowds right, edging away from the center the way that horses shy at phantoms. The darkness in

front of drummer Stephen Morris has the impact of a spotlight. Grim-faced, sober-toned, eyes always straight ahead, New Order wind swatches of sound around the space where Ian Curtis isn't. (Palmer, 1988, p. 86)

What these bands presented was not merely parody. They did not merely represent the 'dark side of life' to make us more 'comfortable' with its presence. When there was no more left to say, when the star and the individual he epitomized were exhausted, they created energy through their own disintegration, their own 'breaking, breaking, breaking'.

Today, I must agree with Joshua Gunn in one respect: that what is most fecund about Gothicism now lies not in what is embraced by those who call themselves Goths, but in what they denounce and what is denounced of the gothic by society at large. In his article on Marilyn Manson (1990b) Gunn discusses the significance of the disavowal of Manson's 'shock violence' by those who now call themselves Goths. Gunn's argument involves the assertion that 'Goth' has survived, not in spite of its sites of mainstream appropriation, but because of the 'memorial struggles' that ensue at these sites, between the 'mainstream' and the 'subcultural identity'. While I do agree that these sites are fecund, I wish to focus on the titled assertion itself, made by self-proclaimed Goths, that 'Marilyn Manson is not Goth'.

While Manson's antics respond to different sociocultural issues, the relationship between Manson and his audience is much more reminiscent of the bands who 'founded' gothic music than those bands which are apparently embraced by contemporary Goths. During Nine Inch Nails' Self-Destruct Tour Part 2 in 1994, for which Marilyn Manson opened, the picture was certainly not of a band who wished to be embraced, nor one that wished to comfort or reassure its audience. The lead singer, in his 'Antichrist Superstar' get-up (which could not be more confrontational), leered at and spit upon his audience as he sang. His words were admonishments, not invitations to join him in a serene contemplation of 'beautiful death'. He invited resistance and, like the vampiric images of earlier Gothic bands, sought to represent the underside of the star (as the band members' choice of names indicates; each chooses a star as a first name and a murderer for the second). Yet unlike earlier gothic bands, Marilyn Manson has survived intact. In fact, the band has recently sat in number one spots alongside many of the 'pop' stars it criticizes. While Manson himself, in a May 2003 e-mail response to a fan, calls this 'irony' (Marilyn Manson, 2003), where is the exhaustion, where the decay?

If gothic music, on the one hand, became mellow and contemplative and allowed for the creation of a peaceful 'subculture', on the other hand its original force had the potential to re-emerge in the figure of the 'Antichrist Superstar'. The fact that Marilyn Manson has been denounced by self-proclaimed Goths should have only lent fuel to this possibility. Yet it seems that, after all, the 'Antichrist Superstar' is one star among others. The band's popularity suggests that the resistance to Manson these days is in the wrong place, at least if one were attempting to characterize the band's music and performances as 'decadent art' in the way in which it has been defined in this paper. The energy of resistance to Manson is somehow lacking; either society is not able to recognize itself in the band's grotesque imagery, or else such a recognition of social decay no longer effects a surge of resistance. In any event, Marilyn Manson seems unable (or perhaps unwilling) to be more than a star, to be more than 'irony', to be able to perform the disintegration of his own image.

The point here is not, of course, whether or not Manson can be rightly called Goth, nor whether or not one can be subversive and also be popular. It is merely to highlight what was original, what was vital, about those 'stars' who donned the dark and critical gothic image, decaying from all aspects of exhaustion – boredom, cliché, parody, apathy, alienation, dissatisfaction, meaninglessness – and infused it with the energy of bare resistance, activating a theretofore dormant resistance of the social itself to the scene of its own disintegration. That it left in its wake only *Disintegration* (the album that would bring The Cure into the mainstream), a disintegration embraced by the very society it was meant to reflect, has sealed its fate as gothic decadence, as a dark and terrible resistance that has been forgotten, abandoned in its very acceptance.

Note

1. While many of us might initially bristle at this apparent condemnation of the discourse of equality and equal rights that we have become accustomed to in the West, none can doubt that, historically, calls for equality and equal rights have always been a sign of decadence and, further, that the danger of total equality (if this were possible) is a levelling down, a spreading mediocrity.

Chapter 14

Straight, narrow and dull: the failure of protest in straight edge rock 'n' roll

Steven Hamelman

Some people say punk is dead. I don't know if that's true – but I do know for sure that protest music lives. (Tomas Squip of Fidelity Jones (1987), quoted in Andersen and Jenkins, 2001, p. 256)

[T]he drug demon has a Janus head, is polarized, divisible into glory and evil. His [disciples] and those potential disciples who, suspecting treachery, are his sworn antagonists will be among the battalions of extremists on drug issues. (Blum, 1970, p. 333)

With a topic such as this, it's a good idea to begin by establishing my credibility, not as a rock scholar with a thesis to argue – that will come – but as a rock musician/fan with a history to explain. For the better part of 40 years, I have been a rock 'n' roll junkie, and every day during those 40 years I have also been a Straight Edger. To be blunt, I am the platonic avatar of an ideology-cum-aesthetic-cum-rock subgenre that, since its beginning, has been marked by conflict and contradiction. During decades of drumming in rock bands and listening to rock music, I have never tasted alcohol or drugs, never smoked a cigarette and never engaged in casual sex – straight edge's three main proscribed habits. Moreover, for 25 years I have refrained from eating meat (a fourth proscription, veganism, was advocated by many second-generation Straight Edgers). No sudden insight on the road to rock 'n' roll Damascus was involved in my choices, no religious inculcation, no talk with God. Choosing the clean life had nothing to do with peer pressure, compulsion disorder, the desire to impress a girl, brainwashing by a cult, rebellion against parents, sexual dysfunction, the need to be different for its own sake, an urge to change the world, a bout with an STD or an epiphany after a struggle with smack, acid, speed, crack or drink. The temptation to swig a beer, snort a powder or 'score a chick' for the fun of it never arose, and so there was never a lapse into pleasures which, unless they become habitual, harmful to others or self-destructive, I have always considered normal for friends to pursue. Moreover, there was no undue difficulty involved in renouncing meat: vegetarianism came in college following my exposure to the transcendentalists, a rite of passage supplemented by a stint cooking in the campus cafeteria. My straight edge credentials are so impeccable that, despite my age and my interest in rock music (voracious, active and openminded, limited to no category, decade, region, nation, medium, age or style), I have more than earned my right to wear a straight edge (sXe) cross, tattoo or T-shirt.

Having said this, I must note three interrelated points. First, despite my straight edge affinities, I don't ever intend to get a tattoo of any sort – certainly not one that would identify my 'membership' in a special interest group – and I rarely buy T-shirts bearing logos or messages. Second, my age is the main reason I didn't become aware of my charter membership in the straight edge club (or cult, clique, subculture, gang, posse, crew) until a good ten years after this movement sprang to life in 1981 in the Ur-songs 'Straight Edge' and 'Out of Step (with the World)' by Minor Threat.[1] In 1981 I was already too old to give much thought to convictions that straight edge kids zealously embraced. Without having made any conscious decision to uphold the three main tenets of this lifestyle, I was, ironically, already a confirmed Straight Edger when the rockers and fans who would grow up to form the official straight edge movement were still in nappies – a movement predicated, with some contradiction, on the individuality of those individuals who happen to fit into it (for you must be an individual to join this group).[2] Third – and this should be obvious to anyone familiar with straight edge theory and practice – I am, of course, not straight edge after all, largely because I'm 'older' (Straight Edgers tend to be between 16 and 21, the age at which drinking in the United States becomes legal and therefore likely to snag many teens tired of straight edge stricture). Furthermore, I don't hang with a straight edge crowd, don't slam or mosh, don't vilify (or, worse, physically attack) carnivores, smokers or drinkers, and don't particularly like the music of any of the official straight edge bands. Not only does straight edge have nothing to teach me about my personal health or my country's substance abuse problems, but I don't even care that the vast majority of my acquaintances enjoy fine wine and other alcoholic beverages, that a few of them smoke cigarettes, that others eat hot dogs and barbecue ribs, that a couple of them adore Fleetwood Mac (those sex-and-drug fiends), and that all the unattached singles among them would happily indulge in a one-night stand with a beautiful stranger.

It would seem easy to stick straight edge into its own unique post-punk category of protest music and leave it there, its bands advocating its three-tiered lifestyle – 'Don't smoke / Don't drink / Don't fuck', in the foundational words of Ian MacKaye, composer of Minor Threat's one-minute and fourteen-second standard 'Out of Step (with the World)' – and its adherents forever stoking the us/them polarity upon which most fanatical causes pivot. But straight edge is bedevilled by enough important inconsistencies striking at the root of its principles that the student of rock – always on the lookout for the fractures that are both the source and the sign of rock's tendency to fall to pieces before our very eyes – will with caution approach, as it were, the edge of the mosh-pit, into which he will insert a foot in order to get a taste of the danger inside the maelstrom, then pull back in time to preserve some degree of objectivity in his account of the experience.[3]

And exactly what is the nature of the pre-eminent fracture in straight edge, the one inconsistency that – even to a person predisposed to live the clean life that straight edge espouses – invites doubt, undermines its doctrines and reveals a mission faltering on naivety (at best) and monomania (at worst)? It's an inconsistency that diverts us from the cliché that since youth are 'supposed' to be rebellious, then youth music (including straight edge, naturally) should reflect this rebelliousness in lifestyle (by enjoying sex and drugs) as well as sound (by enjoying rock 'n' roll). Working from the premise that in its ideal, transcendent state, rock music is a protest against the dull duties of adulthood and related curses like repression, routine, conformity, straight values and monochrome existence in general, we have no choice but to trace the flaw inherent in straight edge to its conclusion; thus, since 1954 rock music has been, to repeat, a form of protest music. Punk rock, commencing in the mid-1970s, was a subgenre of rock music that accelerated the speed, made explicit the content and rendered dissonant the tone of this protest. Hardcore, an offshoot of punk rock commencing in the early 1980s, heightened punk's aggression, in the process rendering its themes of protest even more lethal, by cranking up the volume, increasing lyrical explicitness and picking up the pace (while punk tempos were fast, hardcore tempos were manic). Along with hardcore came a subgenre of a subgenre of a subgenre: straight edge. And it was at this time, in the interior dynamics of rock's ever more narrow, more compressed, more idiosyncratic subgenres that the aforementioned fracture developed.

The birth of straight edge was coincident with the birth of hardcore. Although musically compatible, these two strands of post-punk could coexist for only so long because they weren't ideologically compatible. Straight edge is a subgenre that strains to exist in a realm of mutual exclusivity. Minor Threat is the classic example. This band could be said to define both hardcore and straight edge. Consequently, it's no wonder that, as Michael Azerrad puts it, 'Minor Threat has a comparatively small legacy – two years [1981–1983] and twenty-five songs' (2001, p. 156). Despite this modest output and brief career, over the next 20 years the seeds of straight edge planted by Minor Threat flourished in a small out-of-the-way section of the hardcore/post-punk garden that during the 1980s and 1990s was otherwise overrun with the nettles and weeds of alcohol, drugs and sex. As we have seen, straight edge (whose bands, naturally, tended to burn out quickly) steeled itself against these excesses. In effect, straight edge was (is) a protest against a protest. But if to protest straight society is, by definition, one of the main things that rock 'n' roll does, then straight edge, by condemning (even if they should be condemned!) the sex-and-drug values that permeate rock music, deprives itself of credibility. It negates the essence of rock 'n' roll itself. At once a distillation and dilution of protest (rock → punk → hardcore → straight edge), straight edge is a highly specialized form of rock 'n' roll that founders as much on its self-consciousness (Straight Edgers identify themselves by marking the back of their hands with an X) as its self-righteousness. It might not be overstating the case to say that because of the irony of its (inadvertent) anti-rock attitude, an irony rendered doubly ironical by the intense volume, speed and youth-centred egoism derived from its hardcore origins (in other words, this stuff *does* sound like rock music), nothing straight edge says or does can be taken seriously by anyone who loves rock 'n' roll.[4] Nor would it be an exaggeration to suggest that, for these same reasons, straight edge must also fall flat as protest music.

Let's switch figures by comparing rock music to a pirate ship c. 1550. This ship is crawling with desperate ruffians in flight from the mores of conventional society. In conditions of unfettered riot and debauchery, these mariners (who, not incidentally, play an important economic role in the society that sponsors them) indulge their animal appetites in ways that would scandalize the good citizens back home. Our buccaneers are votaries of sexual depravity, Virginia tobacco and Barbados rum. Somehow finding himself on board this rock 'n' roll Jolly Roger, the Straight Edger is the equivalent of a one- or two-man mutiny – laughable, insane – mounted against the captain and his dissolute crew. He doesn't stand a chance. In short, it's as impossible to imagine a privateer manned by sober, celibate buccaneers as it is to imagine the rock 'n' roll roster peopled exclusively by sober, celibate performers. A mutiny on board the pirate ship of rock 'n' roll could only be termed an aberration, an anomaly, a futile endeavour. Needless to say, the vast majority of rock 'n' rollers (and their fans) are not exemplars of the kind of dissipation we associate with the buccaneers of yore, but the analogy holds insofar as straight edge's extremists are outraged by even the slightest use of the kinds of substances for which any self-respecting pirate would have traded his mother or father. As for unrestrained libido, nothing could stop a band of sixteenth-century pirates from debauching the widows of men slaughtered in a raid. And a post-concert rock 'n' roll party (minus the cutlasses and pikes) without the erotic antics of David Lee Roth, Iggy Pop, Pamela Des Barres, Janis Joplin, The Rolling Stones, Led Zeppelin and The Eagles would be equally unthinkable.

And yet this fanciful image of the Straight Edger bounded by superior numbers of hedonists belies the fact that Straight Edgers will as often as not defend their turf, with physical force if necessary. Photographs of groups such as Cold As Life, Zero Tolerance, Agnostic Front and Unconquered portray burly dudes who, except for their shorter hair, wouldn't look out of place at a summit of motorcycle gangs. Meanwhile, bands such as Strife, Buried Alive and Youth of Today sport an athletic, preppy look not devoid of menace. In sXe circles, to be an animal-loving teetotaller with a taste for hardcore is not inconsistent with aggression, hostility, militancy or even murder. In 1999 *Time* magazine followed straight edge's definitive black-eye story as it unfolded in Salt Lake City, Utah, where three Straight Edgers were being tried for the homicide of a 15-year-old male. The victim 'was attacked with a bat, a knife and police batons ... Local police say [the victim] got into an exchange of taunts with kids on the street. Police insist it was neither gang nor racially motivated, but in the brawl that ensued, Straight Edgers squared off against non-Straight Edgers, and racial slurs were heard' (Lopez, 1999, p. 37). A dead teenager resulted.

Apropos of violence, one Salt Lake Straight Edger with a history of arrests for fighting told Steve Lopez that 'Edgers won't back down if anyone "talks sh—."' But as for cruising around looking to beat people up, he says, "that's a lot of crap"' (1999, p. 37). Perhaps the youngster was protesting too much; the evidence suggests that Straight Edgers are anything but passive in the testing-ground of teen strength. In the same report, Lopez whips up anti-sXe sentiment in his opening paragraph, which introduces American readers to Josh Anderson and Randy Haselton: 'The boys hooked up with Straight Edge, an anti-drug gang of middle-class kids, and discovered new passions [outside their churches]. Josh became a vegan and firebombed a McDonald's; Randy enjoys beating the tar out of people' (1999, p. 36). In 2000 *U.S. News and World Report* zeroed in on another Salt Lake Straight Edge story to go along with the Anderson case. In this instance two Straight Edgers had just been sentenced to five years in prison for bombing a fur supplier's building (Cannon, 2000, p. 30). Bad publicity for straight edge, for sure, but compensating for charges that the national media were exaggerating their fanaticism is Sarah Thornton's argument that '[y]outh resent approving mass mediation of their culture but relish the attention conferred by media condemnation. How else might one turn difference into defiance, lifestyle into social upheaval, leisure into revolt?' (1996, p. 129). It seems that Straight Edgers should thank *Time* and company for their lurid reporting.

It's certain, whether or not Thornton is right when she says '[a] tabloid front page, however distorted, ... can turn the most ephemeral fad into a lasting development' (1996, p. 132), that the media's extreme examples mirror the fact that straight edge is a culture predicated on such extremity that many of its peaceful followers, who are obviously partial to the firebomb instrumentation and vocals of sXe recordings, will be forced to bear the stigma of animosity clinging to the scene. Some insiders bewail this state of affairs. In 1998, having retired from straight edge because of escalating violence in the hardcore community, veteran guitarist Duncan Barlow (Endpoint, Deathwatch, By the Grace of God) told Ryan Downey of *Punk Planet*, 'Straightedge was never about, "I don't drink, I'm going to punch you," it was about, "These are my personal beliefs. I don't need your poison. My mind is clear." But your mind can't be clear if you're addicted to violence' (2001, p. 311). A few years later, speaking with *Punk Planet*'s Daniel Sinker, Ian MacKaye pondered the problem of violence:

I had this idea [in the mid-1980s] that violence was a form of really direct communication and was a way of underscoring the sincerity of the music. But

ultimately what was happening was that people were getting *stomped*. That's when
I said *I* will not fight, and I will not have people fighting at my [Fugazi's] shows ...
I confronted what I felt I had contributed to ... (Quoted in Sinker, 2004, p. 34)

In any event, fighting accomplished nothing: 'During the '80s, people thought
that the way to fight the virus [of ignorance] was to fight the violent people. But
you could eradicate every one of them and there would be a thousand more'
(quoted in Sinker, 2004, p. 35). MacKaye's mature views understate the evidence
that he had been one of a core group of 'Georgetown punks [who as early as
1981] had a reputation as brawlers' (quoted in Andersen and Jenkins, 2001, p.
79). That year, after a set-to at a Black Flag concert in New York City, MacKaye
boasted, 'That made the night so fun for us. Those motherfuckers were leaving
with blood pouring' (quoted in Andersen and Jenkins, p. 83). In his defence,
however, we must remember that MacKaye became embroiled in clashes because
'people wanted to fight me to prove I was wrong' *vis-à-vis* the straight edge creed
(quoted in Andersen and Jenkins, p. 113).

In his analysis of the slamdancing and moshing that define/d New York
hardcore club life, William Tsitsos puts his finger on the ideology of animosity
that permeates straight edge culture. Tied into his thesis that subtle differences in
the dynamics of rebellion are expressed in hardcore dance styles is the insight
that, beginning in the late 1980s, the second generation of Straight Edgers 'began
to see maintaining self-control less as a means to aid fighting the mainstream and
more as an end in itself. ... [T]hey began to advocate not just self-control, but
also control over others. ... [They] were rebelling with the ultimate goal of
becoming agents of control with the power to impose rules on others' (Tsitsos,
1999, p. 404). It's a short step from this point to this one: 'New York City straight
edge shows became legendary for their brutality' (1999, p. 410). Prowling the
clubs to conduct interviews with adolescents who had done the unexpected –
abjured sex, drugs, cigarettes and alcohol – Tsitsos concluded that, for these
youngsters, 'the venting of individual aggression' (1999, p. 410) was the
rationale for participation in the hardcore mosh-pit. But more telling than this
blunt and even predictable observation was this psychological insight: 'In
developing moshing, the New York straight edgers could have maintained the
elements of slamdancing which promote pit unity, but doing so would have
come at the expense of demonstrating power and control. Forced to choose
between strength and unity, they chose strength' (1999, p. 412). In essence, the
moshers believe 'the object of aggression is the disorder and chaos symbolized
in part by the pit itself, and this disorder must be purged' (1999, pp. 412–13).[5]
And purging requires intimidation and assault. Such methods of control are in
keeping with an anecdote about a college student in Utah who found himself
beset with brass knuckles and a sword after he inadvertently asked a Straight
Edger for a match to light his cigarette (Lopez, 1999, p. 37). Mary Pileggi, in her
dissertation 'No Sex, No Drugs, Just Hardcore Rock', shares a similar anecdote

about a boy who invited retaliation for daring to smoke a cigarette at a straight edge show.

On 1984's *The Crew*, 7 Seconds articulates the Straight Edger's willingness to fight (whether defensively or offensively isn't, however, clear). In 'The Crew' vocalist Kevin Seconds yelps, 'We'll raise our voice and blast right through / We'll stop the ones who fuck it up / And show the world that they can't stop the crew.' Even more specifically pugilistic is 'Clenched Fists, Black Eyes': 'We'll keep on fighting, 'Til old ways are dead / ... We're aiming for a different goal / Succeeding where the hippies failed / ... We'll be more than a drugged out threat!' In 'Red and Black' the band threatens vandalism instead of battery, promising to 'attack in red and black [cans of paint] / Cover the buildings, the walls and the street / ... Graveyard graffiti this whole fuckin' city.' The band Gorilla Biscuits has this to say in 'Finish What You Started': 'Want to fight, see the light / Punch him out, he'll just bleed.' Other examples of the fighting spirit crop up in tunes by Minor Threat ('Stand Up', 'Bottled Violence', 'Small Man, Big Mouth'), No Innocent Victim ('Never Face Defeat'), Sumthin' To Prove ('Shallow Grave'), Raid ('Above the Law', 'Words of War'), Earth Crisis ('Smash or Be Smashed'), Judge ('Bringin' It Down') and Youth of Today ('Understand'). Beyond these specific examples of provocation, generally delivered in all but indecipherable barking howls buoyed by ear-splitting guitars and drums, the prevailing tone of straight edge is a confusing blend of fury, accusation, self-doubt, self-esteem, disgust, pessimism and splenetic self-martyrdom.

Still, it's a curious fact that, discounting Christian rock, straight edge – the most judgemental (intolerant, dogmatic, quick to defend/offend with fists) subgenre of rock music – elicits little, if any, counterjudgemental responses from musicologists. As a rule, academic critics of straight edge don't rise to the occasion offered by straight edge youngsters proselytizing from a position that is equal parts arrogance and inexperience, perhaps because, to these scholars, the decrees of straight edge seem to be above question or perhaps because these scholars believe that, to do their work well, they must wear the mantle of *noblesse oblige*. It's also possible that the brunt of straight edge music matters less to them than the subcultural capital that demands explication. Whatever the reason, objective analysis of straight edge precludes counter-opinion. Dick Hebdige probably has this academic lightness of touch in mind when declaring that 'we, the sociologists and interested straights, threaten to kill with kindness the forms which we seek to elucidate' (1979, p. 139). This may be his way of saying that a tough subculture deserves a tough critic.

But what exactly are the critics saying? Mary Pileggi's 1998 study, mentioned above, subtitled 'Using Bourdieu to Understand Straight-Edge Kids and Their Practices', takes an ethnographic approach in the attempt to 'describe, classify and interpret what I observed at [eight] straight-edge hardcore shows in an effort to understand straight-edge practices within that context' (1998, p. 48). Over the course of six months in 1997, Pileggi gleaned much of her data through interviews with 26 straight edge Philadelphian youths. Bourdieu's four-point model of 'field structure' helped her to:

> ... recognize broad behavioral stances regarding drugs, sex and alcohol as the elements of straight-edge *habitus*. Similarly, the acknowledged importance of hardcore music in the straight-edge scene seems to give music and its practice the characteristics of a *capital*. The political stance of straight-edge kids, particularly as it concerns animal rights, is an example of *position-taking* in the field. Finally, the emphasis on DIY reflects the general *strategy* which straight-edge kids employ to operate successfully within the social field. (Pileggi, 1998, p. 86, emphasis added)

Bourdieu also informs Sarah Thornton's classic book *Club Cultures* which, while not addressing straight edge specifically, offers some vital arguments about how to read 'subcultural' capital. Thornton coined this term in an effort to extend Bourdieu's theory of cultural, economic and social capital beyond '*his* social world of players with high volumes of institutionalized cultural capital' into a 'subspecies of capital operating within other less privileged domains', specifically youth dance cultures (Thornton, 1996, p. 11). Deep in the heart of London clubland to conduct her research in/to these domains, Thornton has an experience that can only strike the straight edge scholar as at once amusing and perilous. Trying to gain credibility with a scenester named Kate, Thornton accepts a glass of champagne, then goes into the restroom where Kate divides the contents of a capsule of Ecstasy: 'I put my share in my glass and drink. I'm not a personal fan of drugs – I worry about my brain cells. But they're a fact of this youth culture, so I submit myself to the experiment in the name of thorough research (thereby confirming every stereotype of the subcultural sociologist)' (Thornton, 1996, p. 89). Despite her immersion in a promiscuous, drug-saturated subculture, in the following passage Thornton may as well be speaking about Straight Edgers in addition to clubbers and ravers:

> Subcultural capital is the linchpin of an alternative hierarchy in which the axes of age, gender, sexuality and race are all employed in order to keep the determinations of class, income and occupation at bay. Interestingly, the social logic of subcultural capital reveals itself most clearly by what it dislikes and by what it emphatically isn't. The vast majority of clubbers and ravers distinguish themselves against the mainstream. (Thornton, 1996, p. 105)

We're familiar with what it, straight edge, dislikes, and we know the lengths to which Straight Edgers will go to hold their ground in defiance of what they emphatically aren't.

In their overview of straight edge culture (they cover doctrine, reasons for abstinence, symbols, music, cyberspace), Jesse Helton and William Staudenmeier (2002) use comments posted on sXe websites to conclude that 'conventional alcohol/drug organizations in the public and private sector [may] reach out to use straight edge as a strategic resource for youth abstinence' (2002,

p. 468), suggesting that straight edge's creed of individual self-control may have, despite (or because of) all the evidence of fanaticism and aggression, beneficial social effects. Meanwhile, Robert Wood's article '"Nailed to the X"' examines 600 straight edge songs. '[T]hrough a process of thematic classification', he explains, 'this study utilizes straightedge music lyrics and other subcultural artifacts as means of delineating historical transitions in the norms, values and beliefs which comprise a straightedge frame of reference' (Wood, 1999, p. 136). Thus we learn about straight edge opposition to all forms of intoxication, its militancy, its vegetarian sympathies, its disgust with backsliders and its apocalyptic prophecies. Similar to Pileggi's observation that 'straight-edge kids should not be viewed as a cohesive or monolithic group but as agents sharing interests and beliefs in the field of straight-edge' (Pileggi, 1998, p. 52), Wood backs off from reifying the movement, deciding that straight edge 'is a concept that exists only insofar as individuals subsume themselves collectively within its label and thereby impute it with meaning' (Wood, 1999, 146). All of these writers stress the preliminary, unfinished nature of their research, echoing Darrell Irwin's comment that '[f]urther analysis is necessary before a more mature picture of Straight Edge can be developed' (1999, p. 377). He wrote this in 1999, rather late to be struggling with a definitive account of a fairly simple subgenre.

A less tentative study of the subject is Beth Lahickey's *All Ages: Reflections on Straight Edge* (1997), essentially a collection of interviews with key participants. Too broad to summarize here, it's nevertheless possible to pinpoint major themes, notably the preoccupation with the declining scene. Richie Birkenhead's departure from Youth of Today coincided with signs that this subculture 'had really started to turn into a really ugly jock-like scene. It had become exactly what I thought it had started out as the antithesis of, which was this elitist exclusionary movement full of stupid soap operas between guys and girls' (quoted in Lahickey, 1997, p. 20). Ray Cappo (Youth of Today, Shelter) found that, in the 1990s straight edge became less a matter of 'self-purification' than of 'ego trips and fashion' (quoted in Lahickey, 1997, p. 31). Speaker after speaker bemoans the in-clubbiness, preachiness, insularity, elitism, brawling and image-mongering that infected straight edge. Genuine Straight Edgers had trouble accepting a truth expressed by Dick Hebdige: '[D]ifferent youths bring different degrees of commitment to a subculture. It can represent a major dimension in people's lives ... or it can be a slight distraction, a bit of light relief from the monotonous but none the less paramount realities of school, home and work' (p. 122). Apparently contributing to straight edge's decline was this lack of commitment, the backsliding that occurred among musicians and older fans unable to live up to the dictum 'straight edge for life'. But such lapsing was fated to be the outcome of straight edge's built-in inflexibility. 'For many of the Straight Edgers', writes Jennifer Steinhauer, 'the world is in black and white: the selfish, hateful meat eaters versus those who eat $4-a-box veggie burgers, the sober versus the drunk, with nothing in between. Although Straight Edgers admit that not every drink leads to drunkenness, they will not tolerate the smallest sip' (1995, p. 36). One Straight Edger told Steinhauer, 'You can't be Straight Edge off-and-on' (1995, p. 36).

Self-defeating intransigence isn't universal among Straight Edgers. According to Richie Birkenhead, 'to judge people based on the fact that they live a different lifestyle than you do ... is completely wrong' (quoted in Lahickey, 1997, p. 24). Moreover, Jordan Cooper (owner of Revelation Records) told Lahickey, 'Lines being drawn doesn't make sense to me ... [A] personal choice about drinking, drugs and sex to be an aspect of one's personality or music is fine, but for it to be the basis of it or an obsession is silly' (quoted in Lahickey, 1997, pp. 56, 57). These voices of reason were lost in a discourse of disgust directed at those considered too weak to wear the X without wavering. To repeat, fanaticism didn't help the cause. As Craig O'Hara noted in 1999, 'Straight Edge has become (much like the Skinheads) a place for homophobic, mainstream macho attitudes to be injected into the Punk scene. While it is impossible and illogical to condemn those who choose not to drink, it is necessary to condemn those who choose not to think' (1999, p. 148). Things had become so bad by the 1990s that O'Hara was left saying about Earth Crisis what could have been said about most straight edge music: '[T]he overtly reactionary puritan bullshit they espouse is only good for a mocking laugh at best' (1999, p. 149).

One topic missing from all but a few voices in the literature on straight edge is what its advocates think about rock 'n' roll music made and consumed (as most of it is) by non-Straight Edgers. Could the silence surrounding this topic be a form of denial? Are Straight Edgers afraid to look into the closet where they themselves store compact discs recorded by non-straight rockers? Afraid to suspend their sXe loyalty by enjoying rock music by drug-users, drunks, rakes and bimbos? Afraid to deal with the conundrum of hating drugs and drink and promiscuity but loving the music of, say, Van Halen, the Flaming Lips, Pink Floyd, Jimi Hendrix, Guided by Voices and a thousand other medicated, oversexed burnouts? No, not all of them are afraid; not all of them are completely intimidated by straight edge's either/or ideology. Hedging his opinion, Ian MacKaye at least admitted: 'I like Lou Reed ... The junkie aesthetic is all good and well for intellectual society, but there are a lot of people who follow things on the fashion tip and sometimes don't make it back' (quoted in Lahickey, 1997, p. 106). Kevin Seconds, another prominent Straight Edger, refused to condemn his pot-smoking or drinking friends (Lahickey, 1997, 161). And at age 22, Sterling Wilson (No for an Answer, Inside Out) discovered AC/DC. He confessed to Lahickey that 'those straight edge bands are good, but they just don't drive me the way AC/DC does' (quoted in Lahickey, 1997, p. 220). It should be noted that Wilson 'lost the edge' (by starting to drink) at the same time AC/DC entered his life. That 'allowances' for non-straight culture have been aired by Straight Edgers puts a spin on one of the oldest and thorniest questions in aesthetics. Instead of asking whether or not mind-altering substances (and/or sexual excess) spur creativity, it now asks, 'What are Straight Edgers supposed to do about music made by artists who couldn't care less about clean veins, clean lungs or clean consciences in terms of a carnivorous diet?'

This question is in fact one of the major cruxes in straight edge. Again speaking as a platonic, rather than technical, Straight Edger, let me note that I enjoy – indeed, have been *saved* by – rock played by junkies, drunks and sex-addicts. 'Sister Ray', 'Heroin', 'Street Hassle' and *Berlin* are cornerstones of my music library collection; I have no qualms helping to fund (by purchasing her records) P.J. Harvey's need to chronicle the adventures of her libido; I think a world without The Beatles, The Kinks, The Who and The Rolling Stones would be a much sadder place; I don't fault Kurt Cobain, Arthur Lee, Jeff Tweedy, Nick Drake, Mike Bloomfield, Ian Curtis and 50 other masters for their indulgences and addictions (and let's not overlook jazz masters such as Rollins, Coltrane, Evans, Pepper, Miles, Bird, Dizzy and Lady Day); and if the opportunity arose I would spend the night in the arms of Courtney Love.[6] No drugs or alcohol? No 'Lucy in the Sky with Diamonds', no 'Good Vibrations', no 'Purple Haze'. There would be no *Help!* (a marijuana album), no *There's a Riot Goin' On* (cocaine), no *Blonde on Blonde* (amphetamine), no *Piper at the Gates of Dawn* (acid), no *Tonight's the Night* (heroin), no *Yankee Hotel Foxtrot* (pain killers), no *Taking Drugs to Make Music to Take Drugs To* (who knows?), no Little Feat, Replacements, Butthole Surfers, Ramones, Bob Marley, reggae, shoegazing or Britpop. There would be no Queens of the Stone Age's *[Rated] R* (2000), which opens with this outrageous stoner chant, 'Nicotine, valium, vicodin, marijuana, ecstasy, and alcohol, cocaine'. (Does the song glamorize drugs or demonize them?) And imagine if rock were bleached of sex! Cross off thousands of songs! I like the music of such artists not because it's drenched in sex, alcohol and drugs but because it's good. Whether or not promiscuity and substances make it good is beside the point.

Not beside the point – and presumably no straight edge ideologue would be able to swallow this argument – is that the drug/alcohol element is often what invests rock 'n' roll with its gravitas (think, for starters, of Elvis, Jim, Janis, Jimi, Lowell and Kurt), what lends it tragic depth and what counteracts the genre's mindlessness and hedonism. The bitter struggle with substances and sexual licence that has cursed the lives and careers of artists from Elvis Presley to Layne Staley isn't a peripheral feature of rock 'n' roll artistry. Their successes as well as their failures – the pathos of the fall from youth and promise, the decline into artistic paralysis and then early death – revolve around the tragic flaw of substance dependency and sexual need, as surely as Oedipus's tragedy revolved around hubris or that of Achilles' revolved around rage.

This tragic dimension has its source not merely in human weakness, but also in the yearning to attain utopia. This is the place to trot out Aldous Huxley's famous claims about the wonders of mescaline. In a culture plagued by Oxycontin, binge-drinking and recreational drug use, Huxley may sound hopelessly romantic, as anachronistic as Flower Power or Stephen Stills's 'Love the One You're With', yet his treatise on transcendence reminds us that it was once possible to imagine that spiritual bliss could be gained through natural means:

> To be shaken out of the ruts of ordinary perception [through mescalin or some other drug], to be shown for a few timeless hours the outer and the inner world, not as they appear to an animal obsessed with survival or to a human being obsessed with words and notions, but as they are apprehended, directly and unconditionally, by Mind at Large – his is an experience of inestimable value to everyone and especially to the intellectual. (Huxley, 1954, p. 73)

Implicit in this sentiment, which would be totally lost on the Straight Edger, is the tragic depth to which I referred. Transcendence should, and could, have been the purpose of drug use (and sexual activity too), rather than mere animal pleasure in getting high or 'escaping' one's boredom, exhaustion or loneliness. Huxley – who, significantly, frowned on smoking, bingeing and pill-popping (1954, pp. 66–67]) – realized that '[t]he urge to transcend self-conscious selfhood is ... a principal appetite of the soul' (1954, p. 67). Eternally thwarted in our attempts to transcend ourselves, we human beings 'are apt to resort to religion's chemical surrogates-alcohol and "goof pills" in the modern West, alcohol and opium in the East, hashish in the Mohammedan world, alcohol and marijuana in Central America, alcohol and coca in the Andes, alcohol and the barbiturates in the more up-to-date regions of South America' (1954, p. 67). While Straight Edgers bellow about the power of choice and personal strength, they seem oblivious to the universal and timeless interrelationship between transcendence and addiction. Listen to them: 'I'm a person just like you / But I've got better things to do / Than sit around and smoke dope / 'Cause I know I can cope,' yelps Ian MacKaye in 'Straight Edge'; 'Abusing, misusing, you're out of control / Your mind, spirit and body will take their toll / A slave to your senses, I see nothing more / 'Cause temporary pleasure is what you strive for,' screams Ray Cappo of Youth of Today in 'What Goes Around'; 'Civil soldiers sworn by abstinence to withhold no tolerance / Our war is on, the talk must quit / And all the guilty are gonna get hit / ... I'm a walking protest full of ambition and fueled by relentless resent / ... All users provoke my animosity,' shrieks Steve Lovitt of Raid in 'Words of War'; 'Killing brain cells, wasting away / Killing brain cells, pure misery / Killing brain cells, renounce, relapse / ... Through free will it was chosen, can't pin it on anyone else / Can't pin it on anyone else, except yourself,' howls Karl Buechner of Earth Crisis in 'Killing Brain Cells'.

Bewildered, if not enraged, by Huxley's philosophical defence of certain drugs, Straight Edgers would be no less enlightened by Richard Blum's psychological reading of drug use:

> Pharmaceutical materials do not dispense themselves and the illicit drugs are rarely given away, let alone forced on people. Consequently, the menace lies within the

person, for there would be no drug threat without a drug attraction. ... People are fascinated by drugs – or rather by their own and the mass-media fantasies about drugs – because they are attracted to the states and conditions drugs are said to produce. That is another side to the fear of being disrupted; it is the desire for release, for escape, for magic, and for ecstatic joys. That is the derivation of the menace in drugs – their representation as keys to forbidden kingdoms inside ourselves. The Dreadful in the drug is the *dreadful* in ourselves. (Blum, 1970, p. 335)[7]

Blind and deaf to these complexities, Straight Edgers polarize the issue *ad nauseum* and end up sounding as one-dimensional and fatuous as the religious pamphleteer David Noebel, who in 1969 lacerated The Beatles for what he believed was their leading role in rock's subversion of American adolescents. Deciding that 'any record company or rock and roll group that lends respectability to [LSD, marijuana, amphetamines, and barbiturates] is not only immoral but criminal' (1969, p. 17), Noebel despairs that the Beatles '[are] gods to millions of our teen-agers today' (1969, p. 21). The kids mimic the gods; thus, according to Noebel, sixties kids who liked the Beatles also turned into anti-Christian drug addicts and sex fiends. (Noebel also exposes the Fab Four's alleged promiscuity.) Add to such 'reasoning' Bob Larson's announcement (in 1967) that '[l]yrics of today's rock songs are a large part of the cause of the tidal wave of promiscuity, venereal disease, illegitimate births and political upheaval' (Larson, 1967, p. 22), and two questions arise for the rock fan conversant with straight edge lyrics and lifestyle. First, is it possible that Straight Edgers are as far removed from reality as the two crusaders, David Noebel and Bob Larson? Second, are Straight Edgers capable of having good record collections?

In a 600-page study of psychedelic rock, Jim DeRogatis writes that, with lysergic acid, fabulous 'feelings *could* be evoked – onstage, but even more effectively in the recording studio – with circular, mandala-like song structures; sustained or droning melodies; altered and effected instrumental sounds; reverb, echoes, and tape delays that created a sense of space, and layered mixes that rewarded repeated listening by revealing new and mysterious elements' (2003, p. 12). Quite a recommendation for LSD! And although DeRogatis stresses that stimulants, hallucinogens or depressants aren't needed to create rock or any other kind of music, his list of top psychedelic records suggests the opposite. Most, if not all, of them spell speed, booze, acid, smack, downer and/or coke. In fact, they're standing advertisements to the ubiquity of drugs in the creation of rock 'n' roll. DeRogatis' list would swell if it encompassed bands outside the already broad category of psychedelia (whose main drug, LSD, isn't a creative element in dozens of albums he lists) – bands synonymous with drugs and alcohol (and sex) such as The Eagles, Fleetwood Mac and Nirvana. Derogatis seems unsure whether or not to do a full-bore dance with Dionysius. 'Drugs can be a means to reaching [ecstasy]', he allows, 'but they aren't the only one, and as many psychedelic rockers say that they've taken them as say that they haven't.

Psychedelic rock doesn't mean "drug rock," but rock that is inspired by a philosophical approach implied by the literal meanings of "psychedelic" as "mind-revealing" and "soul-manifesting"' (2003, p. 15). DeRogatis plays coy, even cagey, here, insisting that psychedelia isn't technically a matter of drugs anyway, that it's an attitude – 'accepting no rules, breaking down boundaries, and opening doors whenever possible' (2003, p. 17). The problem is he may as well be describing the attitude of punk rock – that is, the antithesis of psychedelia.

Why is this issue a fatal soft-spot in the straight edge armoury? For aesthetic reasons. Since Straight Edgers condemn the use of acid, alcohol and cigarettes onstage and in the studio too – presumably they also condemn the pepperoni pizzas ordered during late-night recording sessions – then over 90 per cent of rock albums must be tainted for them. Refusing to listen to 90 per cent of music would mean to cram oneself in a corner, there to sneer at the panorama passing by. David Schulz, a Straight Edger from age 19 to 29, had such cramping in mind when, in an interview with me, he addressed aesthetics:

> With the exception of Minor Threat, I don't much like any straight edge music at all. Maybe it has something to do with the fact that straight edge starts with a dogma and then the music is built around that, as if the music itself were an afterthought. For me, Minor Threat was a hardcore band whose members happened to be straight edge. All the others were straight edge bands first and foremost. When I go back and listen to Youth of Today or Judge, I have to laugh because it all sounds very silly, very contrived. Most dogmatic straight edgers, musicians and fans alike, by and large ignore most music outside of their microcosm. I think this is why straight edge, after a couple-few years, began to suck so badly. The 'movement' has suffered under the second law of thermodynamics – in a closed system, things will tend to break down. If all you listen to are straight edge bands that are near duplicates of one another, you're not likely to grow in any direction. (Schulz, 2004, personal interview)

It speaks volumes that no important punk band or performer cites straight edge as an influence on his or her art, and that neither *Magnet* nor *The Big Takeover*, two long-standing alternative rock magazines, published in Philadelphia and New York, respectively, has published articles on straight edge. The subgenre simply doesn't matter. Yet Straight Edgers don't seem able (or willing) to measure the discrepancy between their grandstanding and their low impact on rock music. Worse, it's unlikely that they can gauge the painful irony in the fact that there's no straight edge without hardcore, no hardcore without punk, and no punk without drug lords such as the New York Dolls, Iggy and the Stooges and the Velvet Underground. Although hard to fathom, it's probable that most Straight Edgers have never heard the extraordinary music of these bands. 'Heroin', for example. Too squeamish about heroin to listen to 'Heroin', a pinnacle of rock composition and performance, they will never know that 'Heroin' doesn't celebrate heroin, that it doesn't turn listeners into heroin addicts and that their hardcore straight edge wouldn't exist without it and *The Velvet*

Underground and Nico, an album reeling with vignettes about sex and drugs. How many hundreds of other songs and bands have gone unheeded by Straight Edgers?

Straight edge music failed to develop beyond basic hardcore. Minor Threat was never surpassed. Band after band pummels (with fists marked X!) the listener; guitars burn and screech; drums and cymbals are walloped; voices bark like death-camp Dobermans running after skulking Jews. In hardcore, melody was always already a tentative musical element; in straight edge, it has been annihilated. Straight edge composers eschew melody the way Gestapo parade organizers eschewed flowers, balloons and floats. Like a phalanx of fascists, the music is all hard surfaces, scowls, disapproval and brute precision. Yet one can't help but listen to it in fascination, tracing with awe a given band's single-mindedness. When youngsters are this fanatical, additional fascination lies in the incongruity between age and purpose, between mental development and messianism. These kids are poised to sacrifice everything without having attained the faintest idea of the varieties of human experience or of their own future changes. Consequently, the lyrics, if not dealing specifically with straight edge fetishes, are almost uniformly negative cliché-ridden allegories of the singer's struggles with the evils of modern life.

After all the raging and fighting and ranting and browbeating, perhaps the cruellest irony about straight edge is that its efforts may be in vain. Some anecdotal evidence aside, there's nothing to prove that it has changed more than a few lives for the better – lives that may have been changed in time anyway. Moreover, who can calculate the number of kids who rejected straight edge out of hand, who hastened to rebel against its elitism, dogmatism and self-righteousness? R. Serge Denisoff's comments about rhetorical protest music seem applicable to straight edge: 'This type of song can be ... useful ... in promoting cohesion within the membership of a social movement, but may have very little effect on non-members and in some circumstances may negatively affect non-participants' (1983, p. 61). The last thing most teenagers want to hear is another lecture on the evils of loose sex and alcohol intake, and they'd like to eat their hamburgers in peace. More to the point is Denisoff's discovery, after extensive research, that 'there is little, if any, concrete or empirical evidence that songs *do* in fact have an independent impact upon attitudes in the political arena' (1983, p. 149). And so if Jolanta Pekacz can answer her own question, 'Did rock smash the Wall?' with an unequivocal 'no', along with the indictment that '[s]elf-aggrandizement and self-glorification feed rock mythology by presenting rock as a victorious force against an allegedly monstrous political system' (1994, p. 48), then there's little reason to believe straight edge can have the slightest impact on something much bigger than communism – to wit, the human being's need to medicate him or herself with alcohol, drugs, sex and nicotine. Straight edge's chest-beating is in vain, a major miscalculation in moral and aesthetic terms. Straight Edgers could learn from Joe Pernice's recent comments in *The Big Takeover*:

'I've always thought of art as trying to make something beautiful. Not pretty all the
time, but having a beauty to it without getting too philosophical ... When I start to
write songs that have ventured into the land of politics, it's like I'm swinging a
sledgehammer, there's nothing subtle about it. It still has to be beautiful or you feel
like someone's preaching to you.' (Pernice, 2004, p. 205)

In a recent issue of *Magnet*, letter-writer Dax Riner dressed down a member
of the Strokes for eating *foie gras*. Riner details the torture that ducks and geese
suffer to satisfy the cravings of a pampered rock star. 'All this', fumes Riner, 'so
Valensi can feel like a "viking"' (Riner, 2004). It's a powerful letter, with facts
about the meat industry that are impossible to deny. Proving himself one-quarter
straight edge, Riner could conceivably have written about mindless sex, binge-
drinking, smoking or the drug-*du jour* with equal power. But if Riner's outrage
were turned into straight edge music, he would inevitably come across as one-
dimensional, arrogant and fanatical, in tune with even the best of the official
Straight Edgers. Yes, it's unfortunate, tragic, pathetic, disgusting, shocking and
ultimately senseless that tens of millions of Americans are continually drugged,
drunk, smoke-filled, oversexed and tainted with the blood of dead animals. But
straight edge rock 'n' roll won't make a dent in a problem of such magnitude.
Harnessing rock music to voice their protest against such senselessness, Straight
Edgers paradoxically make crooked (curved?) life look (and sound) a lot better
than it actually is.

This essay is dedicated to the memory of David Schulz.

Notes

1. Ian MacKaye, founder of Minor Threat, penned 'Straight Edge' in 1980 while a
    member of the Teen Idles, and the straight edge movement started at one of TI's last
    gigs: '[T]he Idles were offered an attractive opportunity: a chance to play the 9:30
    Club [in Washington, DC], where Dody Bowers had agreed to try identifying
    underage patrons by putting a large X on their hands. The X quickly became a badge
    of honor, a signifier marking the emerging new scene ... Later the X would become
    a [*sic*] internationally recognized symbol of what became known as "Straight Edge."'
    One should note that '[f]or MacKaye ["Straight Edge"] was – and would remain –
    simply a song, not a philosophy or movement, but for others it would take on a broad
    and lasting significance' (quoted in Andersen and Jenkins, 2001, pp. 70–71, 91).
2. William Tsitsos analyses this paradox at length. He divides the alternative scene into
    three groups: the political, the apolitical, and straight edge, each with their own 'rules
    of rebellion'. He argues 'that different views regarding the best means of rebellion are
    shaped by the tension between individual and communal rebellion. Members of the
    scene confront the paradox of being part of a scene (and, therefore, a community)
    which endorses individuality' (1999, p. 399). A paradox of straight edge in particular
    is that while rejecting external (mainstream, societal) control, its followers tend to
    seek to control others. 'Ironically', writes Tsitsos, 'this places these straight edgers at
    odds with their fellow musicians of the alternative scene' (1999, p. 399).

3. This tendency to fall to pieces before the spectator's eyes is embodied by bands whose members seem to wobble on a high-wire of tension and internal division. Our fascination in watching them sway at such a height with no net beneath them increases in proportion to the brilliance of their work. Think of the Sex Pistols, *Rumours*-era Fleetwood Mac, Uncle Tupelo, Buffalo Springfield, The Verve, Dinosaur Jr, Velvet Underground, Big Star, *Abbey Road*-era Beatles, The Smiths, The Police, Guns 'n' Roses, Jane's Addiction, Oasis and The Replacements. Essentially, we want to see how long such bands can stay on the wire and how their members will fare after the inevitable fall. With straight edge, this voyeurism pertains to the subgenre itself because there are no individual sXe bands in the same artistic league as my examples.

4. This 'youth-centred egoism' is summed up in 'Young 'Til I Die' by 7 Seconds: 'I don't wanna grow up, I'm never getting old / ... I'm gonna stay young until I die.' Giving this song, whose theme is timeless in rock 'n' roll, its straight edge flavour are its swipes at alcohol and the approach of the age 21, at which point many clean kids lose the edge.

5. Jesse Helton and William Staudenmeier reach a different conclusion: 'At shows, the casual observation of an outsider might misinterpret as uncontrolled violence what goes on in the mosh pit with moshing (slam dancing) and stage diving. But within the frame of the participants, the action and body contact are controlled, and complete strangers look out for each other so that no one gets hurt; there are rules to follow, and those who break the rules are punished. This controlled contact is clearly distinguished from fights by the participants' (2002, p. 466). The authors seem so eager to defend Straight Edgers from accusations of violence that they brush aside the supposed solutions to this violence – control and punishment. But what is control if not the threat of violence? And what is punishment of violence but more violence? And why should Straight Edgers be the ones to control the scene in the first place?

6. For more on rock's power to save despite its trashiness and the wasted artists that create much of it, see my *But Is It Garbage? On Rock and Trash* (2004).

7. Like Blum, Jock Young takes a 'social and cultural' view of substance use. 'It is impossible', he writes, 'to make generalizations about the effects of drugs [including tobacco and alcohol] in a vacuum. For the effects of drugs are shaped by the culture of the user and are learned by the novice from the more sophisticated drugtaker' (1969, p. 39). Indeed, 'the detrimental effects of a drug use are closely related to the social factors which surround its use ... Even the question of whether heroin is detrimental to the individual depends on the social setting in which it is used ... Amphetamines taken by people in periods of stress (astronauts and soldiers for instance) are approved of, whereas when the same drug is taken for hedonistic reasons it is deemed socially culpable. Thus I would argue that the distinctions between habituation and addiction are fallacious in that they assume that the same drug in different social settings will have essentially similar effects. Compulsion, tolerance, psychic and physical dependence, social and individual disfunctions [*sic*], are all factors which vary not only with the drug but with the individual or group who have cause to use that drug' (1969, p. 44).

Bibliography

Anonymous (1966), 'Woody's Boy', *Newsweek*, 23 May, p. 110.

—— (1969), 'An Interview with Judy Collins', *Life*, 2 May, pp. 45–46.

—— (1990), 'The Heavy-Metal Image Doesn't Fit Iron Maiden: Vocalist Bruce Dickinson Challenges the Stereotypes with His First Solo Album', *Christian Science Monitor*, 20 August, p. 13.

—— (1992), 'The Dharma Bums: Welcome', *Snipehunt*, **11**, Spring, p. 41.

—— (1992–93), 'Five Eight: I Learned Shut Up Sky', *Snipehunt*, **14**, Winter, p. 36.

—— (1994), 'Various Artists: Live From Sid's Apartment', *Snipehunt*, **20**, Summer, p. 29.

—— (2004), 'Billy Bragg's Modest Proposal', *The Economist*, **370** (8366), p. 58.

Appadurai, Arjun (1996), *Modernity at Large: Cultural Dimensions of Globalization*, Minneapolis: University of Minnesota Press.

Andersen, Mark, and Jenkins, Mark (2001), *Dance of Days: Two Decades of Punk in the Nation's Capital*, New York: Soft Skull Press.

Ankersmit, F.R. (1996), *Aesthetic Politics*, Stanford, CT: Stanford University Press.

Arendt, Hannah (1969), *On Violence*, New York: Harcourt Brace & Co.

Arthur, Jay (1996), *Aboriginal English: A Cultural Study*, Melbourne: Oxford University Press.

Atapattu, Don (2003), 'Songs of Protest and Peace: A Guide to Protest Music, Part One', *Counter Punch,* 1 February, <http://www.counterpunch.org/atapattu02012003.html>.

Audio Evolution Network (1987), 'Advertisement for subscription to *Sound Choice*', *Sound Choice*, **7**, April, p. 6.

Audio Evolution Network (1990), 'Non-profit Cassette Distribution System Set Up', *Sound Choice*, **13**, Winter, p. 11.

Auslander, Philip (1998), 'Seeing is Believing: Live Performance and the Discourse of Authenticity in Rock Culture', *Literature and Psychology*, **44**(4), 26 January , pp. 1–16.

Australians for Native Title and Reconciliation (2004), ANTAR *Newsletter: Third World Health in the Lucky Country*, Sydney: Australians for Native Title and Reconciliation.

Azerrad, Michael (2001), *Our Band Could Be Your Life: Scenes from the American Indie Underground 1981–1991*, Boston: Little, Brown and Company.

Baez, Joan (1987), *And a Voice to Sing With*: *A Memoir*, New York: Summit Books.

Balliger, Robin (1995), 'Sounds of Resistance', in Ron Sakolsky and Fred Wei-Han Ho (eds), *Sounding Off! Music as Subversion/Resistance/Revolution*, New York: Autonomedia, pp. 13–28.

Barrett, Leonard E. (1988), *The Rastafarians: Sounds of Cultural Dissonance* (rev. edn), Boston, MA: Beacon Press Books.

Bartlett, Richard (1993), *The Mabo Decision*, Sydney: Butterworths.

Bastian, Vanessa and Laing, Dave (2003), 'Twenty Years of Music Censorship Around the World', in Martin Cloonan and Reebee Garofalo (eds), *Policing Pop*, Philadelphia: Temple University Press, pp. 46–64.

Baugh, Bruce (1993), 'Prolegomena to Any Aesthetics of Rock Music', *The Journal of*

Aesthetics and Art Criticism, **51**(1), Winter, pp. 23–29.

Bennett, Scott (1989), *Aborigines and Political Power*, Sydney: Allen & Unwin.

Berger, Lawrence M. (2000), 'The Emotional and Intellectual Aspects of Protest Music: Implications for Community Organizing Education', *Journal of Teaching in Social Work*, **20**(1–2), pp. 57–76.

Berlau, John (2003), 'Antiwar Singers Out of Tune With Public: The Entertainers Who Have Crossed the Line in Their Opposition to War with Iraq are Finding There is a High Price to Pay as Fans Reject their Anti-American Rants', *Insight on the News*, **2**(2,) May, p. 30ff.

Bessman, Jim (2003), 'Once Again, Anti-war Songs Proliferate in the U.S.', *Billboard*, **115**(12), p. 35.

Betts, Kate (2004), 'Hey, Big Spenders', *Time: Style and Design*, Fall, p. 5.

Blagg, Christopher (2004), 'Protest Song Is Back – With a Vengeance', *Christian Science Monitor,* 4 June, p. 11.

Blum, Richard H. (1970), 'On the Presence of Demons', *Society and Drugs: Social and Cultural Observations*, San Francisco: Jossey-Bass, Inc., pp. 322–41.

Borneman, W.R. (1986), 'The Cold-Drill Cassette: Oral Poetry, Sound-Text Poetry, Songs and Strange Noises', *Sound Choice*, **4**, Spring, p. 63.

Borneman, W.R. (1987), 'Kevin Campion and Thee Vision-Aires: Hobbies', *Sound Choice*, **6**, January–February, p. 45.

Bourdieu, Pierre. (1984), *Distinction: A Social Critique of the Judgment of Taste*, Cambridge, MA: Harvard University Press.

Bowers, John Waite, Ochs, Donovan J. and Jensen, Richard J. (1993), *The Rhetoric of Agitation and Control*, 2nd edn, Prospect Heights, Illinois: Waveland Press.

Bradby, Barbara (1993), 'Sampling Sexuality; Gender, Technology and the Body in Dance Music', *Popular Music* **12**(2), pp. 155–76.

Brady, Maggie (1992), *Heavy Metal: The Social Meaning of Petrol Sniffing in Australia*, Canberra: Aboriginal Studies Press.

Bragg, Billy (2004), 'Diary', *The New Statesman*, **17**(796), 1 March, p. 8.

Breen, Marcus (1994), 'I Have a Dreamtime: Aboriginal Music and Black Rights in Australia', in Simon Broughton, Mark Ellingham, David Muddyman and Richard Trillo (eds), *World Music: The Rough Guide*, London: Rough Guides, pp. 655–62.

Breiner, Laurence A. (1985–86), 'The English Bible in Jamaican Rastafarianism', *Journal of Religious Thought*, **42**(2), Fall–Winter, pp. 30–43.

Brewer, Cory (2002), Personal Interview, 6 July.

Brinkley, Alan (1987), 'Dreams of the Sixties', *New York Review of Books*, **XXXIV**(16), 22 October, pp. 10–16.

Brown, Samuel Elisha (1966), 'Treatise on the Rastafarian Movement', *Caribbean Studies*, **6**(1), April, pp. 39–40.

Bruno, John-Paul (2003), 'Where Have All the Protest Songs Gone?', *Canadian Content*, 25 February, <http://www.canadiancontent.ca/articles/022503protestsongs.html>.

Burke, Shirley M. (1977), 'Interview with Cedric Brooks', *Jamaica Journal*, **11**(1–2), August, pp. 14–17.

Burrit, Elihu (1868), *Walks in The Black Country and Its Green Border-Land*, London: Sampson Low, Son, and Marston.

Burton, Sarah (2003), 'Truth in the Hands of Artists', *AlterNet,* 24 November, <http://www.alternet.org/story.html?StoryID=17242 2003>.

Campbell, Horace (1987), *Rasta and Resistance: From Marcus Garvey to Walter Rodney*, Trenton, NJ: Africa World Press.

Cannon, Angie (2000), 'The Fur Flies in Utah: Animal Rights Movement Takes a Violent Turn', *U.S. News & World Report*, **128**(12), 27 March, p. 30.

Cantwell, Robert (1996), *When We Were Good: The Folk Revival*, Cambridge, MA: Harvard University Press.

Carson, Tom (1981), 'Joy Division Meant It', *Village Voice*, **26**, February, p. 63.

Carter, David A. (1980), 'The Industrial Workers of the World and the Rhetoric of Song', *Quarterly Journal of Speech*, **66**(4), December, **pp.** 365–74.

Cave, Damien (2003), 'Rockers Unite to Oust Bush: Moby, Henley, Matthews Ask Fans to "Get Involved"', *Rolling Stone On-line*, 26 November, <http://www.rollingstone.com/news/story/_/id/5934457>.

——— (2004), 'Memo to Elton John: Lighten Up, Sir', *New York Times*, 25 July, K3.

Central Australian Aboriginal Media Association (1989), *CAAMA: Prospectus*, Alice Springs: Central Australian Aboriginal Media Association.

——— (n.d.), *From CAAMA* (press release), Alice Springs: Central Australian Aboriginal Media Association.

Chadwell, Sean (2004), 'Inventing That "Old-Timey" Style: Southern Authenticity in *O Brother Where Art Thou?*', *Journal of Popular Film and Television*, **32**(1), Spring, pp. 2–9.

Chang, Jeff (2002), 'Is Protest Music Dead?' *Metro Silicon Valley,* 16 April, <http://www.alternet.org/story.html?StoryID=12880>.

Cheney, Joyce (1976), *All Our Lives: A Woman's Songbook*, Baltimore: Diana Press.

Chevannes, Barry (1988), 'Race and Culture in Jamaica', *World Marxist Review*, **31**(5), May, pp. 138–44.

——— (1990), 'Healing the Nation: Rastafari Exorcism of the Ideology of Racism in Jamaica', *Caribbean Quarterly*, **36**(1–2), June, pp. 59–84.

——— (1994), *Rastafari: Roots and Ideology*, New York: Syracuse University Press.

Christgau, Robert (2000), 'Woody Guthrie's Second Life', *Village Voice*, **45**(22), 6 June, p. 67.

Christie, Ian (2003), *Sound of the Beast: The Complete Headbanging History of Heavy Metal*, New York: HarperCollins.

Chuck D. (1994), Interview with Russell A. Potter, *HardC.O.R.E.*, **2**(3) September, np.

Clarke, Sebastian (1980), *Jah Music: The Evolution of the Popular Jamaican Song*, London: Heinemann Educational Books.

Clayson, Alan (1988), *Back in the High Life: A Biography of Steve Winwood*, London: Sidgwick & Jackson.

Cloonan, Martin and Garofalo, Reebee (eds) (2003), *Policing Pop*, Philadelphia: Temple University Press.

Cohen, Ronald (2000), 'Broadside Magazine and Records, 1962–1988', in Jeff Place and Ronald Cohen, *The Best of Broadside 1962–1988*, Washington, DC: Smithsonian Folkways, pp. 11–16.

Cole, Richard (1971), 'Top Songs in the Sixties', *American Behavioural Scientist*, **14**, pp. 389–400.

Collin, Matthew (1994), 'Interview with Goldie', <http://www.backtotheoldskool.co.uk/goldie.htm>, accessed 12 July 2004.

——— (1997), 'Interview with Goldie', <http://www.techno.de/mixmag/interviews/

goldie.html>, accessed 10 July 2004.

Collins, Andrew (1998), 'From Dagenham to the Dust Bowl', *The New Statesman*, **127**(4375), pp. 30–34.

—— (2003), 'Give Music a Chance: Despite Damon and Ms Dynamite, Today's Protest Singers Can't Match Dylan and Lennon', *New Statesman*, 24 February, <http://www.findarticles.com/p/articles/mi_m0FQP/is_4626_132/ai_98696022>.

Considine, J.D. and Preston, N. (1990), '70s: Led Zeppelin', *Rolling Stone*, **587**, 20 September, pp. 56–62.

Corn, David (2001), 'Where Have All the Protest Songs Gone?' *AlterNet*, 24 April, <http://www.alternet.org/story/10768>.

Coyle, Michael and Dolan, Jon (1999), 'Modeling Authenticity, Authenticating Commercial Models', in Kevin J.H. Dettmar and William Richey (eds), *Reading Rock and Roll: Authenticity, Appropriation, Aesthetics*, New York: Columbia University Press, pp. 17–35.

Cray, Ed (2004), *Ramblin' Man: The Life and Times of Woody Guthrie*, New York: W.W. Norton & Co.

Curtis, Deborah (1996), *Touching From a Distance: Ian Curtis & Joy Division*, London: Faber & Faber.

Cushman, Thomas (1991), 'Rich Rastas and Communist Rockers: A Comparative Study of the Origin, Diffusion and Defusion of Revolutionary Musical Codes', *Journal of Popular Culture*, **25**(3), pp. 17–61.

—— (1995), *Notes from Underground: Rock Music Counterculture in Russia*, Albany, NY: State University of New York Press.

Darsey, James (1991), 'From "Gay is Good" to the Scourge of AIDS: The Evolution of Gay Liberation Rhetoric, 1977–1990', *Communication Studies* **42**(1), pp. 43–66.

Davidson, Vicky (2003), 'Iron Maiden Break the Sound Barrier', *Evening Times*, Glasgow (UK), 9 December, p. 17.

Davies, Jude (1996), 'The Future of "No Future": Punk Rock and Postmodern Theory', *Journal of Popular Culture*, **29**, Spring, pp. 3–25.

Davis, Angela Y. (1998), *Blues Legacies and Black Feminism: Gertrude 'Ma' Rainey, Bessie Smith and Billie Holliday*, New York: Pantheon Books.

Davis, Michaela Angela (2004), 'Quitting Hip Hop', *Essence*, October, pp. 155.

Davis, Stephen and Simon, Peter (1982), 'A Rasta Glossary', in Stephen Davis and Peter Simon (eds), *Reggae International*, New York: Rogner and Berhard, p. 69.

Deleuze, Gilles, and Guattari, Félix (1988), *A Thouand Plateaus: Capitalism and Schizophrenia,* trans. Brian Massumi, Minneapolis: University of Minnesota Press.

Denisoff, R. Serge (1970), 'Protest Songs: Those on the Top Forty and Those of the Streets', *American Quarterly* **22**(4), pp. 807–23.

—— (1972a), 'The Evolution of the American Protest Song', in R. Serge Denisoff and Richard A. Peterson (eds), *The Sounds of Social Change*, Chicago: Rand McNally, pp. 15–25.

—— (1972b), *Great Day Coming*, Urbana: University of Illinois Press.

—— (1975), *Solid Gold: The Popular Record Industry*, New Brunswick: Transaction.

—— (1983), *Sing a Song of Social Significance* (2nd edn), Bowling Green, OH: Popular Press.

—— and Levine, Mark H. (1971), 'The Popular Protest Song: The Case of "Eve of Destruction"', *The Public Opinion Quarterly*, **35**(1), pp. 117–22.

Denning, Michael (1996), *The Cultural Front: The Laboring of American Culture*, New York: Verso.

Department of Employment, Education and Training (1995), *Alive and Deadly: Reviving and Maintaining Australian Indigenous Languages*, Canberra: Commonwealth of Australia.

Derrida, Jacques (1990), *Given Time: I. Counterfeit Money*, trans. Peggy Kamuf, Chicago: University of Chicago Press.

DeRogatis, Jim (2003), *Turn on Your Mind: Four Decades of Great Psychedelic Rock*, Milwaukee: Hal Leonard Corporation.

Dixon, R. (1980), *The Languages of Australia*, Cambridge: Cambridge University Press.

Downey, Ryan (2001), 'Nothing Left Inside: Duncan Barlow', *We Owe You Nothing: 'Punk Planet': The Collected Interviews*, New York: Akashic Books, pp. 304–13.

Doyle, Matthew and Lee, Riley (1993), *Wild Honey Dreaming*, New World Productions.

Dunaway, David King (1981), *How Can I Keep from Singing? Pete Seeger*, New York: McGraw-Hill.

Dunbar-Hall, Peter (1996), 'Rock Songs as Messages: Issues of Health and Lifestyle in Central Australian Aboriginal Communities', *Popular Music and Society*, **20**,(2), pp. 43–68.

—— (1997), 'Music and Meaning: The Aboriginal Rock Album', *Australian Aboriginal Studies*, **1**, pp. 38–47.

—— (2004), 'Alive and Deadly: A Sociolinguistic Reading of Rock Songs by Australian Aboriginal Musicians', *Popular Music and Society*, **27**(1), pp. 41–48.

—— and Gibson, Chris (2004), *Deadly Sounds, Deadly Places: Contemporary Aboriginal Music in Australia*, Sydney: University of NSW Press.

Earle, Steve (2003), 'Woody Guthrie', *The Nation*, **277**(3), 21–28 July, pp. 30–31.

Early, Gerald (1995), *One Nation Under a Groove*, New Jersey: The Ecco Press.

Edmonds, Ennis Barrington (2003), *Rastafari: From Outcasts to Culture Bearers*, New York: Oxford University Press.

Ellison, Mary (1989), *Lyrical Protest*, New York: Praeger.

Epstein, Dan (2003), 'Sing Now, or Forever Hold Your Peace; Where Are the New Protest Songs?', *L.A. Weekly*, 14-20 February, <http://www.LAWeekly.com/ink/03/13/music-epstein.php>.

Epstein, Robin (1992), 'Billy Bragg,' *Progressive*, **56**(8), August, pp. 31–34.

Eyerman, Ron and Jamison, Andrew (1995), 'Social Movements and Cultural Transformation: Popular Music in the 1960s', *Media, Culture & Society*, **17**(3), July, pp. 449–68.

—— (1997), *Music and Social Movements: Mobilizing Traditions in the Twentieth Century*, Cambridge: Cambridge University Press.

Fast, Susan (2001), *In The Houses of the Holy: Led Zeppelin and the Power of Rock Music*, New York: Oxford University Press.

Feingold, Russ (2003), 'Prick Up Your Ears', *The Nation*, **276**(2), 13 January, p. 4.

Fey, Julia Winden (2000), 'Spirituality Bites: Xers and the Gothic Cult/ure', in Richard Flory and Donald Miller (eds), *GenX Religion*, New York: Routledge, pp. 31–53.

Fioretti, Dan (1992), 'What Do You Do With Them Tapes?', in Robin James (ed.), *Cassette Mythos*, Brooklyn, NY: Autonomedia, pp. 18–19.

Fong-Torres, Ben (1998), *The Hits Just Keep On Coming: The History of Top 40 Radio*, San Francisco, CA: Miller Freeman.

Forman, Murray (2002), *The 'Hood' Comes First: Race, Space, and Place in Rap and*

Hip-Hop, Middletown, CT: Wesleyan University Press.

Forsythe, Dennis (1980), 'West Indian Culture Through the Prism of Rastafarianism', *Caribbean Quarterly*, **26**(4), December, pp. 62–81.

Foster, John (1980), 'Letter from the Editor', *Op*, (B), p. 1.

—— (1982), 'Letter from the Editor', *Op*, (L), p. 1.

Foucault, Michel (1984), 'What Is an Author?', in Paul Rabinow (ed.), *The Foucault Reader*, New York: Pantheon, pp. 101–20.

Freeman-Greene, Suzy (1991), 'State of Shock', *The Age*, February, pp. 12–14.

Frey, Hillary (2002), 'Singing to Power', *The Nation*, **274**(3), 17 June, pp. 35–36.

Friedlander, Paul (1996), *Rock and Roll: A Social History*, Boulder, CO: Westview Press.

Friesen, Bruce K. and Epstein, V., (1994), 'Rock 'n' Roll Ain't Noise Pollution: Artistic Conventions and Tensions in the Major Subgenres of Heavy Metal Music', *Popular Music and Society*, **18**(3), pp. 1–17.

Frith, Simon (1987a), 'Copyright and the Music Business', *Popular Music*, **7**(1), pp. 57–75.

—— (1987b), 'Towards an Aesthetic of Popular Music', in Richard Leppert and Susan McClary (eds), *Music and Society: The Politics of Composition, Performance and Reception*, Cambridge: Cambridge University Press, pp. 133–49.

—— (1991), 'Anglo-America and Its Discontents', *Cultural Studies*, **5**(3), pp. 263–69.

—— and Street, John (1992), 'Rock Against Racism and Red Wedge: From Music to Politics, from Politics to Music', in Reebee Garofalo (ed.), *Rockin' the Boat: Mass Music and Mass Movements*, Boston, MA: South End Press, pp. 67–80.

Fudge, Rachel (2003), 'Celebrity Jeopardy: The Perils of Feminist Fame', *Bitch*, Winter, p. 35.

Garofalo, Reebee (ed.), (1992), *Rockin' the Boat: Mass Music and Mass Movements*, Boston, MA: South End Press.

—— (ed.), (1997), *Rockin' Out: Popular Music in the USA*, Boston, MA: Allyn and Bacon.

George, Nelson (1998), *Hip Hop America,* New York: Penguin Books.

Getlen, Larry (2002), 'Michelle Shocked Unlocks Her Musical Cage', <http://www.bankrate.com/brm/new/investing/20020509a.asp>, 9 May.

Gett, Steve (1984), *Judas Priest: Heavy Duty*, Port Chester, NY: Cherry Lane Books.

Giddings, Paula (1984), *When and Where I Enter: The Impact of Black Women on Race and Sex in America*, New York: William Morrow and Company.

Gilroy, Paul (1997), '"After the Love has Gone": Bio-Politics and Entho-poetics in the Black Public Sphere,' in Angela McRobbie (ed.), *Back To Reality? Social Experience and Cultural Studies,* Manchester: Manchester University Press, pp. 83–115.

Gleason, Holly (1988), 'Short, Sharp, Talented', *Rolling Stone*, **538**, 3 November 3, p. 28.

Godwin, Robert (1997), *Led Zeppelin: The Press Reports*, London: CG Publishing.

Gold, John (1998), 'Roll on Columbia: Woody Guthrie, Migrants' Tales, and Regional Transformation in the Pacific Northwest', *Journal of Cultural Geography*, **18**(1), pp. 83–98.

Goldie (2004), 'Autobiography', <http://www.trustthedj.com/Goldie/bio.php?djid=29>, accessed 10 July.

Gottlieb, Martin (1993), 'On the White Side of Crossover Dreams', *New York Times*, 14 February, p. 6.

Grant, Steve (1982), 'Death Will Keep us Together: "Joy Division" and "New Order"

Examined', *Trouser Press*, 9, March, pp. 30–33.

Greene, Graham (1993), *The Lawless Roads*, New York: Penguin.

Gregg, Richard B. (1971), 'The Ego-Function of the Rhetoric of Protest', *Philosophy and Rhetoric*, **4**(1), Spring, pp. 71–91.

Gregorio, Ron (1985), 'Dead Kennedys', *Hard Times* **1**(7), pp. 3–4.

Griffith, D.W. (1915), *The Birth of a Nation*, prod. and dir. D.W. Griffith, perf. Lilian Gish, Mae Marsh, Henry B. Walthall and Walter Long, David W. Griffith Corp.

Groia, Philip (1983), *They All Sang on the Corner*, West Hempstead, NY: P. Dee Enterprises.

Grossberg, Lawrence (1990), 'Is There Rock after Punk?' in Simon Frith and Andrew Goodwin (eds), *On Record: Rock, Pop, and the Written Word*, New York: Pantheon, pp. 112–23.

Grunenberg, Christoph (1997), 'Unsolved Mysteries: Gothic Tales From Frankenstein to the Hair Eating Doll', in Christopher Grunenberg (ed.), *Gothic: Transmutations of Horror in Late Twentieth Century Art*, Cambridge, MA: MIT, pp. 213–158 (backward pagination).

Gunn, Joshua (1999a), 'Gothic Music and the Inevitability of Genre', *Popular Music and Society*, **23**, pp. 31–50.

—— (1999b), 'Marilyn Manson is not Goth: Memorial Struggle and the Rhetoric of Subcultural Identity', *Journal of Communication Inquiry*, **23**(4), October, pp. 408–31.

Guthrie, Woody (1943), *Bound for Glory,* New York: Doubleday.

Guzman, Isaac (2001), 'She's a Defender of Shocked Values', *New York Daily News*, 8 March 8, p. 44.

Hajdu, David (2003), 'Authenticity Blues', *New Republic*, **228**(23), pp. 38–41.

—— (2004), 'Where Has "Where Have All the Flowers Gone?" Gone?', *New Republic*, **230**(24), p. 33.

Hamelman, Steven L. (2004), *But Is It Garbage? On Rock and Trash*, Athens: University of Georgia Press.

Hannaham, James (1997), 'Bela Lugosi's Dead and I Don't Feel So Good Either: Goth and the Glorification of Suffering in Rock Music', in Christopher Grunenberg (ed.), *Gothic: Transmutations of Horror in Late Twentieth Century Art*, Cambridge, MA: MIT, pp. 119–92.

Haralambos, Michael (1974), *Right On: From Blues to Soul in Black America*, London: Edison Press.

Hargus, Billy Bob (1997), 'Greil Marcus: Do Politics Rock?' *Perfect Sound Forever*, June, <http://www.furious.com/perfect/marcus.html>.

Harker, Dave (1980), *One for the Money*, London: Hutchinson.

—— (1992), 'Still Crazy After All These Years', in Bart Moore-Gilbert and John Seed (eds), *Cultural Revolution? The Challenge of the Arts in the 1960s*, London: Routledge, pp. 236–54.

Harrington, Richard (1989), 'Michelle Shocked, Taking Stock: Success and the Singer's Radical Politics', *The Washington Post*, 15 March, B1.

Harris, Alana (1995), 'The Big March', in Irene Moores (ed.), *Voices of Aboriginal Australia: Past, Present, Future*, Springwood, NSW: Butterfly Books, pp. 138–39.

Harrison, Daphne Duval (1988), *Black Pearls: Blues Queens of the 1920s*, New Brunswick: Rutgers University Press.

Hebdige, Dick (1979), *Subculture: The Meaning of Style*, London: Methuen.

—— (1987), *Cut 'N' Mix: Culture, Identity and Caribbean Music*, New York: Methuen.

Helton, J. Jesse, and Staudenmeier, William J.Jr (2002), 'Re-Imagining Being "Straight" in Straight Edge', *Contemporary Drug Problems*, **29**(2), pp. 445–73.

Hilburn, Robert (2003), 'When a Song is Mistaken for an Anthem: Outkast's "Bombs Over Baghdad" is the Latest Song to be Embraced as a Pro-War Anthem. But, as often happens, That's Not What the Author Intended', *Los Angeles Times,* 12 April, E1.

—— (2004), 'Rocker Fogerty Takes on War – Again', *Chicago Tribune,* 14 July, 5.3.

House of Representatives Standing Committee on Aboriginal and Torres Strait Islander Affairs (1992), *Language and Culture – A Matter of Survival: Report of the Inquiry into Aboriginal and Torres Strait Islander Language Maintenance*, Canberra: Commonwealth of Australia.

Howard, Michael (ed.), (1982), *Aboriginal Power in Australian Society*, Honolulu: University of Hawaii Press.

Howe, Stephen (2002), 'Our Critics Choose Their Books of the Year', *The New Statesman*, **131**(4616), 2 December, p. 44.

Humphrey, Clark (1995), *Loser: The Real Seattle Music Story*, Portland: Feral House.

Hunger, The (1983), Tony Scott (director), USA.

Hutcheon, David (2002), 'Interview with Billy Bragg', *Mother Jones*, **29**(2), pp. 82–83.

Huxley, Aldous (1954), *The Doors of Perception and Heaven and Hell*, New York: Harper & Row.

Ingels, Graham (1981), 'Castanets', *Op*, (F), p. 3.

—— (1981b), 'Castanets', *Op*, (G), p. 8.

—— (1983), 'Castanets', *Op*, (O), pp. 18–19.

—— (1984a), 'Castanets', *Op*, (V), pp. 16–18.

—— (1984b), 'Castanets', *Op*, (W), pp. 9–13.

—— (1984c), 'Castanets', *Op*, (Z), pp. 12–18.

Irvine, James R. and Kirkpatrick, Walter G. (1972), 'The Musical Form in Rhetorical Exchange: Theoretical Considerations', *The Quarterly Journal of Speech*, **52**, 272–89.

Irwin, Darrell (1999), 'The Straight Edge Subculture: Examining the Youths' Drug-Free Way', *Journal of Drug Studies*, **29**(2), pp. 365–80.

Jackson, Scott (1987), 'Ice Cream Blisters: You Can Never Step In the Same River Twice', *Sound Choice*, **6**, January–February, p. 53.

Jara, Joan (1983), *Victor: An Unfinished Song*, London: Jonathan Cape.

Jenson, Rich and James, Robin (1992), 'A Sound Mind', in Robin James (ed.), *Cassette Mythos*, Brooklyn, NY: Autonomedia, pp. 41–45.

Jerrentrup, Ansgar (2000), 'Gothic and Dark Music: Forms and Background', *The World of Music*, **42**(1), pp. 25–50.

Johns, Darren (2002), 'Review of *England, Half-English*, *New Musical Express*, 26 March, <http://www.nme.com/reviews/10355.htm>.

Jones, Steve (1992), 'The Cassette Underground', in Robin James (ed.), *Cassette Mythos*, Brooklyn, NY: Autonomedia, pp. 6–13.

Kane, John (2001), *The Politics of Moral Capital*, Cambridge: Cambridge University Press.

Keane, John (2002), *Whatever Happened to Democracy?*, London: IPPR.

Kelley, Robin (1997), *Yo' Mama's Disfunktional! Fighting Cultural Wars in Urban America*, Boston, MA: Beacon Press.

Kemp, Mark (1992), 'Review of *Arkansas Traveler*', *Rolling Stone,* **630**, 14 March, p. 105.

'Kerrville Folk Festival' (2002), *The Handbook of Texas Online*, <http://www.tsha.utexas.edu/handbook/online/articles/fiew/KK/xfkl.html>, accessed 31 May, 2004.

Keyes, Cheryl (2002), *Rap Music and Street Consciousness*, Chicago: University of Illinois Press.

King, Stephen A. (2002), *Reggae, Rastafari, and the Rhetoric of Social Control*, Jackson: University Press of Mississippi.

King, Stephen and Jensen, Richard J. (1995), 'Bob Marley's "Redemption Song": The Rhetoric of Reggae and Rastafari', *Journal of Popular Culture*, **29**(3), pp. 17–36.

Kivy, Peter (1995), *Authenticities: Philosophical Reflections on Musical Performance*, New York: Cornell University Press.

Klein, Joe (1980), *Woody Guthrie: A Life*, New York: Random House.

Klosterman, Chuck (2002), 'The Metal Issue: Robert Plant – Not a Whole Lotta Love', *Spin*, **18**, September, pp. 98–100.

Knupp, Ralph E. (1981), 'A Time for Every Purpose Under Heaven: Rhetorical Dimensions of Protest Music', *Southern Speech Communication Journal*, **46**(4), Summer, pp. 377–89.

Kofsky, Frank (1969), 'Frank Zappa: An Interview', in Jonathan Eisen (ed.), *The Age of Rock*, New York: Random House, p. 256.

Konow, David (2002), *Bang Your Head: The Rise and Fall of Heavy Metal*, New York: Three Rivers Press.

Kot, Greg (2002), 'Few Are Raising Voices for Protest Music', *Chicago Tribune*, 9 December, <http://www.arbiteronline.com/vnews/display.v/art/2002/12/09/3df43ab81abc>.

Lahickey, Beth (1997), *All Ages: Reflections on Straight Edge*, Huntington Beach, CA: Revelation Books.

Lahusen, Christian (1996), *The Rhetoric of Moral Protest*, Berlin: Walter de Gruyter.

Laing, Dave (1985), *One Chord Wonders*, Milton Keynes: Open University Press.

——— (2003), 'Resistance and Protest', in John Shepherd, David Horn, Dave Laing, Paul Oliver and Peter Wicke (eds), *Continuum Encyclopedia of Popular Music of the World*, London: Continuum, pp. 345–46.

Lake, Randall A. (1983), 'Enacting Red Power: The Consummatory Function in Native American Protest Rhetoric', *Quarterly Journal of Speech*, **69**(2), pp. 127–42.

Langton, Marcia (2003), 'Dreaming Art', in Nikos Papastergiadis (ed.), *Complex Entanglements: Art, Globalisation and Cultural Difference*, London: Rivers Oram Press, pp. 42–56.

Larson, Bob (1967), *Rock & Roll: The Devil's Diverson*, McCook, NE: Bob Larson.

Lester, Julius (1967), 'Letter to the Editor', *Broadside*, **84**, September, p. 7.

Lieberson, Stanley (2000), *A Matter of Taste*, New Haven, CT: Yale University Press.

Light, Alan (1991), '*Woody* on Guthrie', *Rolling Stone*, **598**, 21 February, p. 50.

Lippmann, Lorna (1991), *Generations of Resistance: Aborigines Demand Justice* (2nd edn), Melbourne: Longman Cheshire.

Litman, Jessica (1990), 'The Public Domain', *Emory Law Journal*, Fall, **39**(4), pp. 965–1023.

Locke, John (1960), *Two Treatises of Government*, in Peter Laslett (ed), Cambridge: Cambridge University Press, pp. 141–343.

Lomax, Alan (1960), *The Folk Songs of North America*, New York: Doubleday and Company.

Lopez, Steve (1999), 'The Mutant Brady Bunch: Meet Salt Lake City's Clean Cut, Anti-Drug Street Gang – and Tremble', *Time*, **154**(9), 30 August, pp. 36–37.

Lorraine, Renée Cox (2001), 'Recovering Jouissance: Feminist Aesthetics and Music', in Karin Pendle (ed.), *Women and Music: A History*, Bloomington: Indiana University Press, pp. 3–18.

Lowery, Matt Mair (2003), 'Under the Radar', *Tape Op*, **35**, May–June, p. 20.

McClay, Wilfred M. (2001), 'Individualism and Its Discontents', *Virginia Quarterly Review*, **77**(3), pp. 391-405.

McDonald, James R. (1988), 'Politics Revisited: Metatextual Implications of Rock and Roll Criticism', *Youth and Society*, **19**, pp. 485–504.

McGee, Hal (1992), 'Foreword', in Robin James (ed.), *Cassette Mythos*, Brooklyn, NY: Autonomedia, p. viii.

McGee, Michael C. (1980), '"Social Movement": Phenomenon or Meaning?', *Central States Speech Journal*, **31**(4), pp. 233–44.

McGraith, Donal (1990), 'Anti-Copyright and Cassette Culture', in Dan Lander and Micah Lexier (eds), *Sound By Artists*, Ontario: The Coach House Press and Walter Philips Gallery, pp. 73–87.

McGrath, Patrick (1997), 'Transgression and Decay', in Christopher Grunenberg (ed.), *Gothic: Transmutations of Horror in Late Twentieth Century Art*, Cambridge, MA: MIT, pp. 159–62.

Mack, Douglas R.A. (1999), *From Babylon to Rastafari: Origin and History of the Rastafarian Movement*, Chicago: Research Associates School Times Publications Frontline Distribution International.

McKay, George (2003), 'Just A Closer Walk to Thee: New Orleans-style Jazz and the Campaign for Nuclear Disarmament in 1950s Britain', *Popular Music*, **22**(3), pp. 261–82.

McRobbie, Angela (1999), 'Thinking With Music', in Karen Kelly and Evelyn McDonnell (eds), *Stars Don't Stand Still in the Sky: Music and Myth*, New York: New York University Press, pp. 37–49.

—— and Melville, Caspar (1998), 'Amblyssical Chords', *Village Voice*, **17**, February, p. 67.

Mäkelä, Janne (2004), *John Lennon Imagined: Cultural History of a Rock Star*, New York: Peter Lang.

Maley, Patrick (2002), Personal Interview, 29 June.

Maloy, Kathy (1995), 'My Eye', *Snipehunt*, **24**, Summer, p. 6.

—— (1996a), 'My Eye', *Snipehunt*, **27**, Spring, p. 4.

—— (1996b), 'My Eye', *Snipehunt*, **28**, Summer, p. 7.

Mancini, Paolo and Swanson, David (1996), 'Politics, Media, and Modern Democracy: Introduction', in David Swanson and Paolo Mancini (eds), *Politics, Media, and Modern Democracy*, Westport, CT: Praeger, pp. 1–26.

Marcus, Greil (1995), *The Dustbin of History*, Cambridge, MA: Harvard University Press.

Marcus, Tony (1997), 'The War is Over: Interview With Goldie', <http://www.techno.de/mixmag/interviews/goldie.html>, accessed 10 July 2004.

Marilyn Manson (2003), 'Marilyn Manson: The Golden Age of Grotesque', 'The Oracle', 25 May, <http://www.marilynmanson.com/grotesque/>.

Marriott, Robert (2000), 'Blowin' Up', *Vibe*, June–July, pp. 124–32.

Marsh, Dave (1987), *Glory Days: A Biography of Bruce Springsteen*, London: Sidgwick and Jackson.

―――― (2002), 'Alan Lomax: Great White Hunter, or Thief, Plagiarist and Bigot?', *Counterpunch*, 21 July, <www.counterpunch.org/marsh0721.html>.

Marshall, Scott (1995), 'Long Live the Humble Audio Cassette – A Eulogy', in Ron Sakolsky and Fred Wei-han Ho (eds), *Sounding Off! Music as Subversion/ Resistance/Revolution*, Brooklyn: Autonomedia, pp. 212–14.

Mathur, Paul (1988), 'Art of Darkness', *Melody Maker*, **64**, June, pp. 16–17.

Mattern, Mark (1988), 'Cajun Music, Cultural Revival: Theorizing Political Action in Popular Music', *Popular Music and Society*, **22**(2), pp. 31–48.

Maultsby, Portia K. (1983), 'Soul Music: Its Sociological and Political Significance in American Popular Culture', *Journal of Popular Culture*, **17**(2), pp. 51–60.

Meadows, Michael (2002), 'Tell Me What You Want and I'll Give You What You Need: Perspectives on Indigenous Media Audience Research', in Mark Balnaves, Tom O'Regan and Jason Sternberg (eds), *Mobilising the Audience*, Brisbane: University of Queensland Press, pp. 253–65.

Melnick, Jeffrey (1996), 'R&B Skeletons in the Closet: The Men of Doo Wop', *Minnesota Review*, **47**, Fall, pp. 217–29.

Mental, Sam (1987), 'Idiot-Savant: Live 86'd', *Sound Choice*, **6**, January–February, p. 53.

Mercer, Mick (1988), *Gothic Rock Black Book*, London: Omnibus.

Meyer, Gerald (2002), 'Frank Sinatra: The Popular Front and an American Icon', *Science and Society*, **66**(3), pp. 311–35.

Meyer, Thomas (2002), *Media Democracy: How the Media Colonize Politics*, Cambridge: Polity Press.

Meyrowitz, Joshua (1985), *No Sense of Place*, Oxford: Oxford University Press.

Miller, Paul D. (2004c), *Rhythm Science*, Cambridge, MA: MIT Press.

Mills, Fred (1985), 'Letter to the Editor', *Sound Choice*, **2**, Spring, p. 8.

Molenda, Michael (1998), 'Billy Bragg on Woody Guthrie', *Guitar Player*, **32**(9), September, p. 64.

Mondak, Jeffery J. (1988), 'Protest Music as Political Persuasion', *Popular Music and Society*, **12**(3), pp. 25–38.

Moores, Irene (ed.), (1995), *Voices of Aboriginal Australia: Past, Present, Future*, Springwood, NSW: Butterfly Books.

Morris, Charles E. III and Browne, Stephen H. (eds) (2001), *Readings on the Rhetoric of Social Protest*, State College, PA: Strata Publishing.

Morton, David (2000), *Off the Record: The Technology and Culture of Sound Recording in America*, New Jersey: Rutgers University Press.

Mueller, W. (1986), 'Balcony of Ignorance: These Meddling Kids', *Sound Choice*, **4**, Spring, p. 37.

Nagashima, Yoshiko S. (1984), *Rastafarian Music in Contemporary Jamaica: A Study of Socioreligious Music of the Rastafarian Movement in Jamaica*, Tokyo: Institute for the Study of Languages and Cultures of Asia and Africa.

National Board of Employment, Education and Training (1996), *The Land Still Speaks: Review of Aboriginal and Torres Strait Islander Language Maintenance and Development Needs and Activities*, Canberra: Commonwealth of Australia.

Neal, Mark Anthony (1999), *What the Music Said: Black Popular Music and Black*

Popular Culture, New York: Routledge Press.

——— (2001), 'Another Man Is Beating My Time: Gender and Sexuality in Rhythm and Blues', in Rachel Rubin (ed.), *American Popular Music: New Approaches to the Twentieth Century*, Amherst: University of Massachusetts Press, pp. 127–39.

Negus, Keith (1999), *Music Genres and Corporate Cultures*, London: Routledge.

Neill, Rosemary (2002), *White Out: How Politics is Killing Black Australia*, Sydney: Allen & Unwin.

Nemo, Fred (2002), Personal Interview, 11 June.

Nettleford, Rex (1994), Personal Interview with Stephen King, 23 July.

Neuenfeldt, Karl (ed.) (1997), *The Didjeridu: From Arnhem Land to Internet*, London/Sydney: John Libbey/Perfect Beat Publications.

Nietzsche, Friedrich (1967), *The Birth of Tragedy and The Case of Wagner*, trans. W. Kaufmann, New York: Vintage.

Noebel, David A. (1969), *The Beatles: A Study in Drugs, Sex and Revolution*, Tulsa, OK: Christian Crusade Publications.

Norris, Chris (1998), 'Wild Style', *Spin*, **14**, February, pp. 70–73.

O'Connor, Mark (1988), 'Aboriginal Literature Becomes A Force', in Rutherford, A. (ed.), *Aboriginal Culture Today*, Sydney: Dangaroo Press-Kunapipi, pp. 246–53.

O'Hara, Craig (1999), *The Philosophy of Punk: More Than Noise*, London: AK Press.

Orman, John (1984), *The Politics of Rock*, Chicago, Nelson-Hall.

Orris, Michelle (2003), 'Protest Music Thing of the Past', *Badger Herald*, 10 April.

Oswald, John (1995), 'Creatigality', in Ron Sakolsky and Fred Wei-han Ho (eds), *Sounding Off! Music as Subversion/Resistance/Revolution*, Brooklyn, NY: Autonomedia, pp. 87–89.

Owens, Joseph (1976), *Dread: The Rastafarians of Jamaica*, Kingston, Jamaica: Sangster's Book Stores.

Owens, Lynn and Palmer, Kendall L. (2003), 'Making the News: Anarchist Counter-Public Relations on the World Wide Web', *Critical Studies in Media Communication*, **20**(4), pp. 335–61.

Palmer, Robert (1988), 'The Substance of Joy Division: A Talk With New Order', *Musician*, **118**, August, pp. 84–88ff.

Parchment, Clinton (1960), 'Rascally Rastafarians', *Daily Gleaner*, 30 April, p. 8.

Pareles, John (2003), 'Old Message: "No War"', *New York Times*, 9 March, B1–7.

Pasley, Jeffrey L. (1987), 'Right Rock: Rock Music and Reaganism', *The New Republic*, **196**, 23 March, p. 22.

Peddie, Ian (2000), 'Love of Labor', 12 October, <http://www.poppolitics.com/articles/2000-10-12-bragg.shtml>.

Pekacz, Jolanta (1994), 'Did Rock Smash the Wall? The Role of Rock in Political Transition', *Popular Music*, **13**(1), pp. 41–49.

Pernice, Joe (2004), 'Yours, Mine, and Ours for an Hour: Joe Pernice of the Pernice Brothers', *The Big Take-Over*, **54**(25.1), pp. 98–99, 204–05.

Pileggi, Mary S. (1998), 'No Sex, No Drugs, Just Hardcore Rock: Using Bourdieu to Understand Straight-edge Kids and Their Practices', unpublished dissertation, Temple University.

Pollard, Velma (1990), 'The Speech of the Rastafarians of Jamaica, in the Eastern Caribbean: The Case of St. Lucia', *International Journal of the Sociology of Language*, **85**, pp. 81–90.

Pontiac, Ronnie (2004), 'The Golden Age of Rock Activism', *Newtopia Magazine*, **III** (15), <http://www.newtopiamagazine.net/archives/content/issue15/features/rock:php>.

Potter, Russell (1995), *Spectacular Vernaculars: Hip-hop and the Politics of Post-modernsm*. Albany, NY: State University of New York Press.

Pratt, Ray. (1990), *Rhythm and Resistance: Explorations in the Political Uses of Popular Music*, New York: Praeger.

Price, Simon (1993), 'Surely Some Mystique!', *Melody Maker*, **69**, August, pp. 36–37.

Puterbaugh, Parke (2004), 'Sounds of Silence: Pop Music Today Has No Political Edge', *Greensboro (NC) News & Record*, 15 February, H1.

Quantick, David (2000), *The Clash*, New York: Thunder's Mouth Press.

Queens of the Stone Age (2000), 'Feel Good Hit of the Summer', *[Rated] R*, Interscope Records.

Rastafarian Movement Association (1976), *Rasta: A Modern Antique*, Kingston, Jamaica: Rastafarian Movement Association.

Reynolds, Simon (1998), *Energy Flash: A Journey through Rave Music and Dance Culture*, London: Picador.

Rich, Frank (2003), 'Mr Ambassador', in Hilton Als and Darryl A. Turner (eds), *White Noise: The Eminem Collection*, New York: Thunder's Mouth Press.

Richardson, Mary F. (1983), 'Out of Many, One People – Aspiration or Reality? An Examination of the Attitudes to the Various Racial and Ethnic Groups Within the Jamaican Society', *Social and Economic Studies*, **32**(3), pp. 143–67.

Riner, Dax (2004), 'Letter to the Editor', *Magnet*, **64**, August–September, p. 10.

Robinson, Fergus and York, Barry (1977), *The Black Resistance: An Introduction to the History of the Aborigines' Struggle Against British Colonialism*, Melbourne: Widescope.

Rodnitzky, Jerome (1976), *Minstrels of the Dawn: The Folk-Protest Singer as a Cultural Hero,* Chicago: Nelson-Hall.

Rose, Mark (1994), 'The Author in Court', in Peter Jaszi and Martha Woodmansee (eds), *The Construction of Authorship: Textual Appropriation in Law and Literature*, Durham: Duke University Press, pp. 211–29.

Rose, Tricia (1994), *Black Noise: Rap Music and Black Culture in Contemporary America*, Hanover: Wesleyan University Press.

Rosen, Craig (1995), 'Shocked's Suit Seeks Release From Polygram', *Billboard*, **107**(31), 5 August, pp. 10–11.

Rosenthal, Rob (2001), 'Serving the Movement: the Role(s) of Music', *Popular Music and Society* **25**(3–4), pp. 11–24 <http://www.findarticles.com/cf_0/m2822/2001_Fall/Winter>.

Ross, Alex (2001), 'The Searchers: Radiohead's Unquiet Revolution', *The New Yorker*, 20 and 27 August, pp. 112–23.

Sakolsky, Ron and Wei-Han Ho, Fred (eds) (1995), *Sounding Off! Music as Subversion/Resistance/Revolution*, New York: Autonomedia.

Sanders, Rory (1982), 'From the Root of King David', in Stephen Davis and Peter Simon (eds), *Reggae International*, New York: Rogner and Berhard, pp. 59–68.

Schmidt, Annette (1993), *The Loss of Australia's Aboriginal Language Heritage*, Canberra: Aboriginal Studies Press.

Schoenherr, Steve (2004), 'Recording Technology History', <http://history.acusd.edu/gen/recording/notes.html#stereo>, last updated 16 February.

Schulz, David (2004), Personal Interview, 1 July.

Seabrook, Jeremy (2000), 'Goodbye to Provincial Life', *New Statesman*, **129**, 18 September, p. 33.

Seeger, Pete (1965), 'Whatever Happened to Singing in the Unions', *Sing Out*, 15, May, p. 31.

Segal, David (2003), 'Count Me Out', *Washington Monthly*, **35**(10), October, pp. 48-50.

Sheeran, Paul (2001), *Cultural Politics in International Relations*, Aldershot: Ashgate.

Shelton, Robert (1986), *No Direction Home: The Life and Music of Bob Dylan*, New York: William Morrow and Co.

Shirley, Ian (1994), *Dark Entries: Bauhaus and Beyond*, Wembley: SAF Publishing.

Simonelli, David (2002), 'Anarchy, Pop and Violence: Punk Rock Subculture and The Rhetoric of Class, 1976–78', *Contemporary British History,* **16**(2), Summer, pp. 121–44.

Simons, Herbert W., Mechling, Elizabeth W. and Schreier, Howard N. (1984), 'The Functions of Human Communication in Mobilizing for Action From the Bottom Up: The Rhetoric of Social Movements', in Carroll C. Arnold and John W. Bowers, (eds), *Handbook of Rhetorical and Communication Theory*, Boston, MA: Allyn and Bacon, pp. 792–867.

Simpson, George E. (1955), 'Political Cultism in West Kingston, Jamaica', *Social and Economic Studies*, **4**(2), pp. 133–49.

Sinker, Daniel (2004), Interview with Ian MacKaye, *Punk Planet*, 61, May–June, pp. 30–35.

Smith, Danyel (1994), 'Ain't A Damn Thing Changed: Why Women Rappers Don't Sell', in Adam Sexton (ed.), *Rap on Rap: Straight-Up Talk on Hip-hop Culture*, New York: Delta Books, pp. 125–28.

—— (1998), 'She Got Game', *Vibe*, December–January, pp. 113–17.

Smith, Gill (1980), 'Strange Daze', *Melody Maker*, **55**, November, p. 13.

Smith, Rodney (2001), *Australian Political Culture*, Sydney: Longman.

Smith, Suzanne (1999), *Dancing in the Street*, Cambridge, MA: Harvard University Press.

Soghomonian, Talia (2002), 'Interview with Michelle Shocked', *NY Rock*, December, <http://www.nyrock.com/interviews/2002/shocked_int.asp>.

Spector, Ronnie with Waldron, Vince (1990), *Be My Baby*, New York: Harmony Books.

Stark, M. (1998), *Black Sabbath: An Oral History*, New York: HarperCollins.

Steffens, Roger (1998), 'Bob Marley: Rasta Warrior', in Nathaniel S. Murrell, William D. Spencer and Adrian A. McFarlane (eds), *Chanting Down Babylon: The Rastafari Reader*, Philadelphia, Temple University Press, pp. 253–65.

Steinhauer, Jennifer (1995), 'Clean Living's New Look', *New York Times*, 16 July, pp. 36, 38.

Stewart, Charles J. (1999), 'Championing the Rights of Others and Challenging Evil: The Ego Function in the Rhetoric of Other-Directed Social Movements', *Southern Communication Journal*, **64**(2), Winter, pp. 91–105.

—— Smith, Craig Allen and Denton, Robert E. (1989), *Persuasion and Social Movements* (2nd edn), Prospect Heights, ILL: Waveland Press.

Stix, John (1994), 'Black Sabbath: Out of the Blue, Into the Black', <http://www.blacksabbath.com/interviews/tonygeez_0594.html>, accessed 29 September 2004.

Strauss, Neil (1998), 'Recordings: *Saturnz Return*', *Rolling Stone*, **779**, 5 February, pp. 57–58.

Straw, Will (1991), 'Systems of Articulation, Logics of Change: Communities and Scenes in Popular Music', *Cultural Studies*, **5**(3), pp. 368–88.

Strehlow, Theodor (1971), *Songs of Central Australia*, Sydney: Angus & Robertson.

Sutherland, Steve (1981), 'Anarchy in Aylesbury', *Melody Maker*, **56**, July, p. 9ff.

Sweeney, Philip (1991), *The Virgin Directory of World Music: A Guide to Performers and Their Music*, London: Virgin.

Sweeting, Adam (1982), 'The Sisterhood of Terror', *Melody Maker*, **57**, February, p. 11.

Szemere, Anna (2001), *Up From The Underground: The Culture of Rock Music in Postsocialist Hungary*, Philadelphia: The Pennsylvania State University Press.

Talvi, Silja J.A. (2001), 'Billy Bragg: Preaching to the Unconverted,' *LiP Magazine*, 18 March, <www.lipmagazine.org>.

Tate, Greg (1995), 'Motion Thickness: Jungle Changes the Rule of the Drum', *Village Voice*, **49**, 26 December, pp. 73–74.

Temple, Johnny (1999), 'Noise From Underground: Punk Rock's Anarchic Rhythms Spur a New Generation to Political Activism', *The Nation*, **269**(12), 18 October, pp. 17–21.

Thompson, Dave (2002), *The Dark Reign of Gothic Rock: In the Reptile House with The Sisters of Mercy, Bauhaus, and The Cure*, London: Helter Skelter Publishing.

Thomson, D. (1999), 'Talk Talk: Peter Murphy & His Musical Distillation of Isolation', *Goldmine*, **492**, June, pp. 14–15.

Thomson, Irene Traviss (1989), 'The Transformation of the Social Bond: Images of Individualism in the 1920s versus the 1970s', *Social Forces*, **67**(4), pp. 851–70.

Thornton, Sarah (1996), *Club Cultures: Music, Media and Subcultural Capital*, Middletown, CT: Wesleyan University Press.

Tonn, Mari B. (1996), 'Militant Motherhood: Labor's Mary Harris "Mother" Jones', *Quarterly Journal of Speech*, **82**(1), pp. 1–21.

Toynbee, Jason (2000), *Making Popular Music: Musicians, Creativity and Institutions*, London: Arnold.

Tsitsos, William (1999), 'Rules of Rebellion: Slamdancing, Moshing, and the American Alternative Scene', *Popular Music*, **18**(3), pp. 397–414.

United States Department of Labor, Office of Policy, Planning and Research (1965), *The Negro Family: The Case for National Action*, Washington, DC: US Government Printing Office.

Valentine, Penny (1980), 'The Exploding Psychedelic Inevitable', *Creem*, **12**, November, p. 24.

Wall, Mick (2002), Liner Notes, *The Original Black Sabbath: Symptom of the Universe 1970–1978*, AOL Time Warner Company.

Walsh, Michael and Yallop, Colin (1993) (eds), *Language and Culture in Aboriginal Australia*, Canberra: Aboriginal Studies Press.

Walser, Robert (1993), *Running with the Devil*, Hanover (NH): Wesleyan University Press.

Ward, Brian (1998), *Just My Soul Responding: Rhythm and Blues, Black Consciousness and Race Relations*, London: UCL Press.

Ward, Ed, Stokes, Geoffrey and Tucker, Ken (1986), *Rock of Ages: The Rolling Stone History of Rock*, New York: Simon and Schuster.

Warner, Keith Q. (1988), 'Calypso, Reggae, and Rastafarianism: Authentic Caribbean Voices', *Popular Music and Society*, **12**(1), pp. 53–62.

Waters, Anita M. (1985), *Race, Class, and Political Symbols: Rastafari and Reggae in Jamaican Politics*, New Brunswick, NJ: Transaction Publishers.

Watrous, Peter (1994), '3 Women Rap Out Their Independence', *The New York Times*, 30 May, p. 12.

Wiener, Jon (1998), 'Pop and Avante-Garde: The Case of John and Yoko', *Popular Music and Society*, **22**(1), Spring, pp. 1–16.

Weinstein, Deena (1991), *Heavy Metal: A Cultural Sociology*, New York: Lexington.

––––– (2000), *Heavy Metal: The Music and its Culture*, New York: DaCapo.

Weinstein, Michael (2004), 'The Activist in Contemporary Power Structure', *Newtopia Magazine*, **II** (6), January, <http://www.newtopiamagazine.net/content/issue15/>.

Weisbard, Eric (1998), 'The Folk Slingers', *Village Voice*, **43**(2), 13 January, pp. 71–74.

White, Isobel (ed), (1985), *Daisy Bates: The Native Tribes of Western Australia*, Canberra: National Library of Australia.

White, Shane and White, Graham (1998), *Stylin': African American Expressive Culture from its Beginnings to the Zoot Suit*, Ithaca, NY: Cornell University Press.

Wicke, Peter (1992), '"The Times They Are A-Changin'": Rock Music and Political Change in Eastern Germany', in Reebee Garofalo (ed.), *Rockin' the Boat: Mass Music and Mass Movements*, Boston, MA: South End Press, pp. 81–93.

Wielenga, Dave (2002), 'Bio Terrorism: Michelle Shocked's Eccentric Life', *Orange County Weekly*, 7–13 June, pp. 14–15.

Wiener, Jon (1984), *Come Together: John Lennon in his Time*, New York: Random House.

Willhardt, Mark and Stein, Joel (1999), 'Dr. Funkenstein's Supergroovalistic-prosifunkstication: George Clinton Signifies' in Kevin J.H. Dettmar and William Richey (eds), *Reading Rock and Roll: Authenticity, Appropriation, Aesthetics*, New York: Columbia University Press, pp. 145–72.

Wilson, Mary (1986), *Dreamgirl*, New York: St Martin's Press.

Winders, James A. (1983), 'Reggae, Rastafarians and Revolution: Rock Music in the Third World', *Journal of Popular Culture*, **17**(1), December, pp. 61–73.

Woldu, Gail Hilson (2001), 'Contextualizing Rap', in Rachel Rubin (ed.), *American Popular Music: New Approaches to the Twentieth Century*, Amherst: University of Massachusetts Press, pp. 173–91.

Wolk, Douglas (2002), 'Review of *England, Half-English*', *Rolling Stone*, **891**, 14 March, p. 71.

Wood, Brent (1996), 'Resistance in Rhyme', Review of Russell Potter, *Spectacular Vernaculars: Hip-hop and the Politics of Postmodernism. Postmodern Culture*, **7**(1), np.

Wood, Robert T (1999), '"Nailed to the X": A Lyrical History of the Straightedge Youth Culture', *Journal of Youth Studies*, **2**(2), pp. 133–51.

Yorke, Ritchie (2003), *Led Zeppelin: The Definitive Biography*, London: Virgin.

Yamaguchi, Precious (2004), 'Rakan Rocks It with Dilated People's Latest', 10 September, <http://www.chopblock.com/features/dilatedpeoples.cfm>.

Yamma, Frank and Piranpa (1999), *Playing with Fire: Warungku Inkanyi*, CAAMA, 326.

Young, Emma (2003), 'Where Are All the Protest Songs?' *Sidney Morning Herald*, 28 January, <http://www.smh.com.au/articles/2003/01/28/1043534056940.html>.

Young, Jock (1969), *The Drugtakers: The Social Meaning of Drug Use*, London: Paladin.

Discography

Abyssinians (1971/1993), *Satta Massagana*, Heartbeat.

AIDS! How Could I Know? (1989), CAAMA, 203.

Bad Religion (2004), *The Empire Strikes First*, Epitaph.

Bahamadia (2000), 'One-4-Teen', *Bahamadia*, Good Vibe Records.

Baulu-Wah Bushrangers (1998), *Land of Kija People*, no details.

Betts, Kate (2004), 'Hey, Big Spenders', *Time: Style and Design*, Fall, 5.

Black Sabbath (1970), 'Iron Man', *Paranoid*, Warner Brothers.

Black Uhuru (1980), *Sinsemilla*, Mango.

—— (1981), *Red,* Mango.

Blekbala Mujik (1990), *Nitmiluk!* CAAMA, p. 209.

Bowie, David (1995), *Outside*, Sony.

Bragg, Billy (1983), *Life's a Riot With Spy Vs. Spy*, London: Utility/Go! Discs.

—— (1984), *Brewing Up with Billy Bragg*, London: Go! Discs.

—— (1987), *Back to Basics*, London: Go! Discs.

—— (1991), *Don't Try This At Home*, London: Go! Discs.

—— (1998), *Mermaid Avenue*, New York: Elektra.

—— (2000), *Mermaid Avenue Volume II*, New York: Elektra.

—— (2002), *England, Half English*, New York: Elektra.

Brown, Dennis (1978/1998). *Wolves and Leopards*, TKO Magnum Music.

Burning Spear (1980/2002), *Hail H.I.M*, Capitol.

—— (1990), *100th Anniversary*, Mango.

Byles, Junior (2003), *Beat Down Babylon*, Sanctuary/Trojan.

Capitol Steps, The (2003), *Between Iraq and a Hard Place*, Capitol Steps Records.

—— (2004), *Papa's Got a Brand New Baghdad,* Capitol Steps Records.

Carmody, Kev (1991), *Eulogy (For a Black Person)*, Festival Records.

Cash Money (2002), 'Bling Bling', *Cash Money Platinum Hits Vol. I*, Cash Money/ Universal Records.

Coloured Stone (1986), *Black Rock from the Red Centre*, Hot Records.

Compton's Most Wanted (1992), *Music to Driveby*, Sony Records.

Cox, Kerriane (2001), *Opening*, Kerrianne Cox.

Culture (1979/1988), *Cumbolo*, Shanachie.

—— (1979/1988), *International Herb*, Shanachie.

—— (1978/1987), *Two Sevens Clash*, Shanachie.of the Origin, Diffusion and Defusion of Revolutionary Musical Codes', *Journal of Popular Culture*, **25** (3), 17-61.

Da Brat (2000), 'All My Bitches', *Unrestricted*, So So Def Recordings.

Dane, Barbara (1973), *I Hate The Capitalist System,* Paredon Records.

Dement, Iris (1996), *The Way I Should,* Warner Bros.

Dickens, Hazel and Gerard, Alice (1973), *Hazel and Alice*, Rounder Records.

Dilated Peoples (2004), *Neighbourhood Watch*, Capitol Records.

DJ Prime Cuts (2000), *Turntablist Revolution*, DJ Honda Records.

DMX (2001), *The Great Depression*, Def Jam.

Dylan, Bob (1962), *Bob Dylan*, New York: Columbia.

—— (1975), *Desire,* Columbia Records.

Earth Crisis (2000), 'Killing Brain Cells', *Slither*, Victory Records.

Edwards, Kutcha (2001), *Cooinda*, Shock Records.

Eve (2001), 'Gangsta B's', *Scorpion*, Ruff Ryders/Interscope Records.

Gladiators (1977), *Trench Town Mix Up*, Virgin.

Goldie, (1995), *Timeless*, FFRR.

—— (1998), *Saturnz Return*, FFRR.

Gorilla Biscuits (1988), 'Finish What You Started', *Gorilla Biscuits*, Revelation Records.

Hill, Lauryn (1998), 'Doo-Wop', *The Miseducation of Lauryn Hill*, Ruffhouse Records.

Hunter, Ruby (1994), *Thoughts Within*. Aurora/White Records.

Ice Cube (1988), 'I Ain't Tha 1', *Straight Outta Compton*, Priority Records.

In Aboriginal: Aboriginal Music in Aboriginal Languages (1994), CAAMA, 241.

Iron Maiden (1982), 'Number of the Beast', *Number of the Beast*, Harvest-Capitol-EMI Records.

Isley Brothers (1966), *This Old Heart of Mine*, Motown Records.

Judas Priest (1988), 'Monsters of Rock', *Ram It Down*, CBS.

Laughton, Herbie (n.d.), *Herbie Laughton*, Imparja.

Lazy Late Boys (n.d.), *Freedom Day*, CAAMA.

Led Zeppelin (1990), *Remasters*, Atlantic Records.

—— (2003), *How The West Was Won*, Atlantic Records.

Lil' Kim (1996), *Hard Core*, Big Beat Records.

Little Piggies (1997), *Dreaming in Broome*, LPCD1.

Marley, Bob and the Wailers (1975), *Natty Dread*, Island.

—— (1976), *Rastaman Vibration*, Island.

—— (1977), *Exodus*, Island.

—— (1979), *Survival*, Island.

—— (1981), *Uprising*, Tuff Gong.

—— (1991), *Talkin' Blues*, Tuff Gong.

MC Eiht (1992), 'U's a Bitch', *Music to Driveby*, Sony Records.

Mighty Diamonds (1976), *Right Time*, Mango.

Miller, Paul D. (2004a), *Public Talk*, Providence Black Repertory Company, Providence, Rhode Island, October 15.

—— (2004), *Rebirth of a Nation*, Live digital performance, Veterans' Memorial Colosseum, Providence, Rhode Island, 17 October 17.

—— (2004d), *World Hip-hop Mix CD*, No label.

Minor Threat (1981), 'Out of Step (with the World)', *In My Eyes*, Dischord Records.

—— (1981), 'Straight Edge', *Minor Threat*, Dischord Records.

Missy Elliott (2002), 'Work It', *Under Construction*, Warner Music Group.

Nangu (n.d.), *Red Sunset*. CAAMA, 325.

Near, Holly (1973), *Hang In There,* Redwood Records.

—— (1974), *A Live Album,* Redwood Records.

No Fixed Address (1993), *From My Eyes*, Mushroom Records.

NWA (1988), *Straight Outta Compton*, Priority Records.

Orridge, Genesis P. (1990), (as 'Psychic TV'), Liner Notes to *Beyond thee Infinite Beat*, Wax Trax.

Queen Latifah (1989), 'Ladies First', *All Hail the Queen*, Tommy Boy Music.

—— (1991), 'Latifah's Had It Up To Here', *Nature of a Sista'*, Tommy Boy Music.

Raid (1995), 'Words of War', *Hands off the Animals*, Victory Records.

Randall, Bob (n.d.), *Bob Randall*, Imparja, no details.

Rebel Voices from Black Australia (n.d.), Imparja/CAAMA, no details.

Red Star Singers (1974), *The Force of Life,* Paredon Records.

Reeves, Martha and the Vandellas (1998), *The Ultimate Collection*, Motown Records.

Roach, Archie (n.d.), *Jamu Dreaming*, Aurora Recordings.

Romeo, Max (1999), *Open the Gate: 1973–1977*, Blood and Fire.

Roots, The (2004) 'I Don't Care', *The Tipping Point*, Geffen.

Ross, Diana and the Supremes (1997), *The Ultimate Collection*, Motown Records.

Rush (1974), 'Working Man', *Rush*, Mercury.

—— (1981), 'Red Barchetta', *Moving Pictures*, Mercury.

Salt-n-Pepa (1990), 'Independent', *Blacks' Magic*, Next Plateau Records.

—— (1993), 'None of Your Business', *Very Necessary*, London Records.

Scarface (2002), *The Fix*, Def Jam.

7 Seconds (1983), 'Clenched Fists, Black Eyes', *Old School*, Headhunter Records.

—— (1984a), 'The Crew', *The Crew*, BYO Records.

—— (1984b), 'Red and Black', *The Crew*, BYO Records.

—— (1984c), 'Young 'Til I Die', *The Crew*, BYO Records.

Shakur, Tupac (1993), *Strictly 4 My N.I.G.G.A.Z*, Atlantic Records.

Shanté, Roxanne (1989), 'Independent Woman', *Bad Sister*, Breakout Records.

Shocked, Michelle (1986), *The Texas Campfire Tapes*, London: Cooking Vinyl.

—— (1988), *Short Sharp Shocked*, Los Angeles: Mercury.

—— (1989), *Captain Swing*, Los Angeles: Mercury.

—— (1992), *Arkansas Traveler*, Los Angeles: Mercury.

—— (1996), *Mercury Poise: 1988–1995*, Los Angeles: Mercury.

—— (2002), *Deep Natural*, 1001, Los Angeles: Mighty Sound.

Sisters of Mercy, The (1990), 'Doctor Jeep', *Vision Thing*, Merciful Release.

Smalls, Biggie (1994a), 'Juicy', *Ready to Die*, Arista Records.

—— (1994b), 'Me and My Bitch', *Ready to Die*, Arista Records.

SPIN.fx (2003), *Uluparru*, CAAMA, 374.

Stompen Ground (1993), *Highlights from the 1992 Kimberley Aboriginal Arts and Cultural Festival*, ABC Records.

Strong Culture (1998), *Aboriginal Music in Aboriginal Languages* , CAAMA, p. 262.

Sugar Hill Gang (1979), 'Rapper's Delight', *Sugar Hill Gang*, Sugar Hill Records.

Sunrize Band (1993), *Lunggurrma*, ABC Music/Triple J, 518 832–2.

Swift, Rob (1999), 'Modern Day Music', *The Ablist*, Asphodel Records.

Tiddas (1993), *Sing About Life*, Phonogram/Mercury.

Tjapukai Dancers (1990), *Proud to be Aborigine*, Jarra Hill Records.

Tosh, Peter (1977), *Equal Rights*, Columbia.

Toots and the Maytals (1973), *Funky Kingston*, Island.

Trina (2000), 'Da Baddest B***h', *Da Baddest Bitch*, Slip-n-Slide Records.

Twisted Sister (1985), 'I Believe in Rock 'N' Roll', *Come Out and Play*, Atlantic.

Unwankara Palyanku Kanyintjak (1989), *A Strategy for Well Being*, CAAMA, 208.

Various Artists (1993), *Tougher Than Tough: The Story of Jamaican Music*, Island.

Wailer, Bunny (1976), *Blackheart Man*, Island.

Wailers, The (1973), *Burnin'*, Island.

WamaWanti (1988), *Drink Little Bit*, CAAMA, 124.

Wirrinyga Band (1990), *Dreamtime Shadow*, CAAMA, 215.

—— (1996), *Dreamtime Wisdom Modern Time Vision*, CAAMA, 249.

Yothu Yindi (1991), *Tribal Voice*, Mushroom Records.

Youth of Today (1997), 'What Goes Around', *We're Not in This Alone*, Revelation Records.

Index